D1380656

MY LIFE STORY

Central Press Photos, Ltd.

JACK HOBBS IN 1934

MY LIFE STORY

By

SIR JACK HOBBS

Introduction by Benny Green

THE HAMBLEDON PRESS
1981

First Published 1935
Reprinted 1981

The Hambledon Press
35 Gloucester Avenue
London NW1 7AX

DEDICATED TO
MY WIFE
WHOSE LOVING CARE AND DEVOTION
AND INTEREST IN THE GAME
HAVE BEEN A GREAT HELP TO ME
AND THE INSPIRATION OF
MY CAREER

ISBN 0 907628 00 1

Printed and bound in Great Britain by
Redwood Burn Limited
Trowbridge & Esher

CONTENTS

v

LIST OF ILLUSTRATIONS

vi

INTRODUCTION

ONE morning in 1978, "The Times" staged a cultural debate of some profundity, the bone of contention being the literary technique of the well-known author John Berry Hobbs. The argument centred around two of his most popular works, *"The Test Match Surprise"* and *"Between the Wickets"*, originally serialised in that quintessentially chauvinistic periodical *"Chums"*. The indecisivess of the correspondence could not conceal the near-certainty that Hobbs the author was benignly haunted by a company of ghosts, a spectral convocation which indeed flourished so prolifically that the newspaper's literary editor speculated that there may well have been enough of them to raise their own XI. No reference was made during the exchanges to *"My Life Story"*, but it is worth noting that one J. T. Bolton acted as ghost to Hobbs for a period of more than twenty years which ended in 1950; as *"My Life Story"* first appeared in 1935 in the wake of Hobbs' retirement from first-class cricket, the implications are clear enough. But whoever was responsible for putting the book together in its final form, the voice it raises is certainly the authentic voice of Hobbs. Both in its quiet decency verging at times perilously close to Mrs. Grundy, and in a humility so excessive as to be very nearly ostentatious, *"My Life Story"* is clearly a performance deriving from one of the most self-effacing men ever to become a national hero.

It can hardly be said that the prose is bejewelled, or its psychology original, or its disclosures sensational. Hobbs was simply not that kind of an animal. Nevertheless, the republication of the book is a welcome event not just because Hobbs is too important a figure in the evolution of cricket for his image to be allowed to become blurred, but also because the link with a vanished England which the book represents ought to be a priceless asset to the social historian. Perhaps the most demanding challenge facing any student of the past is that of locating and then accepting the validity of the intellectual and moral viewpoint of the people concerned. The sophistication of hindsight can be a very damaging thing, and a great many of the remarks Hobbs makes in his 1935 summation of his life, while they might easily pass for lampoon in our own desenchanted times, were certainly normal enough and worthy enough a century ago. Hobbs was born in December 1882. General Gordon was alive, Sherlock Holmes unborn. Tennyson was Poet Laureate to a monarch still uncorrupted by the idolatry of two jubilees, *"The Mikado"* did not exist, Kipling was a name unknown to any but its owner, and the most successful new book of the season was *"Treasure Island"*. It was a world without the maxim gun, the battleship, wireless telegraphy, X-rays; the message of Charles Darwin had hardly begun to permeate the consciousness of the honest poor. It is against this essentially Victorian background that we have to digest those episodes in Hobbs' boyhood when he sang in the church choir, forsook his amateur status by accepting a fee of threepence for rendering *"I'se a Little Alabama Coon"*, joined the Band of Hope and later enlisted in the cause of Temperance.

So resolutely evangelical an environment for the child was sure to leave its mark on the man, whose brush with Temperance left him with the opinion that the best tipple was soda-and-milk; that when all's said and done, East, West, home's best; that "East Lynne" is "a fine story"; and that however far short of his own ideals he might have slipped from time to time, he has sincerely "tried to be good". But there is an engagingly gastronomic mitigation of all this pietism, especially in the early years, when his consideration of the divine mystery of Creation is influenced by a touching concern for his appetite. One of his choirmasters was in the habit of inviting his young singing birds home to tea, where he would deliver a religious homily in evident ignorance of the fact that what really attracted young Hobbs was the refreshments: "never in my life have I tasted such delicious bread and butter and jam". Again, when is father takes him to see Ranjitsinhji for the first time, what resides in the memory is the hot pork pie devoured in the stands. Later, when he is old enough to help his father perform his duties at the Jesus College ground, what truly animates him is the occasional opportunity to enter the tea-tent and get stuck into the plum pie and custard.

Cricketers may wonder what any of this has to do with Hobbs the master-batsman, although Hobbs himself evidently considered it relevant enough to include in his autobiography. When he claims always to have tried to be good, he is thinking about the cricket field as well as the parish church and the purlieus of Kennington. Hobbs was one of nature's gentlemen, an athlete so pristine in his honorable intentions that he became famous for walking when convinced of the legality of his own dismissal, sometimes absolving the umpires from the embarrassment of an awkward decision. In the thirty seasons he played in first-class cricket, never once was he heard to utter an uncharitable word about a fellow-player, nor ever engage in a brush with authority, nor show dissent, nor aspire to the fleshpots of the Leagues, nor was ever in dispute with his county, nor ever grieved his family through some public indiscretion, nor ever sailed closer to the winds of scandal than the time in Australia when a famous actress chastely kissed him in an impulsive gesture of tribute. But a true gentleman, although he might occasionally kiss, never tells, and Hobbs withheld the actress's name.

He was born into a sporting hierarchy whose administrative methods were a quaint compromise between autocracy and theology. Victorian parallels between Jehovah and the MCC are too familiar to require proof at this late stage; as L.C.B. Seaman has written, "Just as freemasons referred to God as the Great Architect of the Universe, young cricketers were taught to think of Him as the One Great Scorer and almost to regard a Straight Bat as second in religious symbolism only to the Cross of Jesus"; as late as 1921 Lord

Harris could liken a game of cricket to a lesson in God's classroom. It was against this background of cricket as an allegory of Life itself that Hobbs scored more centuries in his career than any other batsman before or since, and more runs, and, until the enchanted summer of Denis Compton in 1947, more centuries in a season than any other player. And although his fifteen centuries for England is a total which shrinks by the year as the proliferation of Test matches between second-rate sides induces an inflationary spiral statistically speaking, it will be duly noted that twelve of those centuries were scored against Australia, a record which is in no immediate danger, and begins to look more impressive than ever when taken into the context of his nearest rivals, Walter Hammond with nine and Herbert Sutcliffe with seven.

But although Hobbs was usually the best player in the England side, and always the best batsman, it never occurred to him to indulge in the fatal syllogism: I am the best player; the captain is the leader: I should be the captain. Hobbs, raised in that climate of Emsworthian pantheistic dottiness exemplified by Harris's theological excesses, accepted the authority of his patrician betters, although not quite without a murmur. There was once a Test match against Australia when the England captain contracted tonsilitis in mid-battle, and Hobbs, being the senior professional, was asked to step into the breach. At first he politely demurred, pointing out that there was another amateur in the side in the person of G. T. S. Stevens. The selectors said that yes, they had noticed that, but would Hobbs lead the side all the same. And so he did, the point being that at the time of the Crisis Stevens, aged twenty five, was playing against Australia for the first time, on that day at Manchester, Hobbs was forty three years old and had appeared for his country on twenty nine previous occasions. And yet the passage in which Hobbs describes the incident is lit with an ambivalence which seems to suggest that Hobbs was not against professional captaincy only captaincy by himself; as he points out, there are moments when the insistence on a Gentleman-leader constitutes both a cricketing absurdity and a social affront to the professionals.

This refusal to take himself seriously as a leader is typical of a man who always appreciated the greatness of others so generously that he never reached the stage where he quite took his own measure. One of the most touching moments in his autobiography comes when he explains why his great hero and cricketing father-figure Tom Hayward was not present among the guests when young Jack took a wife at the end of the 1906 season. Some people thought they detected in Hayward's absence an element of professional jealousy on the part of the junior partner; on the contrary, the bridegroom had all his life gone in such awe of the great Tom that he felt that to send so distinguished a figure an invitation amounted to insufferable pretension. To be sure, 1906 was Tom Hayward's year, his triumphal processional in which he set a new seasonal record aggregate of runs which stood until Compton finally lowered it more than forty years later. Even so, Hobbs too was in the runs that year, nearly two thousand of them, and that so prominent and respected a professional should be too shy to extend a social invitation to his batting partner perhaps tells us as much about the man and his diffidence as all the biographies in the world.

Hayward was, of course, a Cambridgeshire man, like Hobbs, and it was within the boundaries of that county that Hobbs's career was born. Today the student of such affairs may travel to Cambridge and wander across the homely plains of Parker's Piece in the knowledge that it was here, in 1901, under the scrutiny of Tom Hayward's expert eye, that the most complete English batsman of all time first impressed a great cricketer. As in all biographies of extraordinary men, there comes a moment where the tyro is transmuted into the virtuoso, after which the drama of his story tends to fall away. And like every virtuoso, Hobbs can tell us nothing technically enlightening about his art. He was a natural batsman, and any analysis by him of how he did this and that was really a rationalisation after the event of a series of intuitive actions. This is not to say that he never practised, never agonised, never worked, never thought deeply about his cricket, simply that he was born to be a batsman and found his vocation with a swift inevitability to hearten the most abject pessimist. There is in his confessional one moment of rich if unintentional comedy, when he attempts to describe how to extract the sting from a Googly. It will be remembered that Hobbs had hardly begun his first-class career before the sensational arrival in the Garden of Eden of Bosanquet's serpent. At a stroke, the canons of classical batsmanship were overturned, causing those hearty extroverts the front-foot drivers to become so many buckskin-booted Hamlets sicklied o'er with the pale cast of thought. The Googly, harbinger of that Decadence where nothing is quite what it seems, was a gauntlet flung at the feet of the finest classical batsman of the age, and he promptly used those feet to achieve a fresh dimension of mastery:

> When I suspected the googly, I played well forward, so that the break might be smothered, or I played back and watched the ball right on to the bat.

There we have it, the greatest batting technician in world cricket telling how to repel the most cunning challenge of the new epoch. Either play forward or play back. We can derive a little more enlightenment, but not much, for Cardus:

> Immediately the bowler begins his run Hobbs seems to have some instinct of what manner of ball is on the way; rarely does he move his feet to an incorrect position. His footwork is so quick that even from behind the nets it is not always possible to follow its movement in detail.

But if Hobbs is ineffectual as a spokesman for his own batting technique, he is positively mute when it comes to his style as a writer. Neither he nor the best of his biographers, Ronald Mason, ever so much as mentions the works of fiction published under his name, an omission which posterity would surely never forgive me for failing to rectify. Here is an example of how valiantly those journalistic ghosts laboured in the Hobbsian cause on the occasion of the appearance in *"Chums"* of the new serial, *"Between the Wickets"*:

"Fennell", Greystairs said very clearly, "you're the worst kind of cad I've yet met".

Fennell became scarlet as to face. He had no opportunity of replying to the accusation, for just then Greystairs felt a hand on his shoulder. "Trying to freeze you out, old top?", said Drake. "Well, there's two sides to that. I've been talking to Lorimer, the School cricket skipper, about you. He's over at the School net and he wants to have a chat".

Any last lingering doubt that Hobbs was indeed the author of this stirring stuff is dispelled by the italicised sentence at the bottom of the page: "Another topping long instalment soon", buttressed by a photograph of Jack in mufti, "at the desk on which *'Between the Wickets'* was written". What the Band of Hope would have made of that kind of disingenuousness one shudders to think, but it is revealing that when the same publication ran serials by J. W. Hearne, Patsy Hendren, Charlie Buchan and Andy Wilson, every one of those eminent authors seemed to have derived stylistically speaking from Jack Hobbs.

That his world is remote from ours is underlined by incidents like his departure for a Test series in South Africa on a donkey cart, his night out at a

Soho restaurant – gastronomy again – where he exults in eight courses for half a crown, the team outing to the Canterbury Music Hall when the audience called for him and he almost crawled under his seat. The world of Jack Hobbs is a world long-lost, and the devil's advocate might well be justified in asking why we should bother with so ancient a testament as the life of a bygone cricketer. Therein lies one of the several peculiar charms of cricket, the evocative power of its literature. We can never hope to see Hobbs now, moving through time and space to the pitch of the ball as he once did. But somehow, when we become familiar with his conversational nuances, study his photographs, digest his statistics, he begins to swim within the range of our imagination, especially because the game at which he excelled happens to be one which invites long loyalties. Men have been known to grace the first-class game through five decades. Hobbs himself scored half his hundreds when he was past his fortieth birthday, which means that although the young Jack who graduated from Parker's Piece to the great arenas of the world is as quaint to us as a halfpenny bun, the knight who reported cricket in his retirement is no further removed from us than some benign blue-serged, watch-chained great-uncle. More than one of my friends are smug in the knowledge that somewhere at the back of the old wardrobe in the garage is the bat they were bought one red-letter day in childhood at Jack's shop in Fleet Street, and that the great man actually signed the blade for them, shook them by the sticky hand and wished them the joy of many centuries. That shop survived on into the 1960s, a last reminder of the physical presence of a modest virtuoso.

And it is because of this immense span of cricketing lives that the student of the game is able to make contact with epochs otherwise cut off from him. When cricketers like Hobbs perform on the grass over so many seasons, their careers are like great arches spanning the centuries, so that the cricket-lover, like the man who shakes the hand that shook the hand that shook the hand of the Duke of Wellington, is able to arrive, with a hop, a step and a jump back in a distant past which turns out not to be quite so distant after all. In this game of sporting leapfrog Jack Hobbs is a vital figure. More than any other cricketer in the history of the game with the possible exception of Wilfred Rhodes, he is the keystone in the arch of modern cricket history. In his first first-class match he played against Dr. W. G. Grace, who diddled him out of a short single by asking him to tap the ball back to him. In his last first-class game he played alongside F. R. Brown, who captained D. B. Close in a Test match, which means that the unbroken line of succession from 1848, the year of Grace's birth, to 1977, when Close retired, is a route into history. Grace-Hobbs-Brown-Close, a high road from the fall of Metternich to the rise of the Microchip, an odyssey so daunting that were it not for the great symbolic figures we might not be able to contemplate it at all.

In such a way does the unassuming sporting virtuoso retain the affection of generations literally still unborn. Just as Grace was the Great Cricketer, so Jack Hobbs was the Great Professional, a man who mastered the art of batsmanship on the plumb matting of the veldt, but also on wickets misty with English summer rain, a man who scored his last first-class century not long before his 53rd birthday and who retained so powerful a hold on the national imagination that nearly twenty years after his retirement, he was knighted for services to cricket. His life is a proposition, laid out with Euclidean punctilio, that the hired hand may, through application, technical genius and stoic decency, rise as far as he cares to. His age is past and his type extinct. The loss is cricket's. Ours too.

BENNY GREEN.

CHAPTER I

I BEGIN

I AM a Cambridgeshire man. The names of most county cricketers have been conspicuously associated with the county of their birth. Dr. W. G. Grace was always connected in the public mind with Gloucestershire; we think of Yorkshire when we talk about Wilfred Rhodes, George Hirst, Sir Stanley Jackson, or Herbert Sutcliffe; of Notts in mentioning George Gunn and Harold Larwood; of Middlesex when we speak of "Patsy" Hendren. Not so with me; I have always been identified with Surrey, the county of my adoption.

In the year 1882, nine days before Christmas, I first saw the light of this world. It was the year in which Australia won its first victory over England at the Oval—a success not to be repeated on that particular ground until 1930, forty-eight years later. Although I was born with no silver spoon in my mouth, one piece of good luck was showered on me in having Cambridge as the town of my birth, for my father, John Hobbs, was engaged on the staff at the University cricket ground, known as Fenner's, where he used to bowl at the nets and act as a professional umpire.

9

His position there brought me as a small child into touch with the great game.

I have no recollection of the first match I attended, because I was only an infant, carried by my father. The Australians were playing Cambridge University. I was so excited and chirruped so loudly that an Australian fielder near the boundary called out to my father: "Better make a cricketer of that kid, old man." My father was pleased at the time and more than once told me the story later on.

My start in life was in humble circumstances. I was not waited on hand and foot, as is the good fortune of many boys and girls. Knowing what I went through, I determined as a man that my own boys should have a better send-off in life, and I have been fairly able to keep that resolve. My father was of a reserved, quiet type, highly popular with his fellow-townsmen. He was a great hero to me; from childhood onwards I thought the world of him. He was strict, but kind and just. His word was law; to put us on the right road, all that was needed was for our mother to say: "I'll tell your father." The occasional coppers and sixpences he gave me meant a lot. He was a keen fisherman; it was a real thrill to me to take his rod and line down to the station, when he set out on fishing expeditions; and it meant another copper for me. Once, as a great treat, I was allowed to go with him, and I sat for hours watching him fish a few miles up the River Cam.

I was the eldest of twelve, half boys and half girls. My mother's life was all work. I have much to be grateful to her for. She did her best for us, especially after my father's death, and put up a brave fight against adversity. As the eldest, I had to turn to and do my bit of housework. My mother's maiden name was Berry, and, as my father's Christian name was John, I was christened John Berry Hobbs. In spite of lack of money, I never got into much mischief, and, when the time came for me to become a member of a church choir, I mixed with boys of a good sort, whose influence was of great value to me. Keenness for games also undoubtedly helped to keep me right.

My family was fond of dogs and cats and of dumb animals generally. We kept rabbits, and, to serve up a pet rabbit at a meal would have been to us unthinkable. I had a pet kitten, and, when I took it out one day, it was snatched from me by a tall boy down the road and dropped by him over a high fence; I went home shedding tears of grief. My mother, to console me, gave me another kitten. Years later, she had a duck as a household pet; its name was Cyril. The choice of such a pet seemed to me most extraordinary.

The duck followed its mistress wherever she went. It behaved with all the dignity befitting its position, and answered Mother's call regularly and obediently. When Cyril died of old age, she was much upset.

Taking into account all the circumstances, I had a happy childhood. Having never indulged in luxuries, I did not miss them. St. Matthew's Church, at Cambridge, had a small mixed school for infants, and I went there at the age of five. It must have been a relief to Mother, with a family such as ours, to get one child out of the way in the mornings. About a hundred infants attended, and the schooling was free. We were under the supervision of a head mistress, named Miss Bailey, who tried to teach me to knit, but I could never fathom the mysteries of "in, round, catch, off."

On reaching nine years of age, I was sent to another Church of England school—the York Street Boys' School, where the fees were fourpence a week. Mr. Mallet, the head master, was a great sportsman, and any boy like myself, who was good at games, got on famously with him. He joined in with us at football, a small tennis ball being used in that game when we played during the playtime break at ten forty-five and before starting afternoon lessons. The goals were chalked on the wall. Sport was certainly encouraged by this school, cricket and football chiefly. One of the first questions put to me by Mr. Mallet was: "What is a county cricketer's average?" I was able to answer correctly, and he took more notice of me after that; in fact, we sort of chummed up.

He took a good deal of pleasure in the organising of musical plays and sketches, a feature of which was a number of choruses, and he singled me out, as a choir-boy, for some of the solos. In a sketch called "Savages and Sailors," I was one of the sailors. We sailors, on an island, were surprised in a night attack and captured, but a ship came to the rescue, and we fought our way out to freedom and captured the savages in turn. In the second half of the programme, I appeared with a blackened face as a nigger boy, and, holding a doll borrowed from a neighbour, I sang: "I'se a Little Alabama Coon." After the show, as we were changing our clothes, the head master, as pleased as Punch, came into the dressing-room and presented me with a threepenny bit.

I cannot claim to have distinguished myself as a learner of the ordinary school lessons. History interested me. Mechanics and experiments were fascinating; to put hydrogen and oxygen into a bottle and see the mixture pop off was wonderful. I remember being taught such items of knowledge as the pressure of air and of water to the square inch. My chief aversion was free-hand drawing, especially maps, a lesson in which was inflicted upon us on Friday afternoons, and, on that day, I was delighted if I could find an excuse for staying away. No prizes were given at this school—not that I should have won any. Never would I allow school-work or home-work to interfere with games. Fortunately, there was plenty of available time for playing, as the school hours were only nine to twelve and two to four.

Once I obtained some snuff by "swopping" a tennis ball for it. The teacher, discovering me with it, found it awkward to reach me where I sat in the back row of the class-room. In his annoyance, he clambered over some desks, and there was quite a commotion. The tanning on that occasion was the only real tanning I ever got, and even that was only half a tanning, because he was, I think, just a wee bit sympathetic. As he had taken away the snuff, the boy who had given it to me returned the tennis ball to me. I felt a sneak for taking it, but stuck to it all the same.

Some of the playmates of those days have been encountered by me, in after life, in all parts of the country and as far away as Australia. One choir chum occupies a responsible position in Cam-bridge; he and I are still very friendly. I have also run across Mr. Mallet occasionally. He was

EARLY DAYS: HOBBS AND TOM HAYWARD

H. D. G. LEVESON-GOWER'S INVITATION, 1909

a member of the Cambridgeshire Cricket Club. Once I met him at Fenner's and several times in the street. It was a source of great satisfaction to him that I had done so well in my profession.

As regards hobbies, I had a "Bubbles" picture-book, in which I did some painting, and I collected some foreign stamps, but soon tired of that pursuit. One ambition of mine was to obtain a big lot of marbles; I never got beyond the two hundred mark, but to many of the boys the collection of a thousand was a commonplace achievement. Bird-nesting made no appeal to me; I was too fond of birds. I never robbed orchards, probably because I was too scared of the terrors of the law. I can also declare that I rarely broke a window with a hit or kicked ball.

No regular pocket-money came to me in those days; I had only the coppers now and then from Father, and on special occasions he would give me a little bit of silver. Sunday was a great day in our home. We had beef and Yorkshire pudding, and there would be a cake, which we could not afford to have on weekdays. But one cake did not go very far in our large household, and it was soon demolished. Another Sunday treat was an egg for breakfast. Steak and kidney pudding was, and still is, my favourite dish; I never tire of it. I am not sure whether there was any kidney for me in it in those days. Like many other boys, I hated rice puddings. Perhaps they were not so palatable then, for to-day I can eat my wife's rice puddings with relish.

I was always conscious of our humble circumstances. I detested the back road where we lived, and I envied those who had big houses and who could hold up their heads in any company. Certainly I had the inferiority complex to a marked degree.

When I was a kid, Christmas was our jolliest time. We were all at home together. I used to hang up my stocking, but I cannot remember any notable presents; now and again there would be a toy, but mostly oranges and nuts. On Christmas Day, there would be the church choir in the morning, then the feeding, and afterwards games—mostly table games. I loved the spirit of Christmas; it is one of the things that one misses in some parts of the world. On my first tours to South Africa and Australia, I felt homesick at Christmas-time. Somehow I could never associate that season with an atmosphere which resembled what we get on an August Bank Holiday in England.

As a boy, I shunned publicity of any kind. I was shy and nervous, strongly disliked the limelight, and had a hatred of swank, which I still have. Once, when I was very young, I had a fit to save some money. After much self-sacrifice,

I saved up the magnificent sum of sevenpence, putting it into a tin money-box. My mother, being a bit short one day, borrowed it. I never got it back. Whenever I go to Cambridge, I pull my mother's leg about it. She denies it, but I can remember it as if it was yesterday.

In order to have somewhere to go in the evenings, I joined the Band of Hope, the children's branch of the Temperance Society. Cinemas did not exist, but there were magic-lantern shows, in which somebody read a story, and pictures were thrown upon a screen. We only paid a halfpenny for the entertainment, and I enjoyed such evenings tremendously. A circus came to our town and stayed all the summer. I saved up pennies in order to visit it and went three or four times.

In our parish, there was a clergy-house, where young men were trained for the Church, and these excellent fellows had charge of certain organisations in the parish. When old enough, I joined one of them—the Youths' Branch of the Temperance Society—and put in two attendances a week. The games played there alternated; one night it would be draughts or chess or ludo and the next night gymnastics. Sometimes a light-weight champion from the University came to teach us boxing. I recall an occasion on which he knelt down, directing me to aim a

2

left lead to his head and try to hit him in the face. As he slipped his head quickly aside, I failed to bring off a hit, and thought his action wonderfully clever. He said: "Stick out your chest; see if you can stand a blow." I did so; he connected and caught me on a big button. It was very painful, and I remembered it for days.

Some of these training youths of my time became cricket enthusiasts. The Rev. F. S. Girdlestone, of the Old Church Vicarage, Smethwick, was one of them; he has followed my career throughout. We have had many talks together, and I have consulted him as regards my continuing cricket in recent years. I have a great regard for him, and he has been a great help to me.

At ten years old, I joined the choir at St. Matthew's. We were paid half a crown to five shillings per quarter, according to our length of service. At Christmas-time, we sang carols on the vicarage doorstep and were rewarded afterwards by the vicar's coming to the parish-room, where we had choir practice, and sharing out amongst us a box or two of crystallised fruit. Carol-singing was great fun; we played all sorts of jokes. One of the boys would go up to the vicarage garden gate and give a good tug at an inviting bell, and then we all scooted like hares. The choir-master, Mr. A. J. Reed, one of the students at the clergy-house preparing for the Church, was very strict and very religious. Whenever he had an opportunity, he would talk to us on the subject of religion. There were occasions on which he invited a few of us to have tea with him at his home, and never in my life have I tasted such delicious bread and butter and jam. There was cake too, but it was the bread and butter and jam that I revelled in.

This choir-master kept us carefully under his wing. He had strange views about solo-singing. None of us, boys or men, were saints enough, in his opinion, to be permitted to sing solos. Consequently, the solo parts were sung by the combined trebles, altos, tenors or basses, as the case might be.

I loved the singing too much to care about the sermons, which took up a lot of time and seemed dry and quite unnecessary. None of the choir-boys paid much attention to them, and I do not think that they do to-day. The parsons talked above our heads, and the only parts of any sermons that we found any pleasure in were those where the parson happened to tell a story as an illustration.

I think that I have always tried to be good, even if I have failed miserably. That choir-master's influence caused me to try to live up to what he taught. The atmosphere in which I was brought up was distinctly religious. There was Sunday morning and Sunday evening in the choir, and Sunday School twice each Sunday. Tuesdays saw me at the Youths' Branch, Wednesdays at Evensong, and Thursdays at choir-practice. At the morning Sunday School, I had to recite the Collect for the day, a verse of a hymn, and a verse of Scripture. These we had to learn during the week; otherwise we were in trouble. For the most part, I managed to learn mine. We got marks or lost marks in this particular task, and the marks counted for prizes. In most years, prizes came to me.

Sunday School treats were great events. They were held in the grounds of Downing College. All three Sunday Schools in the parish—St. Matthew's, St. James's, and St. Martin's—joined together. The Sunday before the treat was a big day; it was Anniversary Sunday, and we marched round the parish, headed by the Church Army Band. We held aloft in front a number of banners of various colours and sang hymns from leaflets at various stopping-places. I thought myself a real big-wig when asked to carry a choir banner. At the treat, after tea, the big thing was a tug of war between the three schools, and bitterly disappointed was I that St. James's used to win more often than not. There was a fierce competition to get into the Sunday School eight for the tug, and I practised hard in the evenings for the great struggle. Eventually I won a place.

Miss Brown, the oldest teacher in the Sunday School, celebrated her jubilee last year. The dear old soul still writes to me every year for a subscription to the treat.

After quitting the Sunday School, I joined a school for older boys and, later, in my teens, the Ainsworth Bible Class. There the singing was not only hearty, but even ferocious. Each Sunday, some member was permitted to choose the second hymn, and there was keen competition to get in first. We used to call out the title and number of our choice, and the first to catch the speaker's ear had his hymn sung. I got one in now and then. As can be imagined, we had some rollicking tunes, including all Moody and Sankey's.

My first visit to Fenner's, apart from being taken as a child of three, was when I was ten. Father was an attendant on a temporary stand there. I saw the great Ranjitsinhji, Sir Stanley Jackson, and A. O. Jones bat, and the Australians, with Hugh Trumble, S. E. Gregory and C. McLeod, playing against Cambridge University. Little did I realise then that A. O. Jones was to be my first captain in Australia. At that time, I was not old enough to realise what it all meant; I was overawed. It seemed far above me, but it was a very big day for me. I sat at the back of the stand, and, boylike, enjoyed a nice, hot pork pie which my father had sent for. I remember my disappointment when Australia won, for the University collapsed in the second innings.

My first visit to the sea-coast was at the age of eleven, when I went with the Band of Hope to Hunstanton, paying one and fourpence for a day return—not dear for an excursion of 124 miles altogether. For a long time I had looked forward to this trip, and, when I saw the sea, I could hardly believe my eyes. It thrilled me so much that I never moved from the sea-front all day. Hunstanton's cliffs seemed to me marvellous— dark brown at the bottom, then, as they rise, yellow and bright red, with a layer of white chalk at the top.

In the afternoon of that wonderful day I paddled, and in the evening took part in races. I well remember a boot and shoe race. Our boots were mixed up and scattered in all directions; we had to find our own and get back to the winning-post. On my third visit to Hunstanton, for purposes of identification in the races I bought some new laces; very shrewd, was it not? The race started; I was right up amongst the early birds and got home yards in front, very perky. Then I was disqualified, because my laces were not tied tight enough.

CHAPTER II

BOYHOOD

THE Church Choir Eleven at St. Matthew's was the first cricket team in which I played. As I was able to play better than the other boys, I was made captain. I could get twenties, which was not bad for twelve years old. Averages were not kept in that Eleven. The first match in which I ever batted was on Jesus College Close for choir-boys of that College against another side. They were one short, and I was roped in. When I went out to bat, I shook like a leaf, but I had the satisfaction of scoring one or two runs. In my second match, St. Matthew's Choir *v.* Trinity College Choir, my score was three singles. Evening matches followed, in one of which I nearly fulfilled my ambition to score a century, but I was given out l.b.w. when I had hit up 90. My father's joy was tremendous when he heard of that achievement.

During my summer holidays, I had visited the Cambridge Colleges, but now came a great event. It was arranged that I should take my father's dinner to Jesus College, where he had become groundsman and umpire. This was a real delight,

23

for I could watch the cricket on those afternoons. Sometimes there would be an all-day match, and, after the teams had had their lunch, my chance came to go into the tent and enjoy plum tart with custard over it—a fine luxury.

I helped my father at various odd jobs on the Jesus ground during school holidays, such as scouting at the nets, and soon opportunities came of playing a sort of cricket with the college servants, using a tennis ball, a cricket-stump for bat, and a tennis post for wicket. This simple practice laid a wonderful foundation, giving me a keen eye and developing the wrist-strokes which I had seen in the college matches. Boy as I was, I tried to emulate the same strokes, and I was surprised at the number of successful strokes I managed to make. That was the way in which I became a natural batsman. The foot-work came automatically, and the practice became a great source of enjoyment when I recognised how important everything was. The straight stump helped me to sense the importance of the straight bat. Perhaps I tried to over-flourish, but I learnt to appreciate the grace, beauty, swing and rhythm of stroke play and, above all, balance.

Particularly could I delight in the off drive, getting the left leg well across—a drive which to this day is perhaps the most beautiful of all strokes. On one occasion when my father bowled to me on Jesus College Close, he told me to stand up to the wickets. I could see him putting a spin on the ball, and, having no pads, I was tempted to stand a bit clear, but he called out: "Don't draw away." Standing up to the wickets is all important; anyone who draws away cannot play with a straight bat. Moreover, the movement may be the means of your getting bowled off your pads.

One of my choir experiences was a special service at St. Mary's Church, Cambridge, on a public holiday fixed in honour of the marriage of King George, who was then Duke of York. All the choirs were there; my choir helped. I had long had a mania to possess brown rubber shoes, and at last I got a pair, wearing them for the first time at that service. As soon as the service ended, I went off to cricket.

My parents took me on a day-trip to Yarmouth when I was about fourteen. For the first time I went on the sea in a sailing-yacht, and, although I remember getting into the boat, I have no recollection of getting out. So sick was I that I took two hours to recover. I have been a bad sailor all my life, and have made a point of going overland whenever my tours permitted it. At an early age, I used to bathe in the Granta, and I taught myself to swim at fourteen. A lot of us boys were together, and each one helped the others. I remember walking two or three steps from the ladder and then striking out. I shouted: "I've done one stroke." Another amusement of those days was a little harriers' club, formed by the choir-boys. I joined in their night runs. When there happened to be any skating, I was very fond of it. I went to Lingay Fen and to Sturbridge Common, which used to be flooded over. Once I had some skating and sliding on the Cam, but I was nervous at the thought of so much water under me and felt happier on the shallow Fen and Common. I witnessed a championship contest on Lingay Fen; the competitors hardly appeared to be skating, as they took their task so easily with long, easy strides.

The Ivy Club was a boys' club that I helped to form. It served to keep us together, and we played evening matches on Parker's Piece. I was chosen captain. Our meetings were held in a room in a coffee tavern. I was so keen that I used to get up at six in the morning to practise on Parker's Piece. By the time that I had reached seventeen, it might be said that I was either playing or practising morning, noon and night, until the hour when darkness put an end to it.

I was fond of reading serial tales and comic papers. *Chums* and *The Boys' Friend* were real favourites, giving me wonderful thrills and causing me to count the days to their next appearance. I never read in bed, and, if I attempt to do so nowadays, I fail to keep awake. My first novel was *Valentine Vox*, in a paper-covered edition. It gripped me. There was pathos in it, mixed with fun. The ventriloquist hero of the story could throw his voice anywhere. I used to practise talking in my throat without moving my lips.

East Lynne was a book that stuck in my mind— a fine story, with a sentimental side. Of the few other books I read I recall *The Old Curiosity Shop*, *Uncle Tom's Cabin*, *Hereward the Wake*, and *Robinson Crusoe*. Most of what I read were prizes won by myself or by my brothers and sisters; we used to swop them. I did not care for character studies and only wanted nice, readable tales. To-day I am not a big reader. What with sports news, gossip, the wireless and my correspondence, no time is left for books.

I read the Bible in the Sunday School and during the dull parts of sermons. I think that all young people should read it as a great guide to life and a standard of values. There was not much chance for a poor boy like me to visit museums or scientific institutions; the Band of Hope and, later, the Youths' Branch were my only meetings. Two or three times I was asked to become a Sunday School teacher, which meant to take, as an older boy, some of the younger ones. But I was always nervous of speaking to any audience. I detested it, and do to this day. I turn down hundreds of invitations to functions of all kinds where speaking is involved. Never have I tried to overcome this nervousness. I am not gifted that way, and it is not my province.

I used to go to see the college races on the river. When the bumping races were on in May, I was keen that Jesus College should become head of the river. For me it was always Jesus College for cricket, rowing, Rugby, Soccer, golf, and athletics. This interest has stuck to me to the present day, and, whenever I see a combined University side or read about one, I look out to discover if there is a Jesus man in the side. It depressed me when the Light Blue crew lost the boat-race ten times running.

About twelve months before leaving school, I thought that I would add a little grist to the mill and took a situation as Jack of all jobs at a private house. The pay was half a crown a week. I got up early each day and went to the house before attending school. On Saturdays, I stayed longer and got a lunch thrown in.

After leaving school, I worked at Jesus College during the summer as a paid servant. I helped to put up the nets and prepare the wickets, oiled the bats, scouted, cleaned up the pavilion, and took the cricket-bags in a hand-cart to other grounds when matches were being played away. My pay, seven and sixpence a week, was augmented by tips when I fielded at the nets. More "perks" were to be had in those days than now; undergraduates seemed to have more money. In intervals between work duties, I had a knock in the net myself. In fact, I was always practising imaginary strokes with a stump, stick or bat.

I was never very happy with girls, and they did not play any part in my early life. Games were everything. Of my boy chums a special one was a choir-boy named George Harding, who was always regarded as the clever boy of the party. He was certainly a bright lad, and I looked up to him. We played draughts together, and at first he used to beat me as he liked, but I became so keen that it was eventually give and take with us. Curiously enough, he was no good at cricket or other open-air games. George Harding was best man at my wedding.

Apart from cricket, the only game that I greatly liked was Association football, but I had little opportunity for other games. I was never coached at football, any more than at cricket, but I was always kicking a ball about with the choir-boys. My father being groundsman, I had the luck of being able to borrow a football. We played on Saturday afternoons and often in the evenings under an arc-light on Parker's Piece. Not until I came to London to qualify for Surrey did I manage to play football really well. I never made any name or splash at it. Nearly every Saturday I used to go down to Cambridge to play for one of the Cambridge senior teams. They were champions of the League and the best team in Cambridge. I played outside right. The matches were watched by crowds that I then thought enormous—2,000 to 3,000. We played on Parker's Piece, one of the places where I had learned to play cricket. The football pitches there were beautiful. Matches were also played on college grounds.

Parker's Piece stands for a lot in my cricket life. It was divided into four by paths. One part was kept for cricket and never used for anything else. The cricket pitch was sacred; that part was never played on in winter. There is no more wonderful stretch of turf anywhere—the dream wicket of all cricketers. In my mind's eye, I can see Ranjitsinhji practising there, and I can see him being bowled at by the present Jack O'Connor's father. I had a great awe of Ranji. His silk shirts, worn down to the wrists, used to flap in the wind. Dan Hayward used to look after the Parker's Piece practice nets and, on match days, the marquees; and his son Tom was the one real hero of my boyhood. It was for long a popular belief and has been widely asserted that he coached me in my early days. This is not correct. How much Tom Hayward meant to me in those days I shall relate later; but, as a matter of fact, I have never had one hour's coaching from anybody in my life, and the reason why I emphasise this point here is that I am a natural batsman, entirely self-taught. Tom Hayward was idolised at Cambridge. In course of time, he was destined to become my greatest guide and helper, and it was he who recommended me for a trial at the Oval. Whenever Surrey was playing, I used to run up to the library at night, to see how many runs Tom had made. If he had put up a good score, it was a pleasant evening for me.

Amongst others whom I saw play on Parker's Piece were H. Carpenter and W. Reeves. They were playing for Essex. I could see careers in front of them, and I began to feel deeply that there was a career in front of me. Apart from the glamour, the earnings of professionals in those days seemed to my mind very big. I had been told that they were getting five pounds a match. It seemed big money. But even the earnings paled in my imagination in comparison with the glory of playing for a county—say, for instance, for Surrey, the county of my hero, Tom Hayward.

Cricket had become with me an all-absorbing

passion. It was my supreme ambition. It stuck out a mile in my mind beyond anything else. My father's occasional remarks about county players fired my young hopes. Love of the game must have been bred in my very blood. Yet I was a self-made cricketer. The reason why I stress this point again is to give a ray of hope to all young cricketers on the cricketing field. It shows that those who have no great advantages, such as coaching, can hope for success, provided that they possess a certain amount of gumption and natural aptitude, and, next, unlimited perseverance and determination. Ability and a spicing of good luck are excellent ingredients, but neither is sufficient without patience, persistence and perseverance. It is given to few to realise in after life the dreams and glowing aspirations of youth. I am one of those few.

Cambridgeshire Cricket Association

1911 - 1912

To Mr. Jack Hobbs

The Members of the Cambridgeshire Cricket Association and others interested in Cricket in your native Town and County of Cambridge desire to offer you our hearty congratulations upon your participation in a Cricketing Tour in Australia which has restored to the Mother Country those much coveted Mythical Ashes, and to assure you of their high appreciation of the distinguished personal services you have rendered to the English XI and the National Game.

We trust that you may long be spared in health and vigour to continue your successful Cricketing career and sincerely hope that in all your undertakings success may attend you.

Signed on behalf of the Council.

Charles Pigg (President)
Oliver Papworth (Chairman of Executive Committee)
Percy W. Gray (Hon. Treasurer)
A. R. Hill.

A. E. Richford.
A. P. Gray.   Hon. Secretaries
Arthur E. Lofts.
A. B. Diver.
J. Collins.

THE ILLUMINATED ADDRESS FROM THE CAMBRIDGESHIRE CRICKET
ASSOCIATION

CHAPTER III

EARLY MATCHES

THE year 1901 was a big year for me. The first event that I recall in that year was a national bereavement, with which was connected a curious experience for me. Queen Victoria died on January 22nd, and on that day I went with a few chums into a barber's shop to have our hair cut. "What about a shave?" said the barber jokingly. I thought that my chin was pretty smooth. However, in a dare-devil spirit, I replied: "Right. Come on then." The novelty of my first shave is thus linked up in my memory with the passing of the great Queen.

That year I was playing for two clubs—one, the Ainsworth, connected with my Bible-class, and the other the Cambridge Liberals. Having played football for the latter, without, as a matter of fact, mixing in their politics, it naturally came to pass that I played cricket for them when summer arrived. A difficulty arose when a great match between those two clubs was arranged, each wanting to play me. The point was settled by tossing a coin; Ainsworth won. I went in second wicket down and scored 102—the much-desired first century. All cricketers know the glow of pride that comes with a first century. The loud cheers that rang out from all parts of the ground made me very excited, and I shall never forget my feelings as I left the field. It seemed the beginning of great things; I had successfully got over the first hurdle.

In another match, Ainsworth against the University Press, my score was 70 not out, and I took eight wickets. Two other scores for the Ainsworth may be mentioned—51 against the Ivy Club and 44 (including seven 4's) against the Rodney Club. For the Cambridge Liberals I scored 38 against Royston.

It was the habit of Tom Hayward to wind up every season by bringing a team to play on Parker's Piece for the benefit of the local hospital or some other charity. His eleven, mainly county players, met the pick of Cambridge. For years I had watched this match. In 1901, one team was, for some reason or other, a man short, and I was asked to make up. Never before had I played with first-class county players, and here was I taking part in a match against even the great Tom Hayward. I played his bowling quite well, in the opinion of my father, who umpired. My score was 26 not out. Then came another big step; I was asked to play for Cambridgeshire against Herts as an amateur. I went in Number 9 when things were going badly for our side and helped in a big stand with A. J. Rich, notching up 30 whilst he took his score to 92.

In the early Spring of 1902, I applied to the Bedford Grammar School for an engagement, and, on the strength of my cricket performances and character testimonials from friends, I got the job—my first employment as a professional. They engaged me for three summer months. My duties were to attend to the general ground-work in the mornings and to coach at the second nets in the late afternoons after the school-time finished. Harry Coulson, who hailed from Cambridge, coached at the first eleven net, with Cherry the groundsman. In between I got a little cricket, and the engagement served as a highly useful experience to me at that age—nineteen. During the Bedford period, I paid my first visit to London, going up with Coulson to umpire the Bedford School matches against St. Paul's School. He umpired the first eleven match and I the second. I was vastly impressed with the size of the Metropolis and all its bustling activity. The day-trip included an hour or two at the Tivoli music-hall.

At the end of the Bedford School term, I returned home, and soon afterwards earned my first fee for playing in a match. This match was between Royston and the Herts Club and Ground. Playing for Royston, I ran up a score of 119 and was loudly applauded on retiring. My pay was ten shillings and expenses. All Cambridge talked about this score, and my father was in raptures, although on a sick-bed.

A few days after my journey to Royston Heath, my father died. Alas, he never saw me play for a first-class county. Many a time since then the thought has come to me how sad it is that he is not alive to share in celebrating my success. Tom Hayward, generous as ever, collected a team to play a benefit match for my mother, which brought in a few hundred pounds and was a real help at a trying time. I was still in mourning and took no part on that occasion. During that winter, I carried on my father's duties until they fixed up with another groundsman early in the New Year.

My father's friends now recognised, as I did myself, that the time had arrived for me to enter seriously upon the career that I had marked out for myself, and one of those friends, Mr. F. C. Hutt, persuaded Tom Hayward that my record was sufficiently distinguished to justify him in giving me a trial. This was fixed up, and I batted for twenty minutes on Parker's Piece before him and William Reeves, of Essex. They were under no obligation to pronounce any verdict, but I was confident that I had done fairly well. All I gathered was a casual remark by Tom Hayward about seeing if I could have a trial in April at the Oval. The outcome of this remark was that for months I was in a perplexed state of mind, sometimes confident of success and at other times wondering whether anything whatever would result. What kept up my spirits most was a quiet feeling that Tom Hayward's recommendation would be sure to carry weight. In any case, I felt that, if they would only look at me in the nets, I could show enough form to get me a season's engagement.

Whilst I was still a little mystified about the future, Mr. Hutt thought that it would be as well for me to have two strings to my bow, and he very kindly suggested to the Essex County Club that they might do well to engage me. Without giving any reason, Essex declined to let me have even a trial. If there had been a different decision, I might have been playing for Essex for the last thirty years.

My shyness prevented me from worrying Tom Hayward about my future, but I constantly consulted Mr. Hutt, with the result that at last he was able to report that an appointment had been definitely made for me to have a trial at the Oval. The next thing that happened was that Tom Hayward sent for me and gave me full directions as to what I was to do.

The great day arrived. Off I went to London,

with bat and pads in a green carpet-bag. I had also a pair of buckskin boots—the first I ever owned and a present from my father. They were real buckskin and had been made out of a pair of buckskin breeches. I did not do what Bert Strudwick did when he went for his trial. His father insisted on his taking a set of stumps, and he arrived well loaded up. "Struddy" and I often laugh over that episode.

Between Liverpool Street and Kennington I had my first ride on a tube railway and thought its speed remarkable. All the time I was thinking how marvellous it was that I should be on the way to the Oval, the famous ground about which I had read so much. Tom Hayward had told me to ask, on arrival at the gates, for the Surrey coach, W. T. Grayburn. There were a number of other candidates for a trial, some of them nervous and some pretty confident. As it turned out, I was the only one to make good.

It occurs to me to put in here a word of advice to those young chaps who think that they deserve a trial by a county club. I frequently get letters from boys, and sometimes from their mothers, asking what are the right steps to take when one wants to become a county cricketer. They quote averages, some of them really absurd. They set out bowling analyses that represent quite inferior cricket. In their minds is always the notion that

I can engage them at the Oval. One word from me, and they will be straight away taken on—so they think. I was, however, just a servant of the Club and not even a member. I had no say or power. Naturally, if it so happened that I had seen a player in the field and knew all about him from my own experience, a recommendation from me would get him a good chance of a trial. The letters I receive are nearly always from people upon whom I have never set eyes. The best, and indeed the only, method of getting a trial is for a lad to write direct to the secretary of the county club of the particular county in which he was born.

There is no royal road to success in cricket. It is a rough, hard road, and only a few can win through. I always hesitate, when asked, to recommend county cricket as a career. Seek, first, a position in some business, so that there may be something tangible to fall back upon in case of failure at cricket or a dislike of it. It needs not only ability, but good fortune, to come off at the proper time. Luck is essential to success. The unplayable snorter may come along first ball, whereas the lucky man may not get it till he has hit up a century. There is little sometimes between nought and 100. Cricket is too precarious. It is all right if you can rise to the top and get the plums. Otherwise, it is a bare living for a few years, with nothing at the end; one saves a few pounds in the summer and spends them in the winter. Years of hard work are needed, and concentration, self-restraint, abstemiousness, and steadiness.

A youngster who has done well at school obviously cannot get a trial till he is eighteen or nineteen. From school to county cricket is a big step. A boy must practise all he can; he must get quickly into better-class cricket and play against better players than himself. That is the only way to bring out his best. To such a boy I say: "Always have a bat with you and make imaginary strokes until you can bring them off with perfect ease. Practise at the nets and on a good wicket, or even in the back garden with a tennis ball. Above all, watch the best players, either in matches or at the nets. Try always to improve the standard of your cricket."

Lads have a real advantage to-day; there are so many indoor schools of cricket where they can get early coaching, and, even in winter months, keep muscles loose and the eye keen.

I return to that eventful day, April 23rd, 1903, when Mac Jackson, with two or three others, bowled to me at the net at the Oval. I was in quite good form, and was told, after twenty minutes, that I was to play in a trial match the same day. I walked on air; I was really to play at last on that classic ground.

Those two excellent players, J. N. Crawford and N. A. Knox, were captains of the respective trial teams. I played for J. N. Crawford, and was a little nervous on going in. After hitting up 37, I pulled a ball from Mead on to my wickets. It was mortifying to be out, but only one score that day beat mine—53 by R. C. Oliver. Then I was given a turn with the ball, and my analysis was 24 runs, six overs, and no wickets. Evidently the authorities were pleased, for I was told to stay in London and to play in another trial match the next day.

Phil Mead, who was also in this trial match, was already on the staff, but later Surrey let him slip, and he migrated to Hants. In those days, he was not taking batting seriously; bowling was his forte. He afterwards took up batting with the great success that we all know.

I put up for the night with one of the professionals and went in the evening to see a variety show at Sadler's Wells, but thoughts of the next day's match interfered a good deal with my enjoyment of the performance. In this second trial match, I was bowled by Mead when I had reached the unlucky figure of 13. Once again, my bowling analysis was poor; it ran: nine overs; three maidens; twenty-six runs for no wickets. Still it was one of my really luckiest days, for Mr. Alcock, secretary of the Surrey County Club, sent for me and offered me an engagement to qualify for Surrey. At last I was on the first rung of the professional ladder. The offer involved, first of all, that I should reside in Surrey; secondly, that I should be on the ground staff, with a salary; and, finally, it meant that, if I showed promise, I should become a player for the county, thus fulfilling the ambition that had so long fired my blood.

My pay was to be thirty shillings a week in summer, with a pound a week winter retainer and out-of-pocket expenses in all Colts' matches. Small as that salary seems to-day, I felt at the time that it was big money. I went back to Cambridge, and, elated beyond measure, ran off to tell the news to Tom Hayward, who was highly pleased and congratulated me warmly. Later on, without my then knowing anything about it, he told Mr. Alcock what my circumstances were at home, and thus he was the means of obtaining a promise of an additional ten pounds as a bonus at the end of the season. This brought my summer pay to an average of two pounds a week.

It is only fair to professionals and to clubs to say that present-day salaries are much higher. Money, of course, went farther in those days.

I had no extravagances; I found that I had enough to live on and even to send a little home. The same pay and retainer were given me in my second year, and, in addition, a pound a day match money for all club and ground matches. I mention these details to show the difference between the pay then and now.

I took diggings in Fentiman Road, near the Oval, with Joe Bunyan, who was on the ground staff. He was a staunch friend and is to this day. He is still in the game and occupies the post of coach and groundsman at King's College School, Wimbledon.

CHAPTER IV
I QUALIFY FOR SURREY

M Y first season began with a sad set-back—a duck in the very first innings. I had come up to London on May Day, 1903, and played at the Oval on May 12th for the Surrey Colts against Battersea. I was first in and first out, without scoring, but I refused to be scared. When my second innings came, I set my teeth and scored 27 not out. The next day, against Barnes, my scores were 6 and 29 not out.

On May 27th came a match of special interest. It was my first Surrey Club and Ground match; our opponents were Guy's Hospital. I scored 86 and took one wicket for 23 runs, but the special interest was that, for the first time in my life, I saw Bobby Abel bat. He was a great cricketer and a charming, unassuming fellow. At that time, although he hit up 90, his best days were over, by reason of declining health and eye trouble. There is a peculiar story of his scoring 250 one day and then, in the pavilion, illustrating by various strokes how he ought to have played the ball that got his wicket. Most players would have wanted a rest after 250. I am reminded here of a story about Brockwell. Having failed to

44

score with a very excellent new bat, he told the pavilion attendant to bring a chopper, and, in front of several of the Surrey players, he chopped his perfect bat to bits.

Three of the matches in the following month seem worthy of mention. In one, against Heathfield, I scored 21 and took six wickets for 41 in eighteen overs. In another against Epsom College, going in seventh wicket, I scored 52 not out. The Prince of Wales (now King George) was present. In the third of these matches, after I had hit up 61 against Mitcham Wanderers, the ball struck my knee and turned me so faint that water had to be fetched. Before it came, rain stopped play. That season provided one other match of interest to me, in which, against Norbury Park, I had the pleasure of being associated with Abel in putting on 100 for first wicket.

Thus I was getting experience and meeting very good-class players. Some of the new men were putting up a hard struggle. I remember one young professional who was directed to remove his sweater when about to bowl, and was unable to obey because he had no shirt underneath. His one cricket shirt was at the wash.

My Club and Ground average for that first summer of my engagement was: Innings, 9; not out, 1; total, 241; highest score, 86; average, 30.12. My bowling analysis was: Overs, 45; maidens, 6;

runs scored, 131; wickets taken, 9; average, 14·5. I had done even better for the Colts, for my batting average showed: Innings, 10; times not out, 4; total score, 239; highest score, 61 not out; average, 39·83, which put me at the top of the Colts' averages. My bowling analysis for them was: Overs, 36; maidens, 4; runs scored, 139; wickets taken, 10; average, 13·9. It had been a really good season for me; I had every reason to look forward to the future with confidence.

I cannot say that I suffered, in my qualifying days, from any nervousness on my own account, but often I would tremble and shake like a leaf when Tom Hayward went in to bat, so wrapped up in my hero was I and so desperately anxious that he should do well. Although I do not experience what may be called stage-fright, I am highly strung—temperamental, if you like. Beforehand, half an hour, say, before batting, I am apt to imagine the bowlers to be better than they really are; I think of their deadliest balls and of myself being caught in the slips. Nevertheless, directly I am up and doing, these fancies all leave me.

A match that I saw at the Oval during this year, 1903, stands very distinctly in my recollection. The late Sam Hargreave, of Warwickshire, was just getting back from New Zealand. Rain prevented play on the first day; had there been play, he would have been out of the match, as he only arrived on the second day. However, he took six wickets for 40 in the first innings and nine for 35 in the second. Last summer, J. Catton, the well-known sports writer, gave me the ball presented to Hargreave in recognition of his feat. It has the following inscription on a silver band: "Surrey v. Warwickshire, Oval, 1903, 15 wickets for 75 Runs." Every match was a thrill to me then to watch. I rubbed shoulders with all the great players. It took me a long time to get used to the atmosphere, so novel was it to a country lad.

London life suited me to the ground. The streets, the shops, the parks, the theatres, the music-halls, the crowds everywhere, interested me immensely. Sometimes I visited the Camberwell Palace or the Canterbury, in Westminster Bridge Road. I saw all the stars—Little Tich, T. E. Dunville, Harry Tate, George Robey, Joe Elvin, Sir Harry Lauder, Arthur Roberts, Eugene Stratton, Harry Champion, Marie Lloyd, Sam Mayo, Charles Austin and Phil Ray. I liked them all; anything made me laugh. Phil Ray, a keen cricketer, later introduced Fred Holland, who was a Surrey professional cricketer, to the variety stage. On some evenings I listened to the band in Hyde Park. I also went to Madame Tussaud's. Everybody talked about the Chamber of Horrors, and naturally I wanted to see it; it seemed then pretty blood-curdling. Three or four years ago I visited that building to see my own image. It struck me as very funny that I should see myself almost twice my natural size. Such a big Jack Hobbs! The figures are raised on a platform and so have to be made larger than life. When my figure was first put in, I was in Australia, but I was told, in a letter, that they had called at my shop in Fleet Street and bought the best blazer, the best shirt, the best boots, and the best pads, so as to be certain to be correct. The joke of it was that the assistant supplied them with a gorgeous two-guinea white bat, straight-grained, without a flaw. As soon as they got it there, they painted it to make it look like an old bat.

Probably I was more familiar with London in those early days than I am now, for I was constantly strolling about. It was, and still is, to me a most wonderful place, and my experience is that country people get to know more about it than Londoners do themselves. I seldom miss the Boat-race or any Oxford and Cambridge matches. At one 'Varsity Boat-race, years later, I was on the Press launch, doing a report for a Sunday paper. At times I was almost level with the crews; it was a great treat.

I have never seen the Derby. The turf makes no appeal to me. I do not see how one can go

LORD MOYNIHAN

THE GROUND AT BATH WHERE THE 100TH CENTURY WAS SCORED

to the races without having a bet, and I am against gambling on any sport, especially on cricket or football, and try to keep all youngsters away from the betting habit. I play games for the sake of sport. Cricket, according to my experience, is a clean game; I cannot imagine a game that is cleaner. Never have I seen any betting in connection with it.

When the first winter in London came, I joined the Cyprus Club, where I played a little billiards, ping-pong, whist, bagatelle, etc. I kept good hours and never drank much. I got a good deal of enjoyment out of football, playing for the Cyprus Club as centre forward. It was something to look forward to all the week, planning the sides and weighing up positions in the League. We belonged to the Dulwich League and played at Gorringe Park. Our position at the end of the season was not too bad—about half-way in the list.

Mr. King, the Cyprus Club's hon. secretary, took me up West to my first dinner in Soho. It was at the Hôtel d'Italie, in Old Compton Street —eight courses for half a crown. What more do you want? We had no wine. I marvelled how they did it at the price and made a profit. In those days, when I knew that I was going out to dine in the evening, I was excited all day. To-day it is doubtful whether I enjoy my food so much

4

as I did when I was young. To go out to dinner or to a place of amusement I have found an excellent plan, because it helps me to forget the day's cricket. It is always wise to stop thinking about it at night and come back fresh to it next day. After breakfast next morning is quite early enough to worry your mind about your chances.

When the second year of my engagement opened, I had the satisfaction of feeling that I was no longer in a position like that of a new boy at school. I really belonged now to the Oval; I was part and parcel of that famous ground. During that second year, 1904, all the matches were Club and Ground; none were Colts'. Amongst my best scores were 96 against St. Thomas's Hospital and 90 against Wimbledon. In a match against Streatham, I had real bad luck, as I had thoroughly mastered the bowling and had reason to hope for the much-desired century, when I was run out at 73. My season's batting average for the Club and Ground was 43·9 in eleven innings.

At this period I was asked to play a few times for Cambridgeshire and thus got an experience of second-class cricket. In a match against Oxford, I scored 54 and 52—for the first time getting half a century in both innings. More important still was a match against Norfolk, in which I piled up 92, taking two hours and a half over the job.

This was a real test match for me, for I knew that I was being specially watched on behalf of the Surrey authorities. Against Hertfordshire, at Fenner's, I scored 195 and, later on, 129 in the return match against Hertford, which county I came to regard as, for me, a distinctly lucky one. One of these Hertford matches produced the first Press report that caused me to realise that I was getting well into the public eye.

My average of 58 for thirteen innings stood at the head of the Cambridgeshire averages. I mention the averages of that season solely as proof of how I was getting on. In my opinion, the publication of averages in newspapers is detrimental to first-class cricket. A batsman is thus often stopped from playing his natural game. He cannot help visualising in his mind's eye the effect that averages will have on the public and on his friends. Some time or other, he will deliberately or subconsciously play for the benefit of his average, instead of playing to entertain the spectators. A player may fail several times and then come back into the averages with a score of, say, 200 not out against a weak county, whilst some other player, who is getting his 30 or 40 or 50 all the time, with perhaps one failure, is well down on the list. It is a strongly held view of mine that the abolition of the publishing of averages would tend to bring about brighter cricket.

Of course, there is a time for everything. If it is evident that playing "doggo" is necessary in the interests of the side, then it is selfish to go out for runs. It is the side that counts; to play in any other spirit is not to play the real game. I doubt if Frank Woolley, most brilliant of players, has ever been at the top of the averages. Probably he could have been without difficulty if he had elected, after getting 100, to play for safety, instead of trying to hit a few more sixes. In that case, however, he would not have been so popular a favourite on all grounds all over the world. Often he threw his wicket away in his determination to entertain the crowd. No one could accuse him of playing for his average. As regards myself, I have never allowed my average to interfere with my cricket. If I had done so, I could possibly have made a better show in the list of averages. I have sometimes thrown away my wicket in trying to provide bright cricket for the public.

The last event of 1904 that comes to my memory is a match at the Mecca of the game— Lord's ground. I played for George Robey's Eleven against Cross Arrows, which was a Lord's staff team. My score was 55, which was the top score of either side; it included seven 4's. Robey was a great patron of sport; he played cricket and also, for Millwall, football. Many leading actors have been keen cricketers, among them Oscar Asche, who, whenever he practised at the Oval, used to put coins on the stumps.

Amongst those playing on that occasion in George Robey's team were G. L. Jessop and the late Albert Trott. Two of the Hearnes were playing on the Cross Arrows side. They are a wonderful cricketing family. Jessop was a masterly player; no bowling had any fears for him. He was a useful bowler, but as a fielder he was superb. We have had many duels. I am sometimes spoken of as the patentee of short runs, and, on a certain occasion, after I had run a short one, I said to him: "I hope you don't mind." He replied: "Not at all; I reckon it's two to one on me." I said: "I don't think so; I wouldn't attempt it unless I reckoned it two to one on me." A little later, he had a chance of running me out and—missed the wicket. I should have been well out if he had hit it. But there was no bet. Jessop was about the finest cover-point ever seen on a cricket field. Here is a point worth remembering on that subject. When fielding at cover, always, if returning a ball to the wicket-keeper, throw a catch and never a long hop; aim at his chest, just above the stumps.

Whilst the late Albert Trott was a great player, he was disappointing as an umpire. I suffered on two occasions. Once, in a Sussex match, bowling round the wicket, "Razor" Smith sent down an off-spinner to A. E. Relf and appealed for l.b.w. It looked a case, but Trott said: "Not out," much to Smith's disgust. The next delivery was a fast straight one; Smith appealed again. "That *is* out," said Trott. Everyone smiled, except Relf. We still chip Relf about those two decisions.

A story is told of an umpire who disliked too many appeals. A batsman was standing with his knee behind the bat, and the bowler hit him on the leg three times successively and appealed. "Not out," was the umpire's verdict each time. At the end of the over, the umpire said to the bowler: "That's because you always appeal too much." When the same bowler was to begin his next over, the umpire remarked: "I've told that fellow to shift his leg." The bowler got him first ball. Another umpire story concerns T. Oates, of Notts. He was umpiring, and W. Reeves, of Essex, was bowling. The batsman was smartly taken at the wicket. "How's that?" said Oates, forgetting that he was umpiring. "Out," answered Reeves in a second, and the batsman walked off.

One of the best umpires is Chester, who lost an arm in the war and was made an umpire. On the whole, umpiring is very good in first-class cricket. If there are bad umpires, it is partly due to their being put on the list when they are too old. I would not take the post for any consideration. It is hard work, with more kicks than halfpence. The umpire is in the field all the time that the match lasts and gets very little glory out of it.

The value of good umpiring to a player cannot be overstated. The batsman has no qualms; he can go in with all confidence and play his natural game. Moreover, the bowler knows how useless it is to make frivolous appeals. Thus the game becomes much more enjoyable. Bad umpires fray the tempers of players. My sympathy goes out to the Saturday afternoon and club players, who, I am told, suffer from umpiring of a very indifferent character. The unfortunate batsman is given out l.b.w. wherever the ball hits him and wherever it pitches, so long as the umpire cannot see the wickets. Many umpires do not understand the l.b.w. rule and do not attempt to; yet it is so simple that the failure of so many to grasp it is amazing. A mistake by a football referee is seldom fatal—say, for instance, a wrongly given free kick. More often than not, it comes to nothing. In the case of a batsman, it is either out or not out. Obviously, it isn't cricket for a cricketer to take advantage of poor umpiring, when it clearly is a case of "not out." I fear that club cricket is often spoilt by the partiality of umpires, and the remedy would appear to lie in having a properly constituted Umpires' Association.

My season's engagement finished on the last day of August, but there was a later match at the Oval against Leicester, and I fielded in the long field as a substitute, bringing off three catches from "Razor" Smith's bowling. This brought me five pounds from the Club for services as "reserve field." I was also a "sub" for Hants that year in a match that gave me the chance of catching out the captain of my own Club, Lord Dalmeny (now Earl of Rosebery). A hit from him was going straight for the stand when I brought off a catch with both arms extended above my head.

Undoubtedly, I was in good form in that second season. All that second-class cricket, with a little first class, was the stepping-stone towards getting into the Surrey Eleven. I was indeed coming off at the right time. My own idea was that the Club would put me, in 1905, into its Second Eleven, but, as it turned out, I went right past that straight into the County team. Not many professionals are able to say, as I can, that they have never played in their county's Second Eleven.

CHAPTER V

I BECOME A COUNTY PLAYER

APRIL 15th, 1905, was a noteworthy day for me. When I went into the players' room at the Oval, a list posted up caught my eye, and on it was my name as one of the probable team for the opening match of the season on Easter Monday. Imagine my excitement; after thirty years, I can still recall what I felt about it. I also remember the shoals of congratulations that reached me. The match was to be between Surrey, captained by Tom Hayward, and the Gentlemen of England under the captaincy of Dr. W. G. Grace.

As it turned out, Dr. Grace's team was certainly strong enough to terrify any beginner, including as it did G. Beldam, W. Brearley, V. F. S. Crawford, A. E. Lawton, C. Robson, E. H. D. Sewell, and C. L. Townsend. However, I felt fit, keen and happy. To my great astonishment, Tom Hayward took me in with him to open the innings. I looked upon it as a wonderful compliment. Moreover, it saved me the worry of sitting about, fretting for my time to go in. Hanging around undoubtedly causes an anxious state of mind likely to affect run-getting. There is, on the other hand, a real disadvantage in

57

having to face the bowlers when they are fresh and have the use of a new ball, and when the fielders are most on the alert. Indeed, I sometimes thought that I would prefer to bat when the edge had been taken off the bowling. The biggest drawback of all is to have to start batting at half-past five or six o'clock after a day in the field.

As we walked out to the middle, Tom said to me: "We'll go all out for that first single." We did so; each of us got one in the first over. Every batsman tries his best to break his duck, and feels more comfortable when that calamity is escaped. When I had hit up 18, Townsend caught me in the slips off a swinger from Beldam. Tom was bowled by Beldam for 9, and Ernie Hayes knocked up 18. Nothing worth talking about happened in that first innings. We were all out for 86, Hayes and I tying as top scorers. The Gentlemen were all out for the modest total of 115, to which "W.G.'s" contribution was only 12. Then Tom took me in again, to open our second innings, and there was a lively change from the tameness of the morning. After an hour's batting, we were still together at close of play. I had scored 44 and was well content. In the evening, I went to the Tivoli, in the Strand, buying on the way a copy of the old red *Star*, to see what it had to say about my initial appearance for Surrey. The Tivoli of those days was not the large, artistic building of to-day; it was, however, one of the leading variety shows, and its "turns" were on a level with those of the Pavilion and the Oxford. It was the fashion to go to a show in a hansom, as one would to-day in a taxi.

I doubled my score next day; but what the Press described as an "admirable innings" was ended at 88 by a catch at square leg when I tried to pull a ball from Brearley. "I should drop that stroke if I were you," said Brearley, as I went off. I did not, however, quite drop it, but practised at it, until I learnt how to hook. Unless you know how to manage it, it is a dangerous stroke. A ball of good length cannot be pulled; you must wait for a short one. I find it easier to pull when the ball is outside the off-stump, but you must be quick on your feet and get across. The danger of attempting to pull a straight-pitched ball is that it might keep low, and then it is difficult to get the bat to it, and you are not in position to change the stroke. When the ball is outside the off-stump and keeps low, your wicket is not in danger if you miss it.

In his second innings, Dr. Grace got 32, and the match was drawn. The Surrey secretary, Mr. Alcock, told me that he was very pleased with the way in which I had stood up to "W.G.", who, he said, was "very artful at getting out youngsters." To show how cute the Doctor was in that match, I remember that, when I played a ball towards cover and was considering whether I would run or not, he called out in his thin, squeaky voice: "That's right, youngster. Hit it up." That stopped me from running. It was a great pleasure to see the Doctor bat. I played against him a few more times, but never saw him when he was at his greatest. My last sight of him was at Catford, in a charity match, when he was only looking on. He seemed to push his way to come over to say a few words to me, which pleased me tremendously, as he picked me out when many older players were in the pavilion. His kindliness on that occasion caused me to think that he must have had a good bedside manner.

"W.G." was a most remarkable man in appearance, huge in size, with a big, shaggy beard, a high-pitched voice, and the quaintest of tiny caps on his head. Looking at his brawny arms, one realised that there was sure to be a boundary hit if he got behind the ball. Up to the age of fifty he was still good enough to be included in a representative all-England Eleven, and he went on playing till he was sixty-five. He died at sixty-seven, in the same year in which he paid me that compliment at Catford.

I pass over a day or two to the first occasion on which I played in a match against a first-class county. This was a match on May 4th, 5th, and 6th, against Essex at the Oval. Again Tom

Hayward took me in first. My score was 28; but in the second innings I had become more at ease and knocked up 155. To get a century at my debut in first-class county cricket was marvellous good fortune. I had certainly not expected to accomplish that feat at first go-off. My 155 included three 5's and nineteen 4's, and I was batting for three hours. At the end of the match, I caught my old friend and well-wisher, W. Reeves, rather well in the long field, and, as we walked off the field, the crowd were most enthusiastic, greeting me on all sides with shouts of "Good old Hobbs!" As one outcome of that eventful day, Lord Dalmeny gave me my cap; it is a rare occurrence for a cricketer to gain this distinction after his second match. I was evidently beginning to justify the hopes entertained of me by the Surrey authorities.

The bat with which that century was scored is in my possession to-day, but it was not mine then. It belonged to Mr. Hamish Stuart, who brought it to me the day before the match and asked me to use it, saying: "I always bring luck to people." Not caring for it after trying it, I used one of my own in the first innings; but, on the second day, some mysterious whim caused me to ask for Mr. Stuart's bat, and with it I knocked up the 155. Sixteen years afterwards, the bat was generously given to me by Mr. Stuart's widow.

Among those who were impressed by my 155 in my first county match was the poet of the Oval, Craig. His walk in life was to turn the outstanding events of the cricketing world into poetic form, and he was allowed to travel round the ground daily selling his rhymes. My score was duly honoured by him, and I suppose that many of my friends purchased the effort in which he assured them that "Surrey's coming man caused gladness to his clan." Craig went all over the place, even into our dressing-room. In course of time, his scope of action became subject to certain limitations. Though dead a few years, he is still a memory to many Londoners and others.

As I managed to score 102 against Essex in the return match at Leyton, it really looked as if the luckiest county for me was the very one that had turned me down. A Cambridge newspaper remarked at the time: "The more Hobbs flourishes, the keener becomes the regret that he is lost to Cambridgeshire. The regret of Essex must be equally keen, for Hobbs at one time offered them his services, but they failed to discover his talent and so lost a fine cricketer."

On May 11 came a great match against the Australians, whose team was Armstrong, Cotter, Darling, Duff, Clem Hill, A. J. Hopkins, Kelly, Laver, McLeod, Noble and Trumper. "This will be his real trial," said a newspaper, referring to me. Such a comment seemed a little unkind; some of my "trials" to date had been real enough in all conscience. Anyhow, I accepted the challenge, and, wearing my brand-new Surrey cap, went in with Tom Hayward and nearly got a century.

Here is what happened. At 93, I made a hit to the square-leg boundary, ran one and tried to run another. Clem Hill threw the ball in from the boundary, and, although almost square with the wicket, hit the stumps. I was out for 94. Even to-day I still think that I just got home in time, but it was a magnificent throw, and Clem Hill himself, so I am told, felt a pang of pity for his victim. A century in those days against Australia would have meant a collection, and it would have perhaps been a hundred pounds. I was both pleased and disappointed, if it is possible to be both. According to the Press, I gave two chances during the innings; my own idea is that I gave four. The Press treated me very handsomely in its comments on the day's proceedings, one newspaper going so far as to say that I played more like a veteran than like a youngster who had only played in three first-class matches in his life.

The two teams were invited to the Canterbury music-hall that night, and the audience, seeing us, called loudly for Hobbs. I nearly got under my seat. I took my first wicket in first-class cricket on the following day, my analysis being one wicket for 13 runs. I was caught out for 1, but Tom Hayward put up a splendid 129 not out. The match was drawn.

Thanks to that genius, Sam Apted, the groundsman, the Oval pitch was in beautiful condition for that match. He was lord and master there; if a blade of grass were plucked I fancy that he would have missed it. How he stormed at us if we went near the "middle" when we were practising! Once, when some of us were at the nets, a man started to cross the ground. "Look at that chap," we called out. Old Sam was furious and shouted at the man. I said to Sam: "Be careful, that's Mr. Raphael." "Sorry, sir," said Sam to the man, "I didn't know it was you." Then it suddenly dawned on Sam that it was a stranger after all, and not Mr. Raphael, and he became more furious than before, whilst we roared with laughter.

There was a truly sensational finish to the second match against the Australians, which took place in July. Their first innings score was 241, and ours 357, Tom Hayward hitting up 70 and I 58. We thus put on 100 for first wicket. Then the Australians made 271, leaving us 156 to get for victory. In a sporting, but suicidal, spirit, we batted against the clock. I was run out for 4; two others were run out, but Tom scored 52. Ultimately we lost by 22. I have never forgotten the fine way in which we played the true game, instead of going for a draw.

A match against Middlesex followed. They only put up 146 in the first innings, the fiery wicket being the very thing for fast bowlers. We replied with 116. Then Middlesex scored 137, leaving us 168 to get to win. On such a wicket, against a strong attack, we didn't greatly fancy our chances. However, Tom scored 82 not out, and I scored 75 not out; and Surrey won by ten wickets. It was then the custom that any man who captured the ball at the end of a match of that kind was entitled to keep it. I cut the last ball to third man, and, after completing the run, there was a rush for it by Tom Hayward and Albert Trott, I also joining in the chase. Whilst the two were struggling on the ground, I tried to hit it away, but Trott covered it with his big hand, and the trophy was his.

A match against Kent had a sensational finish. Kent scored 202 and 84; as we had only replied with 125, there remained 162 to be got. We reached 161, and Colin Blythe, who was famous for left-hand slows, was bowling to "Razor" Smith, who had, of course, only to obtain one more run for victory. Having called his fielders close in, Blythe sent up a slow, wide ball, and Smith was caught at third man. A less cunning bowler would have sent up a fast ball, but the result proved the

5

wisdom of Blythe's tactics. Sad to say in 1917, the Great War robbed England of poor Colin Blythe.

At last the time came for my holidays. I wanted them badly, for I had worked hard, and the weight of my responsibilities had told upon me. In fifty-four innings I had scored an aggregate of 1,317 runs; I had been three times not out, and my top score had been 155. Nevertheless, my average, 25·82, showed that the high rate of achievement at the start had not been kept up to the finish. In other words, the strain of the task in the course of time had affected me, especially when that task involved two matches a week. As a set-off to my feeling of staleness was the fact that the authorities, so far from criticising, were satisfied with their new recruit.

Although everything was all serene as far as the Surrey Club was concerned, two or three journalists ventured to suggest that my fielding had not been good. This complaint was not fair. The worst that had happened was a little fumbling in the long field on a day when I was not feeling quite up to the mark. To seize on that as an excuse for describing me as a bad field was overdoing the blame. There were two factors that, to a certain limited extent, tended to affect my fielding. One was that my arm used to ache from throwing; the other was that the comments of certain spectators sometimes unsettled me. Surely it is only right that the attitude of the crowd should be one of encouragement, and not of disparaging criticism, to a youngster who is doing his best! I do not pretend that I was as good a fieldsman at first as I was later on; naturally, experience brought improvement. However, all that criticism soon disappeared, and there is a standard book on cricket which maintains that I became "one of England's best covers."

At the outset, any new man has to serve a sort of apprenticeship and is placed in the long field or deep third man, and is general utility man. I had to do my share of chasing round the boundary. Soon after Lord Dalmeny gave up the captaincy, I somehow got to cover point. I was very keen and quickly made that position my own particular play. I was never a long thrower, but was very quick and accurate for short distances. I developed the knack of getting rid of the ball quickly. To be a good cover point, it is essential that you pick up the ball and return in one action; the same rule applies to any position near the wicket.

It is a good tip to be always walking towards the batsman as the bowler delivers the ball. It is also a good idea to lead the batsman to believe that there is a safe run. It might be a good plan to give him an easy single, or perhaps two, in the hope of running him out on the third occasion. Do not show a new batsman all your tricks; let him find out. Do not waste your smartest returns, but reserve them until there is a fifty-fifty chance of running the man out. Some fielders, in playing to the gallery, expose all their tricks; they pick up and return brilliantly when there is no earthly possibility of getting a wicket. Always remember that a run saved is a run made. I was the new cover point in the Australian Tour of 1911–12. The Australian batsmen would keep on running to me, would not be "druve," would not give in to me, and persisted in running. Consequently, during that tour, I ran out no fewer than seventeen batsmen.

It would have been very pleasant if the easy time of that autumn holiday could have lasted without interruption until my second season at the Oval opened. There was, however, an interruption of a most unpleasant nature. I had gone down to Cambridge and had been received there as a popular hero. One day, however, when I was cycling at great speed down Gog Magog Hill, I struck a bank and went over the handlebars. The result was a gash in my knee that took a long time to heal up; indeed, I have the scar to-day. I was laid up for a month.

It was in 1905 that a very unpleasant rumour went the round about me. I happened to be given a rest from a match against one of the

Universities, and from some source a scandalous story was spread that I had got drunk, that I had sworn at Lord Dalmeny, and that I had been sacked by the Club. Some person, pretending to possess a secret, made up this rubbish as an explanation of my absence. The tale was, of course, false in every particular. Although I was not an out-and-out abstainer in those days, I hardly took anything in the way of stimulants. I never had the taste for beer, wine or spirits, and, consequently, it was easy for me to be abstemious. At a later date, I did get to like a glass of champagne when I was dining out; but, after a while, I found that even that did not agree with me and sometimes gave me a nasty headache on the following day.

After my operation for appendicitis in 1921, Sir Berkeley Moynihan, now Lord Moynihan, who had performed the operation, begged me to give up all alcoholic liquor and all smoking. I had occasion to consult him two years later, and he repeated this very strong advice. It was no difficulty for me to stop my very occasional glass of wine, but I have never had the courage to quit smoking. To-day I still smoke more than is, perhaps, good for me. Strudwick is one of those who used to chaff me about my old pipe, which, however, I have often found a true comforter when everything was going badly. George Hirst is a great lover of the pipe. As for cigarettes, if you wish to remain in the pink of condition, keep well away from them. I have always drunk tea, which is said to affect the nerves of some people; it has never made me nervous. Milk I like, and I have a partiality for soda and milk. Ginger-beer is a special favourite, and if of a really good brand is excellent, but a really good brand is not always at hand. My usual cricketing lunch is a joint, cold for choice, salad, fruit and cream, ginger-beer or ginger-ale.

Some cricketers are fond of a glass of beer and believe that it helps them to maintain stamina. Without denying it, and without having any desire to force my opinion upon anyone, I can say with confidence that I have known cricketers to ruin their careers through indulgence, whereas in all my long experience I have never come across any cricketer who has blighted his career through being a teetotaller. I was teetotal all my boyhood and most of my life very abstemious. For twelve years I have been a strict abstainer, for which I take no credit, because I have ceased to care for alcohol. As my friends know that I am T.T., they just don't bother me to come and have one. The man to be admired is, I think, he who, having had a drink, has the strength of mind to say "No" to a second, but the teetotaller's plan is easier and needs no courage, because his pals are aware that he cannot be tempted to have a "wee drappie."

CHAPTER VI

SOME MORE COUNTY MATCHES

I FIND it interesting, in looking back to the events of my second season in 1906, to note the evidence that I was making substantial progress. We started by beating the Gentlemen of England by eight wickets. "W.G." was their captain again, but was not in form, only scoring 21 and 1. My two scores were 29 and 85 not out, which was just the sort of beginning that was calculated to inspire me for the tasks that were to follow. One of my convictions is that a successful start means a successful season. I have many other quaint fancies, such as putting on a particular glove first and a particular pad, walking out from the pavilion on a particular side, disliking to be on certain scores, such as 13, 31, and all scores ending in 9, and hurrying to get off such scores.

Not only am I superstitious, but I am also sensitive. People who know me only slightly sometimes come into my dressing-room and begin chatting to me when I am preparing to go in to bat. They gossip about incidents in my career, how they were present when I scored a duck, how they liked or disliked something else, or some other bit of pestering chatter. If I suggest that I am too preoccupied to discuss any topic whatever, they set me down as churlish. A prominent artist stopped me once just as I was walking out to bat in a Gentlemen *v*. Players match at Lord's and asked me to fix an appointment for him to paint my portrait. I was "strung up" and could not concentrate on anything else than my job. I could not possibly stop to talk or bring my mind to consider dates, and he went off in a huff. I write this protest not because I am thinking of myself, but because I want those who read these lines to show consideration at all times when the thoughts of cricketers must be concentrated on the innings ahead of them.

Of my fifty-three innings in the 1906 season, I will only mention half a dozen. The finish of Surrey *v*. Worcestershire seems well worth recording. We had to get 286 when the last innings began, and, after we had lost four wickets for 112, J. H. Gordon and I succeeded in knocking up the necessary runs, and we won by six wickets. My score was 162 not out, and the crowd in front of the pavilion insisted on a subscription on the spot, the result of which was thirty pounds for my pocket. Yorkshire, which had, along with Surrey, a distinct chance of winning the County Championship, met us next and lost by nine wickets. The game attracted 80,000 people, which was a slice of good luck for Walter Lees, whose benefit it was. I scored 34 and 22. A match against Kent we lost by one wicket, amidst great excitement. When the last man came in, 19 runs were still required. It was a thrilling finish, especially for Kent spectators. This was F. Woolley's first match against Surrey.

Altogether I got four centuries that year—one each in the two matches against Worcester; one against Essex, my favourite opponents; and one against Middlesex. My batting average was 40·70 for the fifty-three innings. As regards bowling, my best feat was against Notts on August Bank Holiday. When the Notts score had reached 349 for six, the crowd at the Oval became tired of the procession of runs. I went on to bowl about six o'clock and took three wickets for three runs. The crowd showed their appreciation by a storm of cheers.

Apart from the centuries, there was a new record in my career in a match against Hampshire that year. It was the first first-class match in which I scored more than 50 in each innings; the exact scores were 79 and 69. In the first innings I ran a 6 to get my 50, and in the second I ran a 5 with the same object in view. A professional, in those days, received as "talent money" £1 extra for scoring 50; £2 for 100; £3 for 150, and so on, together with £1 extra for a victorious match. In a few cases, these amounts were larger, Middlesex professionals getting, for example, a higher rate for beating Surrey. Such increases were invidious, as Middlesex recognised later on by abolishing the system. To-day there is a fairer method of awarding "talent money" by marks, and even 20 runs may earn a mark. There are also marks for fielding, which in the old days brought no talent money.

Professional cricketers are different in one respect from professional footballers; we have to pay our own railway fares and hotel bills when we are playing away from our own county, and buy our own kit. The scorer generally fixed up our hotel arrangements. In the evenings, we have various amusements. Some play bridge; some go to cinemas; I am fond of both. In London, it pleases me most to spend the evening at my own home, varied by a short stroll and winding up with wireless and a little music, in which I take a great delight. As regards exercise in the winter, in order to keep myself in fit condition, I have played football, golf and Badminton. The last-named is a game that calls for much skill in smashing the shuttle with a sharp, downward stroke and also in dropping the shuttle just over the net, whilst one gets plenty of running about.

When not playing for my county, I was invited to play in some out-of-the-way matches in 1906.

For instance, at Luton, I played for the South Kensington Cricket Club against Luton Town, and hit up 116 and 105—two centuries on one day. At a dinner in the following winter, this South Kensington Club gave me a set of silver salt-cellars, in recognition of my assistance to them and as a wedding present. The presentation was followed by my first speech in public, of which I will say nothing here.

A curious experience befell me at that time as the outcome of a visit to Clapham Common, where I went to watch a friend play. Some team or other had failed to turn up, and the rival team asked my friend and his party to make up a match. I was invited to join in, and I hit up a century, knocking some of the balls into the pond. Then I started to bowl and had the ill luck to smash the finger of a detective, who was in the opposing team. I approached to apologise, and, as we were standing around, he exclaimed: "I've got you set; I know who you are." His friends wondered what kind of criminal I might be, but he only told them my name at the end of the game, when they were as delighted as if I had been Crippen!

That reminds me of a small match at St. Quintin's Park, where, after the opposite side had only scored about 75, I went in, and we were expected by the crowd to knock off the runs for first wicket. I was out to a long hop, and the first two wickets fell for 10. On the way to the pavilion, I heard a local supporter say: "That's what some more of you county cricketers will get when you come down here."

This year, 1906, saw my marriage to Miss Ada Ellen Gates, of Cambridge. After I had left the St. Matthew's choir, I continued to go to the church with some of my chums. I met Miss Gates one evening after church. Her early impression of me was that I was very shy, and she had the idea of introducing me to someone else. I started courting very young—at seventeen, to be precise—and it gave me another interest in life. I became even more keen to realise my ambition. I wanted to win her admiration, and it appeared to me that, the more successful I was, the more she would look up to me. In my opinion, courtship smartens up one's ideas all round, and it certainly was a fine stimulus to me in my early career to have somebody to share in my success.

We were married at Cambridge, at St. Matthew's Church, on September 26th, 1906. We wanted a quiet wedding and consequently kept it as much a secret beforehand as possible. The only colleagues of mine who were present were Bill Hitch, with whom I was then lodging, and Tom Rushby, who was staying at Hitch's home near Newmarket. Several Cambridge people wondered why Tom Hayward was not invited, but the fact was that, although I had been associated with him for two cricket seasons, I had not lost that feeling of awe of him. I did not think that the wedding would be grand enough for him or that I should be able to accommodate him in the style that his position warranted. He sent me a very charming wedding present. I was also much pleased with a clock that Lord Dalmeny sent in honour of the occasion, and there were gifts from most of my cricketing colleagues. Telegrams with good wishes arrived at the church on the wedding-day from all parts of the country.

A fortnight's honeymoon at Hastings followed. We were ideally happy, as all people ought to be in early married life. I still had to live in Surrey; so we rented a little flat in Denmark Hill, and there my first boy, Jack, was born on July 29th, 1907. Never have I regretted the step that I took in getting married. It is an ordinary thing to say, but it is said with every justification in my case. I have had a most happy married life, and I still claim to be a happily married man. I am a rare home-bird. Many people who go abroad get the wanderlust, but it has the opposite effect upon me. To-day I am more a home-bird than ever before. I have visited some great countries, have made great friends, and had great times, and still I say: "East, West, Home's Best."

The year 1907 was the year in which I made one of the worst starts in my life. At the annual match against the Gentlemen of England, although we won by nine wickets, I was bowled by R. T. Crawford when I had only made 2. This was my third encounter with "W.G." Again, in a match against Notts on Whit-Monday, my scores were a duck in the first innings and 1 in the second, thus bringing me nearer than at any other time to the calamity of "bagging a brace." However, a match at Edgbaston against Warwickshire gave me a chance to recover my reputation, as on the one day into which the match was compressed, the two previous days being blank by reason of rain, I carried my bat through the whole innings for 60 runs. It was my first innings without dismissal from start to finish, and I had an additional cause to regard it as a good display of batting, as I was at the crease for just on two and a half hours, on a wicket of the consistency of pitch.

June, 1907, brought me a novelty in the shape of a partnership record. Tom Hayward and I for first wicket hit up between us 105 and 125 against Cambridge University, and, in the same week, followed with 147 and 105 for first wicket against Middlesex. To manage these continued first-wicket totals four times running in one week was something out of the ordinary, and has indeed never been repeated in county cricket. Of my other scores in that year I may mention 82 against Northants, which represented my completion of 1,000 runs in first-class cricket; 150 not out against Warwickshire, my first century for 1907, which brought me a telegram asking me to play for the Players at Lord's; 166 not out against Worcestershire, which was my top score up to that date; 135 against Hants; and 110 against Worcestershire, which was quick scoring, as it was all knocked up before lunch on the first day.

Of all the cricket of the year, the Gentlemen *v.* Players match at Lord's every July stands first and foremost. For more than seventy years a similar match has been played at the Oval, and there have been nearly fifty matches of that kind at Scarborough in its Festival Week at the end of the season. None of these, however, has the prestige of the Lord's match, which represents the game's high-water mark. I had been asked to be one of the Players at the Oval contest, but now at last I was one of the Eleven really representing the professionals of the land.

What was the result? Failure! In the Gentlemen *v.* Players match at the Oval I scored 5 and 19. At Lord's my score was 2 and 9. And this was the annual match in which I was in later life to score centuries four years running. The tale of my disgrace at Lord's is soon told; a ball from W. Brearley, which kept low and which I tried to hook, proved my downfall in the first innings, and, on the second day, I was caught at the wicket from a ball of Brearley's which rose sharply. Wisden's comment ran as follows: "Hobbs on his form fully deserved the compliment of being picked for the professionals, but he failed."

I have more of a liking for Lord's ground to-day than I had then. It used to seem to me uncomfortable as regards watching the game, and the lunch served to us was very poor. I always felt at Lord's that a professional was looked down upon. However, about thirteen years ago, arrangements were made for the professionals to lunch with the amateurs, and the catering is excellent. Things all round have so much improved that I would as readily play there as on any ground outside the Oval.

The disappointments of that July were all cleared out of my mind when the following letter reached me in August from Mr. (now Sir) F. E. Lacey, secretary of the M.C.C.:

"DEAR SIR,
"The Committee of the M.C.C. are sending an England team to Australia in September. I have been instructed to invite you to accompany the team. The terms of engagement are

FIRST TEST PARTNERSHIP WITH SUTCLIFFE, BIRMINGHAM, 1924

HOBBS AND D. R. JARDINE GOING IN TO BAT; "WILL HOBBS HIT THOSE 9?"

P. G. H. FENDER TAKING OUT A DRIN AFTER THE EQUALLING OF TI RECORD

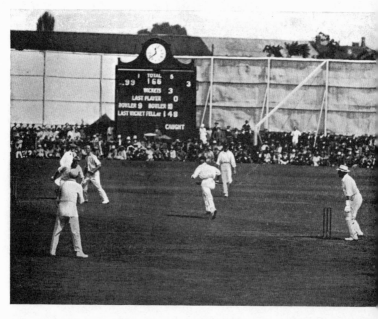

THE ACTUAL RUN THAT EQUALLED GRACE'S RECORD OF CENTURIES

embodied in the enclosed agreement. If you accept the invitation, please sign and return the agreement."

This was, of course, far and away the greatest honour that could be showered upon me at that time.

I will not deny that I had some sort of hope that I might be selected. There were hints in the Press that I stood a chance of getting into the team for "down under." One sports-writer boldly advocated my inclusion. He wrote: "Hobbs might with advantage be taken to Australia this winter. He has the proper temperament for cricket and is always seen at his best upon the very fast wickets which have usually to be played on in the Antipodes." Cheering as it was to read the suggestion in various newspapers, the fact remained that Tom Hayward and three or four others had claims stronger than mine. Some of them were, however, not satisfied with all the terms of the agreement and were not prepared to go. So it all came right, and here was I, whose highest ambition had been to play for Surrey, suddenly promoted to be a member of an England touring team.

There was only one fly in the ointment; the prolonged separation from my wife was the disturbing factor, especially in view of the fact that a son and heir had come to us a few days

6

before the invitation. This difficulty, however, was surmounted by my wife's recognising at once that to go was to obey the call of duty. So I accepted and began to make arrangements for the first of the series of big overseas trips which were to be my lot.

The 1907 season had embraced a few failures, but a great many successes. Four centuries stood to my credit, and on the list of county averages my name stood number eight. Here are the figures: Innings, 63; runs, 2,135; times not out, 6; highest score, 166 not out; average, 37·45.

At the end of the season, I went to Scarborough to play against the South Africa team in the Festival Week. Here I knocked up 78, which was quite a decent finish to my aggregate for the year. A week later, the Orient liner *Ophir* was carrying me down the Channel on the way to Marseilles, Naples, Port Said, Colombo and Perth, where the first Australian match was to be played.

CHAPTER VII

OFF TO AUSTRALIA

WE had a hearty send-off from a big crowd of friends and admirers when we left St. Pancras Station on September 20th, 1907, and many of them went on to Tilbury to see the *Ophir* sail and wish us a prosperous voyage. Our party consisted of five amateurs and nine professionals, the list being: A. O. Jones (captain), J. N. Crawford, F. L. Fane, K. L. Hutchings, R. A. Young, Syd Barnes, Colin Blythe, Len Braund, Arthur Fielder, Joe Hardstaff, Ernie Hayes, Joe Humphries, Rhodes and myself. Mr. Jones had his wife with him, but my wife had gone off with her baby to Cambridge, where she stayed whilst I was away, as we gave up our London home for the period of the tour. As it so happened, our team in the first matches played under the captaincy of F. L. Fane, because A. O. Jones became ill. George Gunn accompanied us for the benefit of his health and was not one of the chosen team, but he afterwards played in every Test match. In the first of the series, he knocked up 119 and 74, and those scores led to his being included in the subsequent matches.

Although the *Ophir* was quite inferior to the

83

ships used in the present day for pleasure-cruises, it possessed the distinction of having taken the Duke of York (now King George) to Melbourne in 1901, to open the first Parliament of the Commonwealth. I had never been before on a liner, and the novelty of everything was most delightful until sea-sickness put a damper on my enjoyment. Ernie Hayes shared a cabin with me in a forward part of the ship, where the motion of the vessel could be experienced to the full. I am the world's worst sailor. During the whole voyage I was ill, except for brief periods when I went on shore at ports where we called and when going through the Suez Canal and the Red Sea.

Friends who knew the ropes advised me what to get for the trip in the way of summer flannels, suits and deck shoes. I bought evening-dress so that, for the first time in my life, I could present myself spick and span in "glad rags." There were plenty of amusements on board, the best being deck quoits. I could have had a shot at the competitions in that game if I had mastered the beastly oscillation of the vessel. Nowadays, the liveliest of games on board is, of course, deck tennis. At Plymouth, our first stop, we had a chance to land for half a day, and my *mal-de-mer* began from that point and lasted all the way to Gibraltar.

The sightseeing on shore broke the monotony

of the voyage. The view of the magnificent Bay of Naples, with its amphitheatre of hills at the back, was delightful. The old tag: "See Naples and die," seemed appropriate for me, for my sight of the beautiful city might well be the preliminary to death from any further doses of sea-sickness. Charming as Naples appears from the sea, the place itself in its oldest parts is full of squalid streets, narrow alleys and tiring climbs up lanes of tumbledown houses. The smoking mountain of Vesuvius was most impressive to one whose knowledge of high altitudes had been largely confined to such eminences as Hindhead and Box Hill. In the year before my visit, 500 people had been suffocated or killed in some other way by a Vesuvius eruption, and a town of nearly 10,000 inhabitants had been destroyed. We rode over to Pompeii to have a look at the excavated ruins, but to explore the place properly takes four or five hours—much more than we had at our disposal. Some of the restorations have, since my first visit, been carried out with such thoroughness that it is almost possible to imagine that the occupants have gone for a stroll and will be back shortly. It struck me, incidentally, that guides can be too voluble and too greedy.

Port Said was our next port of call; it is quite modern, with trams, electric light and golf links.

We were not permitted to land until we had been medically examined. Here, as at Colombo and most parts in the East, the authorities are always scared at the risk of the arrival of somebody importing smallpox or cholera. We dined at a Port Said restaurant and I noticed that food on a ship, however good in quality, never tastes so appetisingly as a meal ashore. Then came the Suez Canal—very interesting. The ship made only quite slow progress along that narrow strip, and at many points the natives came alongside on the sandbank. Small vessels have to pull in to the side to allow liners to pass, and, for this purpose, bays have been cut in the canal. A pilot takes charge of each liner from Port Said to Port Tewfik at the other end of the Canal. The heat of the Red Sea, its humidity, and its glare rendered this part of our trip uncomfortable. On a more recent tour, one of our party, baked and almost unable to breathe, exclaimed: "I wish somebody would hit me on the neck with a snowball."

From the Red Sea, past Aden, and across the Indian Ocean, we travelled until we came to Colombo. Here was a paradise of palms, coconut and cinnamon trees, with elephants bathing in pools, and tourists riding about in rickshaws. We tried that quaint kind of vehicle and had a run round the town. When I was young I loved to gaze through a kaleidoscope; the variations of colour astonished me. Colombo reminded me of that toy of my youth; whichever way one looked, the most marvellous reds, blues, greens and yellows were mingled in a panorama. Everywhere were to be seen the gayest tints of turban and shawl. I would spend a holiday in Colombo every year if I could only reach that resort by train.

From that harbour to Australia was a long stretch, and I was consistently sick as before. Fremantle gave me my first sight of the land of our doughty opponents—the British cousins, who had learnt cricket from us in long past days, who had since taught us some points in the game, and who had established friendships with us that had a perpetual value.

Fielder, Gunn and I went straight on to Adelaide, but the others got off at the former port to play a match against a Western Australia team at Perth, about eight miles away. The Australian climate, with its cloudless skies and brilliant sunshine, was a pleasant surprise to me, and it was a splendid experience to rest and revel in the sun after the trying time that I had gone through, which had left me in a washed-out state. As I was considered to be still unfit to play, I stood out when the second match was played. This was against South Australia, on the Adelaide ground, with the temperature standing at 94 in the shade.

South Australia went in first, scored the decent total of 343, and yet were defeated by an innings, because England piled up 660, and then got the South Australians out for 134. Jones, Braund, Crawford and Hardstaff all got centuries. Altogether, there were six matches before the first Test match, but I only played in two of them. The impression was created in my mind that A. O. Jones had not the highest opinion of my capabilities, and I could not help harbouring the thought that the right course would have been to play me. If I was worth sending, I was worth trying, to see how I shaped. Here was I, a youngster with my spurs to win; surely it would have been wise policy on the part of our captain to have "blooded" me at an early stage so that I could adapt myself as quickly as possible to Australian wickets and conditions. How in all conscience could I be expected to "come off" in the Tests, if denied practice in the State games? However, when the day came that circumstances compelled them to play me, I determined to give a good account of myself, and I succeeded. From that time onwards, I have always been an England player.

I come now to my first match in Australia, one of the six fixtures before the Tests started. England was playing Victoria at Melbourne. I scored 3 and 26. My second match was against

Queensland; I scored 21. The time came for the first Test, which was played at Sydney. As I have already stated, A. O. Jones was an absentee through illness. Indeed, he played in no Test for two months. George Gunn, although he was not an official member of the team and had not played in any of the preliminary State matches, yet was chosen as one of England's eleven in this first Test, and I was twelfth man. In the first innings England's score was 273, and I was the first to congratulate Gunn on his fine contribution of 119. Let me make it clear that no friction existed between Gunn and myself, either then or at any other time. I admire him as a splendid cricketer. We were real friends throughout the tour and have remained on the best of terms down to the present day.

The Australians then scored 300. Strange to say, 300 was also our score in our second innings. It looked like a close finish; but, when the Australian wickets fell so rapidly as the end approached that their last three men had to get 88, we looked like winning. Then Carter's wicket fell after he had hit up 61, and there still remained 56 to be got. Nevertheless, they managed the task, Cotter and Hazlitt getting the 56 in forty minutes. Thus Australia won by two wickets.

Next came a match between England and Victoria, in which I scored 77, and Ernie Hayes hit up 98. We then played a Bendigo Eighteen, and I scored 58, Hayes again doing well with 53. Thus the question arose whether Hayes or I should be selected for the second Test match, and the choice fell on me. Australia went in first and got 266. I opened the innings for England with F. L. Fane. It was an exceedingly critical innings for me; I was fully alive to the importance of doing my best and of maintaining the defensive in the most careful fashion. As it turned out, I was at the wicket for three hours, and, when I was ultimately bowled by Cotter, I had compiled 83. That first Test score was followed by some of the gladdest moments in my life. Not only did I think that I had pleased the Australian crowd, but I knew that in the homeland far away there would be rejoicings. I could almost hear the thousands of voices joining in the chorus of "Well done, Jack."

This second Test match was destined to be famous for all time, because of its sensational finish. To Australia's 266 we replied with 382, our top scorer being Kenneth Hutchings with 126, and then Australia scored 397, leaving us with the job of getting 282 for a win. We tried our best, but no big scoring followed. I scored 28, Gunn got a "duck," and progress was slow. Towards the end, the hope of winning faded, and 73 runs were still wanted when only two wickets were to fall. With the dismissal of Humphries, 39 were needed. Could Barnes and Fielder do it? Run by run the scoring continued, until actually level scores were reached; we wanted only one more. The two batsmen must have suffered terrors from the extreme tension. We in the dressing-room dare not stir a foot or a finger for fear of changing the luck. Then Barnes hit a ball a few yards towards cover, and they started to run. Hazlitt, at cover, threw the ball in so excitedly that it went wide, and a huge cheer broke out over the ground; England had won by one wicket. Had the ball been returned accurately to the wicket-keeper, it would have meant a run out and the match ending in a tie. The Melbourne crowd was thoroughly sportsmanlike and gave Barnes and Fielder a reception worthy of the occasion.

We started well in the third Test match, scoring 363 in the first innings to the Australians' 285, my score being 26. In the second innings, they lost seven wickets for 180, and, if their three last batsmen could have been got out for something small, there would have been only a little over a hundred for us to hit up in our second innings. What those three batsmen did was a marvellous performance; they took the score from 180 to 506, thanks to 160 from Clem Hill and 116 from Hartigan. How could we get 429 on a wicket several days old? Actually we hit up 183 (only 23 not out from me), and Australia won by 245. I was injured during the early part of our innings and had to retire until next day.

One of the very best innings that I ever played was in the fourth Test match. The Australians had scored 214 on a thoroughly good wicket, and rain poured down immediately afterwards, making the wicket that we were to bat on terribly sticky. In little more than an hour I hit up 57 on this demoralised pitch, and then was bowled by Noble. Our total was 105. Next day, the wicket having improved during the night, Australia scored 385, and our reply was only 186, my score being a "duck." Victory went to the "Aussies" by 308 runs.

In order to provide us with a healthy sort of outing, to break the spell of the arduous work entailed by the Tests, we now took a sea-trip to Tasmania. As far as I was concerned, the first part of the programme included a judicious retirement to my cabin to study the motion of the steamer in private. Once on land, the charm of the scenery, some of it mountainous, gave me all the delights of an ideal holiday. At Launceston, we defeated a Tasmanian Eleven by 120 runs. Teams from the Mother Country had played Tasmania before, but this was the first time that matches there were given the status of first-class cricket. One incident of this holiday was a climb by coach up Mount Wellington; it was a somewhat nerve-racking experience, as the narrow roads were on the edge of a precipice, and the coach sometimes had only about a foot of space as the margin of safety.

The disgrace of my "duck" in the second innings of the fourth Test match was partly wiped out by my score of 72 in the final match. Australia had started the day with 137, Barnes's bowling being the main cause of their modest total. Our reply began with 116 for one wicket, and, at close of play, Gunn was 50 not out and I was 65 not out. I was soon dismissed on the following day, but Gunn went on to 122 not out, the highest of our team's scores during that winter. Our total was 281, and we led by 144. Yet we lost that final match. In Australia's second innings 422 was scored, to which we could only reply with 229, which left Australia 48 in front. They had won all the Tests except the second.

My averages worked out as follows: Innings in Test matches, 8; runs, 302; times not out, 1; highest score, 83; average, 43·14. In Test matches and other matches taken together, my averages were: Innings, 23; runs, 934; times not out, 1; highest score, 115; average, 42·45.

Before starting for home, we played a football match against Western Australia, and won it by three goals to two. Most of us played in cricket boots and didn't bother about spikes. There was a big crowd to see us at a game at which we played moderately well; one of us, however, Joe Hardstaff to wit, was a professional football player. I played inside right and did not score, but I obtained my cap for International Soccer!

Our voyage home was entirely enjoyable, with a smooth ocean, no sea-sickness for me, and pleasant days at Colombo and Naples on the way. When I reached England, I had a most cordial welcome from the Cambridge Cricket Association, who entertained me, and, during the evening, there was a surprise for me in the shape of a gold presentation watch from the Cambridge friends.

CHAPTER VIII

TEST MATCHES IN ENGLAND

OUR arrival home from Australia coincided almost exactly with the opening of the 1908 cricket season. I opened the season with a "duck." This was on April 20th, at the annual fixture between Surrey and the Gentlemen of England. W. Brearley got me that "duck," and, just after it had happened, Tom Hayward, who had arrived too late to open with me, came into the dressing-room and exclaimed: "What's this about somebody getting a blob?" A few minutes later, he was out for a blob himself. That was the last match in which I played against the veteran of cricket, W. G. Grace. We defeated the Gentlemen by an innings and 41 runs.

It was to be a comparatively quiet year, with no team over here from Australia or South Africa or any other part of the Empire, a condition of things that is wholesome for county cricket in one way, because Test matches tend to rob the inter-county matches of some of their importance and interest. These Tests, on the other hand, confer financial benefits, because the exchequers of the county clubs receive a share of the gate-money, and sometimes it amounts to a sum large enough to turn a club's deficit into a profit.

Looking back on that 1908 season, my pleasantest recollections are my score of 81 at Lord's in the Gentlemen v. Players match; my 161 against Hants; my 106 against Kent at Blackheath; and my 155 against Kent at the Oval. Other centuries of mine that year, making six in all, were against Northamptonshire, Notts and Oxford University. Although we did not manage to win at Blackheath, I was particularly pleased with my 106 there, because the Blackheath ground was regarded as a mysterious hoodoo for Surrey, casting its spell over us whenever we went there. I have no complaint to make against the ground as a ground; the accommodation is poor, but the wicket is excellent, and we never minded playing there; but, year after year, when we were carrying all before us elsewhere, rain would fall at the Blackheath fixture, turning the pitch into a glue-pot—a dream wicket for the spin bowlers, where Kent had a great advantage, but to our batsmen a perfect pig. Certainly Blackheath was a thorn in Surrey's flesh.

In 1909, the Australians came to England with a team consisting mostly of Test players I had met out there. Noble was captain, and the others were Armstrong, Bardsley, Carkeek, Carter, Cotter, Sid Gregory, Hartigan, Hopkins, Laver,

CONGRATULATIONS OF THE SOMERSET TEAM (AT THE END OF THE OVER) ON THE 126TH CENTURY

FIRST APPEARANCE AT THE OVAL AFTER BEATING GRACE'S RECORD

Hammett & Co., Printers, Parade, Taunton.

COUNTY CRICKET GROUND, TAUNTON.

Saturday, Monday and Tuesday, August 15th, 17th and 18th, 1925,

SOMERSET v. SURREY

SOMERSET.

	First Innings.		Second Innings.	
1	J. C. W. MacBryan b Holmes	6	b Fender	109
2	Young c Sadler b Lockton	58	c Strudwick b Sadler	71
3	T. E. S. Francis b Sadler	0	c Strudwick b Lockton	12
4	J. C. White b Sadler	1	c Strudwick b Sadler	30
5	P. R. Johnson c & b Lockton	30	c Peach b Fender	16
6	E. F. Longrigg b Sadler	5	run out	4
7	R. A. Ingle b Fender	22	c Shepherd b Peach	23
8	Hunt b Lockton	4	b Fender	59
9	J. Bridges c & b Shepherd	25	b Fender	26
10	R. G. R.-Glasgow c Jardine b Lockton	4	c Sadler b Fender	5
11	M. Ll.-Hill not out	0	not out	1
	b, 1-b8, n-b, w4	12	b9, 1-b5, n-b4, w	18

	Total	167		Total	374

1-11 2-12 3-16 4-93 5-110 6-112 7-118 8-126 9-163 10-167
1-184 2-203 3-228 4-262 5-268 6-268 7-310 8-352 9-373 10-374

SURREY.

	First Innings.		Second Innings.	
1	Hobbs c Hill b Bridges	101	not out	101
2	Sandham c Longrigg b Bridges	13	not out	74
3	D. J. Knight run out	34		
4	Shepherd b White	0		
5	D. R. Jardine run out	47		
6	E. R. T. Holmes c Hill b Glasgow	24		
7	P. G. H. Fender st. Hill b Young	59		
8	Peach b Young	20		
9	J. H. Lockton absent			
10	Sadler c Johnson b Young	25		
11	Strudwick not out	10		
	b15, 1-b8, n-b3, w	26	b7, 1-b1, n-b, w	8

	Total	359		Total	183

1-50 2-146 3-148 4-170 5-221 6-260 7-322 8-325 9-359 10-
1- 2- 3- 4- 5- 6- 7- 8- 9- 10-

Scorers—Trump & Boyington.   Umpires—Draper & Young.
Lunch Interval 1.30 p.m.   Tea Interval 4.15 p.m.   Stumps Drawn 5.30 p.m.

BOWLING ANALYSIS.

SOMERSET.

	First Innings.				Second Innings.			
	O.	M.	R.	W.	O.	M.	R.	W.
P. G. H. Fender	13	3	39	1	35.5	8	120	5
E. R. T. Holmes	8	2	32	—	17	—	56	—
J. H. Lockton	16	4	36	4	9	2	15	1
Sadler	16	4	28	2	21	5	59	2
Peach	3	1	19	—	20	7	48	1
Shepherd	4	1	19	1	21	5	60	—

Sadler bowled 2 wides.
Mr. Fender and Mr. Holmes bowled 1 wide each.

Mr. Fender bowled 8 no-balls.
Mr. Holmes bowled 1 no-ball.

SURREY.

	First Innings.				Second Innings.			
	O.	M.	R.	W.	O.	M.	R.	W.
J. C. White	29	13	51	—	14	6	34	—
R.-Glasgow	26	1	144	1	6	—	42	—
J. J. Bridges	37	8	115	2	11	3	27	—
Hunt	4	1	14	—	8	4	15	—
Young	5.3	1	9	3	15.5	1	39	—
E. F. Longrigg					3	—	18	—

Mr. R.-Glasgow bowled 3 no-balls.

Creating Two Records by J. B. HOBBS.

126th and 127th Centuries.

13th and 14th Centuries in One Season.

THE FINAL SCORE CARD SHOWING THE 126TH AND 127TH CENTURIES

MacAlister, Macartney, O'Connor, Trumper and Whitty. Our match against that team at the Oval resulted in a victory for us, but only just. At the end, when Australia only needed 20 for last wicket, the position became truly sensational. They still went on scoring run by run at a slow pace, when suddenly MacAlister tried to pull a short one from Walter Lees and was easily caught by Hitch. It was a win for us by the narrow margin of 5 runs. My scores were 44 and 4.

Now I come to a match in which, for the first time, I scored a century in both innings. It was at Birmingham, against Warwickshire. I had often hoped that the day would soon come for me to accomplish that feat, to which, indeed, all batsmen look forward. Not only did these two centuries give me pardonable pride, but their importance can be judged from a delightful sequel in the shape of the following letter from Mr. H. D. G. Leveson-Gower:

"MY DEAR JACK,

"Please be at Birmingham on Thursday to play if wanted for England. I am so pleased; no one deserves the honour more than you do. A thousand thanks for your wonderful innings last match.

"With very many congratulations,

"Yours very sincerely,

"H. D. G. LEVESON-GOWER"

7

A letter in such cordial terms was highly encouraging to me.

Later on, I discovered that H. D. G. Leveson-Gower, who was on the Selection Committee, had strongly urged my inclusion in the England team when A. C. MacLaren, the captain, was inclined to favour another player. The difference of opinion led to a discussion, which was ended by A. C. MacLaren saying to H. D. G. Leveson-Gower: "You know more about his cricket than I, and, if you really think that he is a Test player, let us give him a chance."

I have known many exciting experiences in my career, but one of those that stand out clearest in my memory is the scene at Birmingham when I played in my very first Test match in England, which, unfortunately, was marred by rain. There were scores of fine cricketers in the country, and yet here was I, a youngster of twenty-six, about to be given my chance. Enormous crowds had arrived from all the districts round; thousands of eyes were ready to watch intently every ball sent down and every stroke of the bat; and we knew that the whole nation was yearning for an English victory. The hopes of our side mounted when Australia was all out for 74 in the first innings, and then A. C. MacLaren took me in with him to open the innings for England. I was up in the clouds with eager expectancy, and then, in a few seconds, all my dream was shattered. I was out first ball l.b.w. to Macartney. Can you see me walking away crestfallen? I almost wished that the ground would open to let me collapse into Australia. The rest of the day was a misery, to be followed by a night of remorse and wretchedness.

Next day Colin Blythe presented me with a statuette representing a boy with a bat in his hand and bearing the inscription: "The Hope of his Side." He said, as he gave it to me: "Here you are, Jack. Cheer up; this will bring you luck." And so it did. Our reply to the 74 had only been 121; so we were 47 ahead when the "Aussies" went in a second time. They hit up 151, and we required 105 for a win. A. C. MacLaren sent me in first with C. B. Fry, who had also got a "duck" in the first go-off. What a strange choice—starting with the two who were in such dire disgrace, joint candidates for a double blob! His decision, was, however, justified to the full, for C. B. Fry and I knocked up those 105 runs for first wicket. My score was 62; C. B. Fry's was 35; and, with 8 extras, the deed was done, the victory won. The thousands who were privileged to witness this thrilling finish went mad with enthusiasm; the uproar was tremendous. Everybody was shouting for A. C. MacLaren or for C. B. Fry or for Hobbs! So persistent was the crowd that W. Brearley hurried into the dressing-room, lugged me out, and compelled me to get on to the pavilion's balcony to acknowledge the cheering. I felt overwhelmed, and was so absolutely excited that I just managed to stand there three seconds, waved my cap, and dashed back to the professionals' room. I much preferred the ordeal of facing Australian bowling to that of facing a jubilant English crowd.

When I was getting near my London home that night I thought to myself how delighted my wife would be, how she would be standing at the door to welcome me as a hero returning from the battle-field, how she would be longing to hear all about my performance. It didn't come off like that at all. To my surprise, she wasn't in; she was out shopping. Moreover, when she returned and I spoke of our wonderful victory, she didn't know whether I had made a "duck" or a century. As far as she was concerned, I might just as well have not played.

Just before this great Test day, I played at the Oval against Essex and scored 99, which was one run short of what I needed to be able to claim three centuries running. I also very much wanted to score 1,000 runs before May was out. There was a chance to get them if I could put up a good score on the last day of the month at

Nottingham. The wicket there was excellent, and I felt in good enough form for 80 runs—the number that I was short of 1,000. No such luck, however, for Nottingham won the toss and batted till close of play. It was a feat that I was keen on, for such a total by the end of May means play of extraordinary consistency and a mixture of good luck. My hero, Tom Hayward, had done it, and why not I? I wished to emulate him and to walk in his footsteps. As it turned out, it was not to be. I had only 920 runs to date. It was disappointing to be so near and yet so far. Still it was better to have tried and failed than never to have tried at all.

I was fortunate enough to be invited to play in the second Test match. This was at Lord's in June. We won the toss and scored 269, of which my share was only 9. Australia hit up 350, including 143 not out by Ransford. We then scored 121, so that Australia had only to get 41 for a win; that was no task for them, and they beat us by nine wickets. It was the last Test match in which Tom Hayward played, and his score was only 6 in his last innings, which was a grief to me, his fervent admirer. So he passed from the field of international cricket. He was a great figure, a man always looked up to by his fellow-cricketers, and one of the finest players of fast bowling of all time. He was not quite at his best against slow spinners or against "googlies," the mastering of which developed later. A strange habit of his used to amuse the spectators— the nearer he got to a century the farther his cap travelled to the back of his head. He certainly left his mark as a great player for many years. Surrey had no greater batsman, nor had England.

The third Test was at Leeds; we were beaten again. An unpleasant wrangle occurred in that match. I had hit the ball nearly to the leg boundary, and, in starting to run, I slipped and knocked the bails from the wicket. Thinking that I was out, I was starting for the pavilion when it occurred to me that I had finished the stroke before my foot dislodged the bails. So I appealed, and the umpire gave me "Not out." Then the row began. The Australians were very cross and gathered together on the field. A big argument was carried on, Warwick Armstrong having the most to say, and he was, in my opinion, unduly argumentative. After all, what had I done wrong? I was quite convinced in my own mind that I had dislodged the bails after I had completed the stroke.

Therefore, I had exercised what every cricketer knows was my legitimate right in the circumstances and appealed to the umpire. He was the sole judge; he had witnessed what had happened. I thought that that should have ended it. The umpire's decision might have gone against me. I should have accepted it; I should not have started a discussion, if I disagreed in my own mind with his verdict. When it was recognised that the umpire's decision was final and the game continued, the upshot was that I was so much upset that, two balls later, I was bowled, not even trying to play a ball.

I hit up 30 in our second innings and was third man out. I went off to have a bath. There was some sort of loud commotion outside just as I was drying myself, and I poked my nose to ask what was happening. " Somebody out?" I inquired. "Only the rest of England," was the reply. I nearly tumbled back into the bath. It was the fact; we were all out for 87, and the "Aussies" had won by 126. As it so happened, that disastrous finish was the occasion of my last appearance in Test matches that season, as I damaged a finger at Old Trafford when trying to catch a ball from Brearley and was out of all cricket for four or five weeks. As the following Tests were drawn, the nett result was two wins for Australia, one win for England, and two drawn games.

The Australians in those days stood out in my eyes greater than they do to-day. I was younger; they impressed me more. I think that the finest captain I have struck in my career was Monty

Noble. I thought so years ago; that view has stuck to me all through, and I have seen no reason to change it. In the first place, he was a great all-round cricketer, which would help him enormously to weigh up other people. It was undoubtedly a great asset. He could place himself in the batsman's position or the bowler's. He was a man of very sound judgment and always seemed to adopt a wise policy. As all great captains should, he knew when to change his bowlers and had the uncanny knack of putting on the particular bowler that a batsman disliked. What stands out in my mind foremost of his qualities was his placing of the field. When I have been playing against him, he has saved his side scores of runs by blocking the batsman's favourite shots.

He was a fine, big-built, tall fellow, with a commanding personality and a cheerful disposition. He was never disagreeable and went about everything in a quiet way, with no fuss. He had the respect of his men and was, at the same time, a disciplinarian. Even to-day I like to read what he says, for invariably he shows the same good judgment that he did on the field.

I would probably have bracketed P. G. H. Fender with him if it were not for the fact that he likes a gamble and is content to pay too big a price for a batsman's wicket. He again is a

great all-rounder. I cannot help thinking sometimes how unfortunate he is, for, if he had had
his just deserts, he would undoubtedly have
been an England captain and in my view, would
have ranked with the greatest.

The cricket season of 1909 was important to
me, apart from my first home appearance for
England. My first double century was obtained;
this was in a match against Hampshire, in which
I scored 205. Surrey on that occasion knocked
up the extraordinary score of 742, and won by
an innings and 468. A short time before, when
we were about to play a match against Northamptonshire, a certain gentleman, unknown to
me, brought a bat to the Oval and said: "If you
will use this bat in this coming match and score
a century with it, I will give you a five-pound
note." I agreed; the same offer was made to
Ernie Hayes and accepted. We both failed in the
Northamptonshire match, and, when the gentleman made the same offer for the match against
Hampshire, I was willing to try again, but Ernie
thought that the bat was responsible for his
poor score on the previous occasion and would
not take on the proposal. Well, I scored the
205 with it, and the strange visitor presented
me with ten pounds. Ernie was terribly vexed;
he had actually beaten my big score on that day
and hit up a splendid 276! That selfsame type

of bat became known as the "Force" bat ; it was placed on the market and is a good seller.

Amongst the other events of the 1909 season, the most extraordinary was an August match at the Oval against Yorkshire. Rain stopped nearly all play on the second day, and, on the third day Surrey scored only 62 in its second innings. As Yorkshire had only to get 113, they stood apparently a good chance of winning. Such was the state of the wicket and the skill or luck of our bowlers that they were all out for 26. The top score was 6 by Drake; Mr. Extras came second for 5! Our bowling showed as follows: Smith, wickets, 5; runs, 9; Rushby, wickets, 5; runs, 12. Didn't the Oval crowd enjoy themselves! Somebody arranged for the score to be printed on silk, and I keep a copy as a curiosity. I was myself no hero; my scores were 8 and 0.

Most of the stories that I have been telling concern myself; here is one in which I played no part. After a match at Sheffield, on the way to the station, "Razor" Smith purchased a child's ball, and the team played "head ball" to one another down the road. They travelled from Sheffield to Chesterfield to play Derbyshire, taking this ball with them, but I left them, making for Leeds for the third Test match. It appears that, at Chesterfield, they "headed" and kicked the ball again on the way to their hotel, with the result that a constable asked Alan Marshal for his name. As he wouldn't give it, he was taken to the police station, and then the others who followed him had their names and addresses taken. They also gave the name of Walter Lees, who had not gone with them at all. However, when the matter came before the Chief Constable, he proved to be a true sport, and next morning there was an end to the business without anybody being brought into court. If you ever hear that the Surrey team was once arrested, you will be able to supply a correct explanation of the whole affair.

My batting average for the 1909 season worked out quite well, as follows: Innings 54; runs 2,114; not out, 2; highest score, 205; average, 40·65. No other player had made so many centuries; there were five scored by Denton, Rhodes, and J. Sharp (Lancashire) respectively, but, as I have already reported, there were six to my credit.

CHAPTER IX

TO SOUTH AFRICA

A LITTLE while after the Leeds Test match, an invitation was sent to me to join the team that was to tour in South Africa in the winter.

There were two reasons why I should wish to stay in England; in the first place, I had now two children, and, in the second place, I had come to dread the sickness that sea-voyages generally caused. I talked it over with the wife, and we both came to the conclusion that my duty was to accept the invitation.

Early one morning in November of that year, 1909, Bert Strudwick, who lived next door to me and who was to be one of the team, started out with me from our road, with the intention of joining the others at Waterloo Station, and we nearly missed the whole party. The bulk of our luggage had been sent on in advance, but we each had a suit-case, and no cab could be found. We had to walk; there was no time to lose and our anxiety became serious, as our heavy suit-cases were delaying us. Suddenly a donkey-barrow came round the corner, and the man agreed with us to transport the suit-cases to Tooting Station. We walked briskly behind, and this undignified procession was the start of our trips to one of the Empire's great Dominions.

A very big crowd assembled at Waterloo to see us depart, and we found on board the train any number of telegrams wishing us luck. It was an almost uneventful voyage; but a tribute must be paid to Colin Blythe for helping to make things bright and cheerful. He was very clever at card tricks, and he was so good a musician that he played the violin in the ship's orchestra each morning.

At Cape Town, we had our first view of South Africa; the sight of Table Mountain, of which I had often heard, with Cape Town spread out below it, was most impressive. The authorities gave us a reception and a lunch, and we put up at a beautiful spot a few miles away from the town. Here we practised on a fine ground, on wickets consisting of matting over turf. My performance at the nets, which was being carefully observed by newspaper reporters, was not at all brilliant, and one paper had the audacity to advise me to go back home. " Hobbs," it declared, "will never be of any use on our matting wickets." In the first match, however, I scored 110; so the criticism of that journal was quickly shown to be out of place. That first match was against Seventeen Colts of the Western Province; then against an Eleven of the Province I hit up 114.

In the first Test match against South Africa, we began with the very respectable score of 310 against 208, Rhodes and I putting up more than 100 for first wicket. The South Africans, however, replied with 345, and we ultimately lost by 19. We also lost the second Test by 95; my scores were 53 and 70. This second Test was played at Durban, and the ground was turf round an ant-hill wicket, with matting over it. Ant-hill soil, which is the soil thrown up by ants, is carted to the ground and is laid down for the wickets. It soon gets very hard, almost as hard as concrete, and plays very true. Green matting is stretched over it—the same kind of matting as is sometimes used in England. At Cape Town, the matting was laid over turf, ant-hill soil not being necessary there. Matting over turf plays much slower than matting over ant-hill soil. Consequently, we were up against the difficulty of playing on wickets of varying pace, and some of our players found it by no means easy to get used to this variation. The outfield at Cape Town and Durban was turf; elsewhere it was just soil, hard, and trying for the feet, and causing the ball to travel very fast to the boundary. It is not advisable on soil to wear long spikes, as on English turf wickets; we wore rounded hob-nails. For batting on matting, however, rubber soles are best, for spikes get held up in matting. To-day, natural turf wickets are, I believe, the vogue in most of the centres; I think this a very wise and essential move, greatly assisting the development of cricket in South Africa and likely to enable its teams to cope better with teams in Australia and England, where all matches are played on turf wickets. It was undoubtedly a big handicap to South Africans to play in England or Australia on turf wickets, after having been brought up on matting wickets and having learnt their cricket in that way.

Our spirits were restored by the result of the third Test, a highly exciting encounter at Johannesburg. As South Africa knocked up 305 and our team 322, we had 17 in hand at the opening of the second innings. I went in a bit later than usual, having got a touch of the sun whilst fielding, and only scored 11. Against South Africa's second score of 237, we wanted 221 to win. Next morning, I went in after three wickets were down, and our task looked difficult when six of our wickets had gone for 93. My old form, however, came back to me, and 95 runs were put up by M. C. Bird and myself. Dashing play was out of the question; I set my teeth and decided to play carefully. When M. C. Bird was run out for 45, H. D. G. Leveson-Gower joined me, and, after a few runs had been scored, the position was that two more runs would give us the match. I played a ball to cover, and we ran 1; the ball was fumbled, and we ran another. Victory! The match was ours, and my score was 93 not out. The spectators in their excitement rushed on to the field, collared me, and carried me off on the shoulders of two or three of them. They insisted on a collection, and nearly £90 was handed to me. Curiously, they had already subscribed £50 for Vogler, when they thought that his bowling was bound to bring success to his side. At the Johannesburg station, on our departure, there was another scene of the wildest enthusiasm, and speechifying was demanded. A telegram from Lord Methuen was brought to me in the train; he was then Governor-General of South Africa. His message ran:

"Heartiest congratulations on your splendid performance, and all good luck to you in remaining matches."

Not good luck, but downright depression, was to be my fate in the next Test, which was at Cape Town, and not my fate only, for Rhodes and Denton were in as bad a plight there as I. The scores of the three of us in the fourth Test only amounted to 16 in the whole game. So that the reader may judge how unhappy we felt.

I set the scores out here. Mine were 1 and a duck; Rhodes's, a duck and 5; Denton's, a duck and 10! We lost by four wickets. What a contrast for me with what was to come! On the one hand, only 1 and a duck; on the other hand, in the very next match, my first century in international cricket. These ups and downs serve the purpose of keeping you near to earth. Cricket is a grand preventive of swollen head. One day you are in the seventh heaven, and next day there is a "blob" for you.

The story of the fifth and final Test makes more cheerful reading; in fact, it was a triumph, but it came when the rubber was lost beyond recovery. To begin with, one of the records in all International matches up to date was beaten by our score of 221 for first wicket. Next, I hit up 187—my first century in any Test match anywhere. I was batting for three hours and fifty minutes. The long array of first-wicket partnerships of Rhodes and myself had their beginning in this tour. Nobody with whom I ever batted excelled him as a run-stealer. Even when I was about to play a ball, he would be three or four yards up the pitch, ready to run for anything I called for. Just a word, or even nothing at all, and off we ran. The secret of our success was confidence in each other. This practice of short, sharp singles was continued by the two of us in

8

England and in the next tour in Australia. Later on, my partnership with Rhodes changed into a partnership with another Yorkshireman, Herbert Sutcliffe.

We captured that fifth Test by nine wickets, and thus the series finished with three wins for South Africa and two for us. My Test batting average worked out at 67·33. Of the non-Test matches, my highest score was 163 against Natal; Rhodes and I hit up 207 there for first wicket. I was able to feel that I had really done well on the tour, and even to-day I can bring back to mind my elation when I had completed that 187 in the last Test. Compliments were paid to me in many quarters. Sydney Gregory, interviewed at Cape Town on his way to Australia, said to a newspaper representative : "I believe Hobbs to be just about the finest bat in the world to-day. Moreover, he is the prettiest to watch."

My recollections of South Africa are of the pleasantest nature, with one exception—namely, that the climate was sometimes trying, rendering the train journeys hot, dusty, and thoroughly uncomfortable, which was a serious matter when the journey from Cape Town to Johannesburg took three days and two nights. The hospitality shown to us was delightful. At Groote Schuur, which had once been the home of the famous Cecil Rhodes, but is now Government

House, we were entertained by the steward, Mr. Garlick, and I had the luxury there of resting for hours in a hammock. Two lions were born in the Zoo attached to the magnificent grounds whilst we were there, and they were given the names of "Strudwick" and "Hobbs." We were also the guests of Sir Abe Bailey, who has been a most generous supporter of South African cricket. He put his foot into it, however, on one occasion. He was giving a dinner to us and to a Transvaal team at a club, and, patting M. C. Bird on the back, he said: "You are the type of man we want out here as a coach, not the professional cricketer." That was a nasty remark for some of us, and I have reason to know that our amateurs were also annoyed at so unfortunate an observation. He certainly put it badly, but I am convinced that he never meant to say anything unkind. Professionals are not accustomed to be unfavourably compared with amateurs, nor is there any justification for a comparison of that kind. At another dinner, we had as host a local mayor who knew nothing about cricket. He said nothing to annoy us, but something that amused us mightily, for, in proposing the toast in our honour, he called us the W.C.C. team and expressed a fervent hope that the best side would win; he was oblivious of the fact that the match had finished that day!

We had opportunities of visiting several interesting places during our stay. One was Kimberley, where we saw the wonderful De Beers diamond mines. Some of the objects shown to us were great curiosities—amber diamonds that resembled bits of amber, diamonds with letters inside them, and so forth. I held in my hand diamonds of an enormous total value, and not one stuck! Magersfontein was another spot visited—the lofty battle-ground of the Boer War at the beginning of the century. We found it difficult to understand how our troops stormed the heights with a hot sun beating down upon them and the enemy in force at the top. It was quite an arduous climb for us, even with no equipment to burden us. Another sight that seems to me worth recalling was the great Karoo desert, which skirts the railway northwards from Cape Town. Nothing green is visible there, not a blade of grass, and yet we saw cattle feeding.

As a treat for Christmas Day, we were taken to see a Kaffir war-dance near Johannesburg. The dance began at a slow pace, and gradually accelerated until it developed into the wildest fury. They were all leaping about, banging their tom-toms and yelling like mad. Perspiration streamed from their half-naked bodies, for Christmas there is far hotter than our hottest July. What was most alarming to us was the continuous brandishing of knobkerries and spears; we thought that any moment might bring one of us a terrific clout on the head. If they got paid for all that hard work, they certainly earned it.

It was in the course of this tour that I played golf for the first time. "Struddy" and I had a round at Port Elizabeth, but it was interrupted by a violent thunderstorm. We beat a retreat helter-skelter into the club-house, and we were gazing at the lightning flashes when, with the most tremendous bang, down came the flagstaff from the roof just under our noses. I sometimes play golf to-day, but my games are humdrum compared with that round when I first began as a golfer.

No description of the tour of 1909–10 can be regarded as adequate without reference to that bogy of cricket, the googly. The bowling of googly balls came under my notice when the South Africans visited England in 1907, and, although I did not understand it at the time, I knocked up 78 when I encountered it for the first time. That was at Scarborough. Now, in this tour of ours, we had any amount of it on the matting wickets. K. J. Key, who captained Surrey at one time, wrote to me many years ago an interesting letter, in which he stated that the googly was invented in 1885 by H. V. Page, captain of Oxford. Mr. Page, he wrote, used to bowl it constantly when a wicket fell, whilst waiting for the next man to come in; he never really perfected it, not bowling it in a first-class match, but only in some college matches. He undoubtedly invented it, added K. J. Key, and it was perfected by B. J. T. Bosanquet early in the present century. It is generally understood that Schwarz, before he went to South Africa, learnt the googly from B. J. T. Bosanquet, and he in his turn taught it to Faulkner, Vogler and Gordon White. So it came about that, on this first visit of mine to South Africa, I had a lot of experience of the "wrong 'un," as the googly is often termed. Schwarz bowled nothing else except for an occasional fast straight one; Faulkner was the most successful at it, and White's were the most difficult to detect. There were some of our team who had hardly ever met the googly before, and that fact goes a long way to explain the defeat that we suffered. A googly is not delivered below the wrist, but above it, so that one method of spotting it is to watch the wrist action carefully. When I suspected the googly, I played well forward, so that the break might be smothered, or I played back and watched the ball right on to the bat.

Our opponents in South Africa not only distinguished themselves as bowlers, there was also some excellent batting. Faulkner's batting average in the Tests was: Innings 9; runs 545; average 60·55. Aubrey Faulkner will go down to history as South Africa's greatest all-rounder; and indeed in an article that I wrote in 1910, I declared him to be the greatest all-rounder in the world. He was a really splendid googly bowler, keeping an immaculate length, much faster than Grimmett, and perhaps the best of the googly bowlers with the exception of Arthur Mailey. Faulkner did not spin the ball as much as Mailey, but was more consistent in his length. As a batsman, he was not what I should call brilliant, but undoubtedly great. He had rather a crouch at the wicket and watched the ball right on to the bat. His chief stroke was an elegant drive through the covers.

In our team, Frank Woolley was playing in International cricket for the first time in his life; he did not, however, display on matting wickets the great powers that he showed on turf wickets.

Strudwick had strange experiences with us— an extraordinary mixture of high spirits with serious illness. First of all, on starting out, he had the comic beginning with the donkey-barrow, which I have recorded. Next, on the way out, he was a great success at a fancy-dress ball held on the ship, being garbed in the skin of a chimpanzee, with G. H. Simpson-Hayward as his master, an Italian organ-grinder. Leaping on tables and chairs in the saloon at dinner, he sent everybody into roars of laughter. In the second Test, however, he had the misfortune to be hit in the face so severely that he had to retire, and, finally, he contracted malaria. It was a question of leaving him behind when we were arranging for our departure, but he thought out a clever trick that enabled him to accompany us. The doctor was taking his temperature, and Blythe attracted the doctor's attention from the patient. Immediately, Struddy removed the thermometer, only replacing it just as the doctor returned to examine it. Naturally, no grave increase of temperature was recorded, and the doctor gave him permission to leave for England. He had run a serious risk with his ingenious scheme, for he was unconscious during most of the voyage. On our arrival at Southampton, however, he had recovered to some extent.

I believe that Strudwick was the finest wicket-keeper that England had in my time, and I do not say that because he was a Surrey player, a teammate and a bosom friend. I have seen him perform in England, Australia and South Africa. He was plucky to a degree ; in fact, many a time in the early days I have known that he could not sleep at night owing to bad fingers, but next day he would be taking his place at the wicket and would be going about his work as though nothing was wrong with him. I could name half a dozen efficient England wicket-keepers during my time, but I put Struddy as the best. His work on the leg side was always magnificent. From time to time a lot has been said about a wicket-keeper standing up to the wicket to fast bowling, and all cricketers can doubtless recall H. Martyn standing up to N. A. Knox and W. Brearley at Lord's in a Gentlemen v. Players match. Struddy could have done that at any time, and I have no doubt that many other wicket-keepers could have done the same. The real answer to that is that there is more to be lost than gained by doing so. Strudwick is really a great character—modest, unassuming, always ready to try to help others and to do a good turn.

We had two most delightful welcomes on reaching England—first, at Southampton, where our wives had assembled in strong force, and, secondly, in London, where a multitude of friends were gathered on the platform. I was glad to be home once more, but also mightily pleased to have seen such a wonderful Dominion as South Africa. We had had a magnificent welcome there, and I think that I have justification in testifying that the spectators there showed as much cordiality and true sportsmanship as would be found on any ground in England. It is a little different in Australia, because there the rivalry is so keen that they hate being beaten. I was once criticised for saying something on those lines, but I like to speak as I feel. Certainly the Australians have become very friendly to me.

If I had at any time a doubt about my success on South African cricket grounds, it would have been dispelled by the high compliment paid me by H. D. G. Leveson-Gower, when he came to write about the tour that he had captained. " Without any question," he wrote, " the feature of the tour was the batting of Hobbs. I have never seen better, either in England or anywhere else. It was magnificent."

CHAPTER X

TWO SEASONS AT HOME

THE home cricket season of 1910 began soon after our arrival from South Africa, for it was already April. It was a very wet season, and, thanks largely to that fact, it was "Razor" Smith's big year. He took 247 wickets at a cost of 13·05 runs per wicket, thus coming second in the bowling averages, whilst J. T. Hearne finished top with 119 wickets at an average cost of 12·79 runs. "Razor" was a great bowler on wet wickets. He could make the ball run away like a leg break; many a time have I seen him pitch a ball on the leg stump and hit the middle and off.

Surrey was due to play Derbyshire in May at the Oval, but the ground on the Thursday was too soft, and King Edward's death caused Saturday to be also a blank day, so that play was restricted to the Friday. A week later, we met Essex at the Oval, and this time the King's funeral on the Friday made it a two-day match. I remember getting up early on the Friday morning and setting out with the wife for Hyde Park. We found a good position near the railings to see the funeral go by, and there we stood for hours, until, becoming tired and exhausted with the long waiting, we went off and sat on the grass. That is where we were when the great procession passed—too far off to get the view for which we had come.

I was not quite so successful with centuries this season. My best score was 133 at Derby against Derbyshire, and I hit up two other centuries. In the Gentlemen *v*. Players match at the Oval, I scored two 50's. The more important Gentlemen *v*. Players match at Lord's resulted in a fine win for the Players by ten wickets. We hit up 209, of which I scored 35, and the Gentlemen could only get 114, "Razor" Smith taking five of their wickets for 18 runs. Their second score came to 95, which made them exactly level with our total for two innings, and we wanted for victory only one run, which was secured by a hit for 4 from "Razor" Smith. My batting average for the season was: Innings, 63; times not out, 3; runs, 1,982; average 33·03.

During the winter of 1910, I returned to the pastime that had been so dramatically interfered with at Port Elizabeth and attempted to learn golf seriously. I do not, however, think it a sensible policy for young professional cricketers to play golf. The swing and the follow through are quite different in the two games—so much so that golf is apt to be detrimental to a young batsman. Cricket upsets golf more than golf upsets cricket; but, all the same, I am of opinion that for a cricketer to play golf in the early stages of his career is most unwise. In cricket you must carry the bat right through in the direction of extra cover, and your body comes through with it; whereas, if you do that in golf, you slice the ball to blazes. It is a totally different swing in golf, for in the drive the club finishes over your left shoulder, and you must not let your body come forward.

A feature of the next season, 1911, was the adoption of a new method of arriving at the final choice of the team that was to tour Australia in the winter of 1911–12. A number of Test trial matches were arranged in England, so that the Selection Committee might have additional indications of the capabilities of our cricketers. Not only was the visit to Australia under consideration in these trials, but also the composition of an England side for the summer of 1912, when both Australians and South Africans were to come over here for what were to be known as the Triangular Tests. Looking back to those days, my view is that Test trials are not a very great help. There is something to be said for them in getting a side together, settling the positions in the field, and arranging for them to blend as a team—in other words, team-work.

They mean, however, very little to the stable player. He is playing against his own colleagues, and it is impossible to get the Test match atmosphere. There is nothing hanging to the result. For instance, if Herbert Sutcliffe or Wally Hammond failed in a Test trial, who would think of leaving them out of an England team? On the other hand, if a promising youngster hit up a century, it would be by no means a certainty that he would be included in the next English side. Temperament is the great thing in Test matches, and a cricketer must actually play in a Test match to prove that he has the right temperament. The pre-war matches at Lord's between Gentlemen and Players were, to my mind, bigger than any Test trial that I played in, and were superior as a testing method. Amateur cricket has, however, greatly fallen off in post-war years.

In future, a far better baptism would be, say, three North v. South matches each year. The spectators would be more keen, especially in the north, where they are more clannish. The players for North and South would be able to overcome that feeling of antagonism on the part of the crowd—a feeling that conveys itself to the player on the field. It would provide a better test of temperament, and it would make the players themselves tremendously keen. There would be more in it, and the selectors would be better able to judge whether a particular fellow was of the right calibre.

The year 1911 was a much more satisfactory season for me than 1910. I accepted invitations to play in the Gentlemen v. Players match at the Oval and in the similar match at Lord's. After accepting these invitations, I had rather a lean time for a few matches. In fact, I struck a bad patch. My scores in the Oval match were only 12 and 38, and, during this match, it was suggested to me that I should stand down for the Lord's match. There were at that period any number of really great cricketers worthy of the honour. I indicated that I saw the justice of the suggestion made to me and that I was willing to stand down. Nevertheless, at the last moment, they decided to stick to their original selection. The Players had certainly a wonderful side on that occasion. Here is the list in batting order: Tom Hayward, J. B. Hobbs, J. T. Tyldesley, H. T. Hardinge, F. A. Tarrant, W. Rhodes, G. Hirst, J. Iremonger, E. J. Smith, S. F. Barnes, and C. P. Buckenham. Although that clearly constituted a really great side, the Gentlemen beat us by 130 runs.

In the first innings I got only 18, but in the second innings I did one of my best performances, carrying my bat right through the innings for

154. It bears out the point that last-minute selections are very often most successful. That was the first century that I had scored in a Gentlemen *v.* Players match. It did not, however, save us from defeat. One of the newspapers wrote of it as follows : "Hobbs batted gallantly to win the game, but his fellows were incapable of backing his splendid efforts up." Another paper went so far as to declare my innings to be "worthy of a place among those that can be legitimately called great."

About 18,000 people paid for admission to that match during the three days. Some of the elderly supporters of the game will tell you that you do not see the crowds to-day that you saw a quarter of a century ago. They also imagine that the game is not the game it used to be. No game, however, which you keep on playing can go back for any length of time. It moves in cycles. Perhaps, in the old days, when I first started, there were more outstanding person-alities, and certainly there were more really fast bowlers. I do not think that the game has gone back to any great extent. There has been an all-round levelling up; new styles of bowling and new methods of attack have been introduced.

Possibly we do not get the same big crowds in county matches. This may be accounted for by the fact that there is much more cricket played.

Then there are many counter-attractions, with which in olden days we did not have to contend. On the other hand, for any specially attractive match the crowd will turn up in far greater numbers than it used to, as is proved by the fact that it was almost impossible to get a seat at the last three series of Test matches against Australia.

For the sake of argument, it may be said that cricket is not so bright nowadays. Allowing all credit to the Jessops, the Fenders, the Chapmans, the Carrs, and fast scorers of that class in former days, it must be remembered that bowlers to-day bowl more with the fixed idea of keeping the batsman quiet. I do not detect any marked falling off in the rate of scoring. We have of late years certainly seen some very bright and remarkable finishes, thrilling enough for any-body—one side trying to get runs against the clock and another trying to bring about a definite result. Matches have been packed full of excitement, with the crowd held breathless and spell-bound.

This has undoubtedly been brought about by the changes in the method of scoring in the County Championship Table. To-day 15 points are counted for a win outright, and $7\frac{1}{2}$ points if the match ends in a tie. If a match be not finished, 5 points go to the side leading in the

9

first innings, and 3 points to the opponents. In
a three-day match, if there is no play on the first
two days, the match is played under the laws for
one-day matches, except that Law 54, which gives
the right of declaration at any time in a one-day
match, does not apply for this competition, and
no side can declare its first innings closed until
it has batted for at least sixty minutes. When a
match is decided by the first innings, the winning
side counts 10 points and its opponents 3 points.
Should there be no result on the first innings or
should a match not be finished and the scores be
equal on the first innings, each side scores 4 points.

Cricket has always had its slow scorers as well
as its hitters. We are apt in these days to compare cricket with football and other fast games,
where one sees both start and finish in a short
period of time. In this respect, cricket is, of
course, at a disadvantage, because people cannot
afford a lot of time; but, if I may judge from the
letters I receive, there are still thousands of
enthusiasts to whom cricket is their first love
and the only game that matters.

Wickets have not improved since my time as
much as is so fondly imagined. In these days of
finance, it is necessary that wickets should, if
possible, last three days, and methods have to
be adopted to ensure this, such as covering the
wicket. Where I do notice a marked change is

in the fact that you seldom see a really sticky dog of a wicket, as was the case in my early days. This is due to the dressing introduced.

There is nothing wrong with the game, but the Press is constantly singing out for brighter cricket, and the public is upset. Some of our writers are too ready to indulge in destructive criticism. Cricket in no way stands in need of "brightening" by mixing it up with military bands, Aunt Sallies, coco-nut shies, and miscellaneous side-shows.

It was in this year, 1911, that my best bowling feat in first-class cricket was achieved. On the Parks ground at Oxford, against Oxford University, I was bowling unchanged throughout the second innings and captured seven wickets for 56 runs. The trees all round the ground made the atmosphere tense and heavy, which enabled me to make the ball swing through pretty well the whole innings. A new ball always swings in England, but it swings very little in Australia or South Africa, where the atmosphere is so thin. The biggest swinger of my time was George Hirst. As a memento of this Oxford bowling of mine, our skipper, H. D. G. Leveson-Gower, presented me with a silver ink-well in the shape of a bell, a replica of a famous bell in Oxford. It had the nature of my performance and the date inscribed upon it.

Of the other events in that season, I may mention my score of 93 against Cambridge University, which pleased me particularly because it was hit up amongst my old friends in the town of my birth. In July, I accepted the invitation that came to me to join the team that was to visit Australia in the winter. During the Festival Week at Scarborough, this team selected for Australia played Lord Londesborough's Eleven, and I was fortunate enough to carry my bat through the whole of the first innings for 117, and scored 84 in the second innings. A match at Darlington followed, against Mr. Bucknall's Eleven, mostly Yorkshiremen; I scored 175. An extraordinary match came at the end of that season. Warwickshire, as Champion County, played against the Rest of England and was defeated by an innings and 365 runs. The Rest got 631 for five wickets, including 244 from P. F. Warner, 102 not out from C. B. Fry, 101 from Mead, and 97 from me. P. F. Warner's score was his best in first-class cricket. Warwickshire gained the County Championship that year, thanks in great measure to the splendid bowling of F. R. Foster, who well earned his place for the first time in the team for "down under."

CHAPTER XI

AUSTRALIA AGAIN

ONCE more I was to meet Australia's giants of the game whose names stood for so much in the great world of cricket. Once more I was to play in those grand enclosures and on those shirt-front wickets. I should see again the magic of my name on the mammoth scoreboards, the like of which are not to be met with anywhere in the world, and I should encounter again the hillites and the barrackers in full cry. Last but not least, I was sure to be overwhelmed again by the most wonderful hospitality, for the Australians are the most generous of hosts.

The team finally chosen, after the Test trial matches, to which I have already referred, consisted largely of players who had not been to Australia before—namely, J. W. H. T. Douglas, F. R. Foster, J. W. Hitch, S. P. Kinneir, P. Mead, E. J. Smith and Joe Vine. Of those who had been included in previous tours, there were Gunn, the invalid of 1907, and Strudwick, who had formerly been "down under," but not in 1907.

The usual demonstrative farewell from innumerable supporters marked the team's departure from Tilbury in September. I was there, but did not go on board, for Strudwick and I had preferred to set out a few days later and have a rail journey across France, escaping the rough Bay of Biscay, and catching up the others at Marseilles. Just as had happened on starting for South Africa, "Struddy" and I were within an ace of being left behind, thanks to an unreliable watch, which stopped for half an hour and then went on. It was the morning of our setting out, and I thought that the postman was calling earlier than usual, but did not suspect my watch. When we reached Victoria, with the comfortable notion in our heads that we had loads of time, we asked a porter to take our cases to the boat train. "You've only got three minutes," said the porter. It meant a sprint for the tickets, a rush through the group of friends who got in my way, and a scramble for a seat in the train. My last view of the scene was that of a porter walking along the platform with my suit-case and peering into each compartment for me and not being able to find me. The suit-case thus left behind contained spare collars, shaving-tackle, brushes, combs, etc., so "Struddy" had to supply me with all such requisites for the journey, until the contents of the suit-case turned up, which did not happen until we reached the port of Taranto, where the ship stopped after leaving Marseilles.

Before the team's departure from Tilbury, I

had had a bet of half a crown with Bill Hitch that he would be sea-sick before he had got through the Bay of Biscay. As I was going on board at Marseilles, Hitch leaned over the gangway and paid up. We had a bit of a scare at Taranto, because Italy was then at war with Turkey, and the harbour was surrounded by mines laid by the Italian naval authorities to keep invaders away. We were piloted into the bay and were not permitted to land, but a band came out on a boat to give us a serenade with our National Anthem. I tried to spot mines in the sea around, varying that occupation by aiming pennies and fruit into the large brass instruments of the band.

At Colombo, where I had enjoyed myself so much on my previous visit, a cricket match was arranged for us on a beautiful ground, and we played a Ceylon team, which included two county cricketers living out there—V. F. S. Crawford and W. T. Greswell. Our score was 213 (including 45 from me), and theirs was 61; they took their defeat in a very sporting spirit, and we thanked them for their hospitality. Topees had to be worn by us during the game to protect us from sunstroke. The sun's glare made it difficult to follow the ball. As for the wicket, it was excellent.

Adelaide was reached on November 4th.

What a treat to see oranges growing in the sunshine and to picture the fogs and chilly air of London, which just then was getting ready for the Fifth of November's guys and squibs. Our reception was delightfully cordial from J. N. Crawford, Clem Hill and other friends. J. N. Crawford was living out there at the time. The attitude of the general public was friendly, but there was a little contemptuousness on the part of a section, and already at Fremantle, the first port at which our vessel stopped, we had heard the local urchins jeering, advising us to go home, and telling us that we hadn't a dog's chance. "Trumper is scoring hundreds," they shouted. "Armstrong is knocking them out of the ground; Cotter is doing the hat-trick every match."

As regards the attitude of the populace to me personally, it was most cordial. An England player only becomes really a favourite on a second visit. Some of the young boys treated me in a very familiar fashion. A firm of batmakers had printed post cards with my portrait on them, and I handed out a few to some youngsters who pestered me. Later, as we were watching the game, a boy poked his head through the dressing-room window and asked: "Got any more post cards, Hobbsey?" Jack Hearne has often since then greeted me with: "Got any more post cards, Hobbsey?"

During the four days that preceded our first match, we had some quite stiff practice, relieved by a charming drive to Mount Lofty, a range of hills ten miles distant. The road was unprotected at the side and overlooked in parts a yawning chasm. Consequently, it was dangerous, and P. F. Warner had to tell the drivers to keep well away from the edge.

A new scoring-board of immense size had just been set up at Adelaide, and a prize was on offer for the first century inscribed on it. The winner was J. N. Crawford, who hit up 126 for South Australia against Victoria, in a match played two days after our arrival. Prominent Australian firms have a habit of offering prizes to their own Test players for such successes as centuries or the capture of a certain number of wickets. At a later date—1920, to be exact—the English players were allowed to share in these prizes, and I was one of the recipients. These prizes are indications of the enormous interest in cricket that characterises the Australian public.

Although my own score was only 36, we put up the big total of 563 in our first match in the Dominion, which was against South Australia, centuries being scored by Messrs. Foster, Warner and Gunn. We won by an innings and 194. The match had a most unhappy sequel. P. F. Warner became ill immediately after his splendid

151 in that match, and took no further part in the tour. He was not even able to come and watch the game until the fourth Test. References in most kindly terms were made to him in the columns of the Australian papers, and he received an ovation from the crowd when, during that fourth Test, he walked round the ground one morning just before play started.

It was great joy to the Australians to win the first Test match. This was played at Sydney; the scores were: Australia, 447 and 308; England, 318 and 291; victory for Australia by 146. One of the features of the match was Victor Trumper's 113, his last century in International cricket. I managed to knock up 63 in my second innings.

The place fixed for the second Test was Melbourne. On our arrival there a few weeks previously, a reception took place at the Town Hall, and J. W. H. T. Douglas, now our captain in place of P. F. Warner, had to respond to the words of welcome addressed to us. He was a good boxer, but disliked public speaking, and his reply was somewhat as follows: "I hate speeches. As Bob Fitzsimmons once said: 'I ain't no blooming orator, but I'll fight any man in this blinking country.'"

Our defeat in the first Test had not unduly depressed our spirits, and the second Test put quite a different complexion on the condition of affairs. At the very outset, six Australian wickets fell for 38, giving us reason to believe that they could hardly recover from so disastrous a beginning. However, they managed to score 184 in all, to which our reply was 265. In the second innings, Australia put in 299, after which we hit up the 219 needed and won by eight wickets. My first score was of no importance, but I had the satisfaction of getting 126 not out in my second knock.

In this second Test, Barnes was magnificent. When the first six Australian wickets were down, his bowling showed: Overs, 11; maidens, 7; runs, 6; wickets, 5. This was on a perfect wicket, and I look back on it as the finest bowling that I have ever witnessed. In my opinion, Barnes was undoubtedly the greatest bowler of my time. It amazes me when I find newspaper correspondents suggesting world teams and omitting Syd Barnes. He had the advantage of being tall and used his great height to bring the ball well over. He could bowl both the leg and the off spinner, and he kept a perfect length, with clever and subtle variations of pace and flight. He never needed any loosener. Many bowlers are afraid to send down the leg break until they have bowled an over or two, but he could start by sending down a leg spinner the very first ball. The more aggressive the batsman the more determinedly Barnes would bowl. On matting he was *par excellence*. I have seen him beat good batsmen three times in an over. He would have reaped a rare harvest if the bigger stumps had been the vogue, for most of his balls lifted a little too high.

Although P. F. Warner was confined to his room, he retained authority in matters concerning the tour, and, when he heard that complaints were being made about J. W. H. T. Douglas's methods of procedure, he sent for half a dozen of us and discussed with us the question of allowing Douglas to continue as captain. The trouble arose from a delay in putting Barnes on to bowl. J. W. H. T. Douglas had preferred to use the new ball himself, and had, with F. R. Foster, started the bowling, allowing Barnes to follow later. I took the view that a change in the captaincy would produce friction and a lot of unpleasant remarks outside. Our meeting was not unanimous, but J. W. H. T. Douglas was left in command, and subsequent results point to the wisdom of the decision then taken. It was at Melbourne, by the way, that the crowd began the joke of translating the initials of J. W. H. T. Douglas into the form of "Johnny Won't Hit To-day."

On the day after the second Test, I had to go to the dentist's to have a tooth drawn, but the fact that I had scored 126 not out the day before—

my very first century against Australia—made me quite indifferent to the discomfort. It is pleasant to relate that another century was to come quickly, for in the third Test, at Adelaide, I reached 187, my highest score in all Australian matches. The England total came to 501. Australia had led off with only 133, but hit up a fine 476 in the second innings. The few we then wanted were got easily—a win by seven wickets. This was the first Test match won by England at Adelaide for twenty years.

The fourth Test match was very remarkable in many ways. In the first place, our score of 589 was a Test record up to that time; and, secondly, the 323 of Rhodes and myself, besides being a first-wicket record for Tests, was a first-wicket partnership record for all first-class cricket in Australia. Rhodes's score was one more than mine; he hit up 179, and I was caught for 178. I had now secured three centuries in three successive matches, and no other member of any touring side had done it up to that time. Captain Campbell, our honorary scorer, was so gratified with my performance that he presented me with a silver cigarette-case, on which the figures of my three centuries were inscribed, and I have that much-appreciated gift to this day. We won that fourth Test by an innings and 225 runs, and thus the "Ashes" came into our possession after belonging to the "Aussies" for six years.

When this match was ended, we were all invited to honour the occasion by drinking wine in the office on the ground, and a number of speeches followed, in one of which Clem Hill was polite enough to admit that his side had had a fair and square licking. We also as a team stood ourselves a dinner to celebrate the victory. The printed menu contained such dishes as turtle soup *à la* Douglas, Woolley lamb, Hobbled asparagus, and *pêche* Warner, winding up with Ashes on toast.

There was yet a fifth Test, although the rubber was ours. This was played at Sydney and ran into seven days. We won by 70 runs, thanks largely to a fine 133 not out by Woolley. My scores were 32 and 45, which brought my average down a peg. Nevertheless, the averages showed me easily top, and the first three were as follows: Hobbs, 82·75; Rhodes, 57·87; Woolley, 48·16. That 82·75 average brought me several presentations, including a silver rose-bowl showing my average in an inscription and gold cuff-links from Lord Richard Nevill with my three Test centuries engraved upon them. Years later, my wife sent those cuff-links in my shirt to the laundry, and they were lost. In a conversation with Lord Richard Nevill, I mentioned the loss of them, and he most kindly gave me another set.

The return to England was not marked by anything that lends itself to much description. There was a lunch at Colombo in honour of our victory, and, during the voyage, a charming lecture by Mr. Warner was delivered on the subject: "How we Recovered the 'Ashes.'" Naturally a great reception awaited us in London, and my own friends in Cambridge arranged in my honour a dinner, concert and illuminated address.

Before I quit the account of my second Australian tour, I must put on record an experience that I shall always remember, in connection with Adelaide. We had all been invited to lunch with the Governor at his residence in the hills a few miles away. After we had travelled by car a little distance, we saw clouds of smoke and were told that it was a bush fire. This news aroused our interest, but we only understood how serious such a fire can be when we got to the entrance to the drive leading to the Governor's house. Here we could see flames through the dense smoke and hear the crackling of burning wood. Some of the trees were pillars of fire, and scorched chickens lay in our path. We had to cover our faces with our arms as we rushed through the flaming forest. At the Governor's house, the staff were fighting the fire, trying to save the building, and we started at once helping to keep a chain of buckets at work. The windows were breaking from the intense heat, and even the creepers on the side of the house got alight. It was like a great fireworks display. In time, however, the fire was got under, and we enjoyed a lunch that we had done something to earn. Four of our party were missing at the lunch; they had turned back at some point on the road, deciding that it was safer to lunch by themselves at Adelaide than to venture into the fire zone that they could see ahead. Next morning the four found white feathers on their plates at breakfast.

MEMENTO FROM THE SURREY TEAM ON THE OCCASION OF THE BEATING OF GRACE'S RECORD

BALMORAL CASTLE.

20th. August, 1925.

Dear Mr. Hobbs,

The King has heard with much pleasure and interest of your unique cricket achievement in scoring 127 centuries, thus exceeding the number made by the late Dr. W.G. Grace, and also attaining a further record of 14 centuries in the course of one season.

His Majesty warmly congratulates you upon this remarkable success, whereby you have established a new and greater record in the history of our National Game.

Yours very truly,

Stamfordham

J. Hobbs Esq.

THE KING'S LETTER

CHAPTER XII

THE TRIANGULAR TOURNAMENT

A NOVELTY in the cricket world was introduced in 1912, in the shape of Triangular Test matches, both Australia and South Africa sending teams over here. There were two or three points in favour of this experiment, but the disadvantages outweighed them. True, it was something quite new, and many people enjoy innovations as a change from what they have been experiencing for years past, and the matches had a certain importance of their own, as will be seen from my summary of the results. On the other hand, the enlarged programme interfered very seriously with county cricket, and anything that has that effect cannot be good for the game. Whilst you could get a crowd for England *v.* Australia or for England *v.* South Africa, it was obviously not so easy to attract one for a contest between Australia and South Africa. The truth is that we are ready to welcome either the Australians or the South Africans, but not both. Nine Test matches in one season cut too much into the county cricket programme—the backbone of the game. There is no room for them, and I do not think that they will be played again.

Before the actual Tests began, two Test trials were arranged. The Eleven who had been to Australia played the Rest of England at Lord's, and there was a match at the Oval between an England team and the Rest. In the latter match, England won by an innings, my score being 68. The trial at Lord's was more exciting, the score for England mounting up to 509. P. F. Warner reappeared and knocked up 126, which aroused much enthusiasm amongst his colleagues and the general public. The Rest were again defeated by an innings.

Manchester saw the first of the Triangular Tests, Australia beating South Africa by an innings and 88 runs. It aroused no particular interest; indeed, the only problem that concerned the public was whether England would defeat Australia. When the South Africans came out against us at Lord's, they started in a most miserable fashion, being all out for 58, with Mr. Extras as top scorer for 17. Our bowling showed: Foster, 5 wickets, 16 runs; Barnes, 5 wickets, 25 runs. It has to be said in excuse for them that rain had fallen the whole of the day before. Frank Foster was in strong form at that time. His left arm round the wicket bowling was always much faster than it looked, his pace off the pitch being equal to that of a fast bowler, although he was only looked upon as medium. He always maintained a good length, made the ball swing in, and occasionally made it turn back like lightning, which was, I think, more due to body swing in delivery than to genuine finger spin. There was never any question of body line (that ugly term) with him, for he never bowled short.

When I batted in that Lord's match, I hit a full toss for 4 and then played on to my wicket —out in the first over. We won by an innings and 62. During the match, C. B. Fry put me on to bowl. I had bowled a few overs for England in Australia and South Africa, but this was the first time that I had ever bowled at home for England.

Rain spoilt our encounter with Australia at Lord's, only allowing us three hours of play on the first day and less than half an hour on the second, so that it is not surprising that the match was drawn. Rhodes and I put on 112 for the first wicket. We were opening the innings so often that we were given the name of "The Old Firm." One commentator wrote about us in the following terms: "Hobbs and Rhodes kept the bowlers and fielders in a state of continual anxiety. If they hit the ball only three yards, they ran, and they got their stolen singles easily. The runs they stole amounted to some fifteen per cent of the total, and the effect of their audacity upon the enemy was at once noticeable."

I went to 107, and that century was specially

pleasing to me, because only three centuries had ever been scored at Lord's against Australia. England declared at 310 for seven wickets, and, at the finish, the "Aussies" were 282 for seven. In spite of the bad weather, no fewer than 35,000 spectators assembled at Lord's during the three days, and amongst them was the present Prince of Wales, whose eighteenth birthday fell that week.

In July, at Leeds, came our second match with South Africa. We scored 242 to their 147 and followed with 238 to their 159—a win for us by 174. Our scores included 82 by R. H. Spooner and 55 by me. Spooner, the prettiest player of his time, was what might be called a wristy batsman. He was more supple than anybody I could name; he would stand back and, by sheer wristwork, he would hit to mid-on with a most beautiful shot. Macartney once got out for 99 in a Test match, and, when he was at a distance from the wicket, Spooner ran after him to pat him on the back in sympathy. "Reggie's" personality was as delightful as his cricket.

After Australia had defeated South Africa at Lord's by ten wickets, the time arrived for our second tussle with Australia. This was at Manchester at the tail-end of July. Rain again, and no chance of any result but a draw. Play began about 3 p.m. on the first day, about 5 p.m. on the second, and not at any time whatever on the third. We were in during nearly the whole of such time as play was possible and scored 203, which included 92 from Rhodes and a trifling 19 from me. The Australians had just the smallest look-in—14 for no wicket—when all was over, except the rain!

Another draw followed when Australia met South Africa at Nottingham. Rain was again the cause, and it was rough luck for South Africa, who were getting the best of the encounter.

For a different reason, our second match against South Africa, which was at the Oval, also stopped abruptly, but it was because we finished them off in two days, and took a holiday on the third day. Against their scores of 95 and 93, we hit up 176, and then Jack Hearne and I soon finished off the 13 runs required, winning the match by ten wickets.

Our last encounter with the Australians provided more interest. It resulted in a big final victory for England. J. W. H. T. Douglas, who then made his first appearance in the "Triangulars," had a marvellous ovation when he went to the wicket, the spectators seizing the opportunity to cheer to the echo the great captain who had retrieved the "Ashes" in Australia a few months previously. Perhaps he could still hear those cheers in those heroic moments, eighteen years later, when he went down in the *Oberon* in the

North Sea with his father. Rhodes and I started with 107 for the first wicket, and my score of 66 was most important for me, because of the necessity that I always feel of doing myself justice before an Oval crowd. I have heard that particular crowd criticised, but there is in my view, no better crowd in England. We were all out for 245, and the unfortunate Australians could only manage 111 against the superb bowling of Barnes and Woolley. We added 175 in our second knock. Hazlitt had the marvellous bowling average of seven wickets for 25; in fact, he actually finished us off by capturing five of our wickets for 1. It was now the task of the Australians to get 309 to catch us up. They scored only 65, leaving us winners by 244, and winners not only of that final match, but of the whole Triangular series.

One of the incidents in this last of the three matches against Australia caused much talk at the time and was also discussed afterwards a good deal. I was fielding, and, because of an injured leg, was behind point, instead of at cover as usual. Bardsley cut the ball towards me; I seized it, threw it in towards the end to which he was running, and the stump flew out of the ground. Vociferous cheers rang out when the umpire's finger went up, but Bardsley looked very much surprised and remained at the wicket as if challenging the decision. Some onlookers in the pavilion thought that he was not out, one well-known cricketer taking that view very emphatically. Barnes was convinced that Bardsley was out, and I thought so also, but was not near enough to judge very well.

The fact of the matter is that there are too many pavilion and ringside critics who express opinions when they are not in a position to form an accurate judgment. Many examples of their mistakes have come under my notice. Let me give a case in point. I was run out at Birmingham in 1923, but, when I reached the pavilion, I was told by one of the players there that it was a bad decision and that I had not been out. "I was well out," was my reply. "From here," he said, "you looked to be well in." The pavilion is not a reliable place from which such doubtful points can be judged.

Each of the three competitors in the series had now played six matches, with the result that England had won four, Australia two, South Africa none, and three matches had been drawn. In other words, England had beaten Australia once, had drawn two matches against her, and had beaten South Africa three times, whilst Australia had beaten South Africa twice and had drawn once with her and twice with us. The deplorable position of South Africa at the bottom of the list, with only one drawn game to show for nine matches, had the unfortunate sequel of depriving our next tour in South Africa of some of the interest that might have been taken in it otherwise.

The Australians and the South Africans, whilst in this country, played the usual games, in addition to the Test matches. One game out of the ordinary was when a mixed team of Surrey and Middlesex players met the Australians and defeated them by ten wickets. Then Australia defeated Surrey by seven wickets, my score being 81 and Macartney knocking up 100 for Australia. A match between South Africa and Surrey was left unfinished on account of the rain. The greatest interest attached to a second match between Australia and Surrey. When the visitors' second innings opened, they were 328 behind, and our victory seemed assured, but a magnificent stand by Jennings and Smith put the issue in doubt. In less than an hour they hit up 176 between them, and, finally, Australia only needed 41, with four wickets in hand. However, thanks largely to Hitch's bowling, the Australians collapsed at the critical moment, and Surrey won by 21.

The county matches of this year were not only overshadowed by the Dominions invasion, but also much upset by reason of its being such a wet season. In the Gentlemen *v.* Players match at the

Oval, my score was a "duck" in the first innings, but I determined to have a go for the bowling in the second innings and scored 50 in twenty minutes, mostly off W. T. Greswell. I was caught by him at 54. Next day the following letter came to me, apparently from a schoolboy:

"SWANKER,

"You thought yourself very clever for getting a few fours off Greswell, and you only did it to pander to the Oval mob, which you are always doing. They applaud anything Surrey there, even if Hobbs, Esq., misfields a ball! You had not so much side on Friday when Foster bowled you for a duck! England would fall to pieces without you—I don't think."

I have quite a collection of all sorts of letters; only at very rare intervals are they of an uncomplimentary type.

I did better in the Gentlemen v. Players match at Lord's, scoring 94 and 55. My temperament for once showed itself to some disadvantage, for I tried in somewhat reckless fashion to hit a 6 to turn my 94 into a century and got stumped. As regards other county matches, my best score was 111 against Lancashire. Although the season was assuredly not one of my best, my position in the averages was not one to complain about. It worked out at 36·17; Ernie Hayes was top with 44, and I came second on the Surrey list.

Since the year 1904, I had never played for Surrey Club and Ground, but this year, 1912, I was specially asked by H. D. G. Leveson-Gower to play for the Club and Ground against Godstone. He told me that I should be an attraction. We played on the village green in front of a picturesque inn, in which Queen Elizabeth is supposed to have once slept. We scored 421 for four wickets and dismissed Godstone for 54. Sandham's score was 175 and mine 172; the two of us hit up 300 for first wicket. Although I had made centuries in very important matches before vast crowds, it was a special joy to me to knock up that particular century on that ancient green. Why? Because it was the first century that I had scored for the Surrey Club and Ground.

The Godstone team and ourselves were to dine together, and we passed the time before dinner in playing a sort of pitch and toss, oblivious of the fact that what we were doing could be seen in the police station opposite. A constable marched across, but we were too intent on our coin-throwing to observe that he was coming, until suddenly he was amongst us. We felt a bit sheepish and expected to have our names and addresses taken. However, he only said: "Having a good time, ain't yer?" So we carried on, and he carried on watching us. And that was that!

CHAPTER XIII

SOUTH AFRICA AGAIN

WHEN I hear any mention of the year 1913, it brings to memory my last visit to the country where cricket on matting wickets was played in blazing sunshine. Before, however, I tell the tale of my second and final South African tour, let me deal with some of the happenings at home. To my supreme delight, Tom Hayward, in June, hit up his hundredth century, a feat that had not been accomplished up to then by any player except the illustrious Grace. It was at a match between Surrey and Lancashire, and the latter county started off with the big score of 558, against which we only mustered 345, and, following on, added 219 for six wickets. When I, at a later date, reached my hundredth century, I was batting far from home, but Tom, more fortunate than I, brought off his great achievement at the much-loved Oval. How the crowd cheered and cheered again!

The Gentlemen *v.* Players match at Lord's that year had a thrilling and exciting finish. At first go off, the Gentlemen knocked up 232; rain prevented play on the second day; and our reply was 212 on the third day. It seemed impossible that anybody could win in the time available, but the unexpected happened. The Amateurs, batting again, were dismissed for 102, leaving us to score 123 to win, with 105 minutes in which to do it—in other words, at a rate of more than a run per minute. We accepted the challenge and decided to go for the runs. Rhodes and I set about the bowling—so much so that, when the second wicket fell, only 36 runs were needed in forty minutes. Woolley was splendidly "caught and bowled" by H. L. Simms, and there remained only half an hour to play. The Gentlemen were well on their toes, making a most determined effort, by clever bowling, to prevent runs, but our score mounted up, and at last we tied. Then I cut a ball off G. L. Jessop to the boundary, amidst great excitement. We won a marvellous victory against the clock, with the bare margin of six minutes in hand. My score was 72 not out.

One curious feature of this match was that G. L. Jessop had not been selected originally, and it was only arranged at the last moment that he should be in the team. In the previous Gentlemen *v.* Players match at the Oval, he had scored 81 and 107, and A. C. Johnston, of Hampshire, offered in a true sporting spirit to stand down for him. So little did he expect to play that he had to borrow trousers, shoes and cap to start with. In his first innings, he hit up 63, and he was responsible for a splendid throw-in that put a stop to a fine stand that Rhodes was making with Tarrant.

Here is the story, or part of it, of a close finish that season between Surrey and Hampshire. H. K. Hesketh Prichard was last man in. He was one of those batsmen whose plan of campaign can be easily detected. Before the ball was bowled, he would decide how he would play it. If he intended to hit, he would shift his hands almost to the top of the bat-handle. I watched him and drew in to within three yards. He let the ball hit the bat and I fell on my knees, taking a catch almost off the end of the bat, and Surrey had won by 5 runs. He told me afterwards that I had prevented him from sleeping a wink all that night.

The year 1913 was one of my good years. My average was 50·09 for 57 innings (5 times not out), and, for the first time, I took second place in first-class averages—a position in the list that I secured again in 1914, 1920 and 1922. As for centuries, I got nine, of which the highest was 184 against Worcestershire. Sandham in that season hit up his first century for Surrey.

There was a fine one-day match that year at Wimbledon, which was organised for charity. I have taken a team there for several years, and we have raised over £1,000 on eight occasions and nearly £16,000 in all. It is not known to every-body how willingly the leading cricketers give their services to matches in aid of hospitals and of funds for useful public objects. Such play is more than play: it is a work of love.

The time came in due course for me to leave home for South Africa. On the day of my departure, I ordered a taxi, and, as it happened, on my way to the station, I passed Strudwick's taxi, and it amused me to recall the donkey-barrow that carried our suit-cases on a former occasion. There was a patron of cricket on the liner, who offered a prize for the best bowling that should be accomplished by us in South Africa, and another prize for the best batting. J. W. H. T. Douglas took charge of these prizes, and later on, the bowling prize went to Barnes, and the cup for the best batting stands in my dining-room to-day.

We played five Test matches in South Africa, won four, drew one, and played in seventeen non-Test matches. As regards our team, which was captained by J. W. H. T. Douglas, the important changes from our previous tour were the inclusion of S. Barnes, who was now seeing Africa for the first time, and of the Hon. Lionel Tennyson (now Lord Tennyson), who had not been a Test player anywhere before. The South African side had lost some of the players who had proved most formidable on our previous visit: Faulkner, Schwarz, Vogler and Gordon White were not to be in the field this time. Faulkner's absence was explained by the fact that he had decided to live in England. Blanckenberg was one of their new men, and there were other young recruits who, though not, perhaps, in the same category as our men, showed considerable promise.

Their captain, Herbert W. Taylor, was to my mind South Africa's greatest batsman. He was very quick on his feet, never put them in the wrong place, wielded a perfectly straight bat, and was always well up on his toes when playing back. He had all the strokes in the book, and it was a delight to watch him. I was particularly impressed by the way in which he shaped against Syd Barnes, when the latter was bowling so magnificently. Indeed, I cannot recall ever seeing any batsman play Barnes so effectively as Taylor did throughout the tour, and nobody in the South African team except Taylor could tackle Barnes at all. I will go so far as to say that, if a world team were being selected at that period to play on matting wickets, Taylor would be number one batsman.

J. W. H. T. Douglas was one of the best bowlers with a new ball that I have ever batted against. He could swing in and out. It was difficult to distinguish his in-swinger from the away-swinger. He was one of the greatest triers and wholehearted players I have ever met—all in and all out, all the time. Every match was a battle to him. Moreover, he was a marvellous companion on tour.

Our first match was against Western Province. It was played on the beautiful Newlands ground, near Cape Town, where I had practised at the nets and played on my first arrival in the Colony in 1909. I scored 72 and 80. This match was drawn. A local newspaper just then wrote about me in a very kindly manner. Its comments ran as follows: "Hobbs says that he cannot understand what he has done to deserve the kindness shown to him. I think I know. He, first of all, lays us under an obligation by showing us the greatest of all batting, without ever being in danger of requiring bigger-sized headgear. That's why we like you and your pals, Mr. Hobbs."

We played a local Fifteen at Robertson, and I scored 107, and then at Port Elizabeth against Cape Province I hit up 170—one of my best innings. These figures prove that I had, without any delay, found my form of 1909. According to the newspapers, I was not rlaying with the old *abandon*; it would have been more correct to say that I knew more about it; my value to my

HOBBS AND THE GRAND OLD MAN

THE TEST TEAM BEING PRESENTED TO THE KING, AT LORD'S, 1926

side was more obvious to me, and I recognised my responsibilities. Other centuries of mine were scored against an Eleven of Transvaal at Johannesburg; against Fifteen of Transvaal at Vogelfontein; against Griqualand West at Kimberley; and against Transvaal for the second time at Johannesburg.

Durban was the scene of the first Test. We won by an innings and 157. Our best scores were 119 from J. W. H. T. Douglas and 82 from me, and their top score was hit up by Taylor, who went in first and was last man out for 109. Johannesburg saw the second Test. Barnes took eight wickets for 56 and then nine for 103. To capture seventeen wickets in a Test match is a most extraordinary exploit; and he would have had a better analysis had not the matting made the ball sometimes just clear the top of the wickets. Their first innings produced 160, and Rhodes opened with Relf for us, J. W. H. T. Douglas keeping me for next day. Rhodes hit up 152 and was more than five hours at the wicket. Such steady play was not to the liking of some of the spectators, but the resentment that they indicated made no difference to him. He is always dour and imperturbable. An earthquake might shake the pavilion; it would not alter his style of batting. Mead, who helped Rhodes to put on 152 for third wicket, had the

11

satisfaction of scoring his first Test century. We won by an innings and 12 runs.

In the third Test we gained another win and the rubber. This game was also played at Johannesburg, and the South Africans put up a gallant fight. J. W. Hearne took five wickets for 49. This was good, but, taking the tour as a whole, he did not shine to the extent that I had anticipated. Unless you can find your length quickly when you are bowling leg breaks, the outcome may be costly. That is the penalty for googlies and other "funny stuff." Our two totals were 238 and 308, against which our opponents put up 151 and had to get 396 for a win, which was no light task. However, they were 124 with no wicket down when the adjournment came from Saturday evening to Monday. That fine beginning was not kept up, and Monday's play only took them to 304, leaving us the winners by 91.

Right in the middle of this procession of victories came a distinct smack in the eye. We went to Durban for the last but one of our seventeen non-Test matches, and Natal put a strong team in the field against us, including Taylor and Nourse. I have only seen Strudwick fielding on two occasions; each time he was a substitute, and each time he missed a catch. In this Durban match Taylor, early in his innings, was missed by him at mid-on and then scored a century. Natal won by four wickets, mainly by reason of a magnificent stand by Taylor and Nourse, which added 135 for third wicket. During the whole tour, this was our sole defeat.

When the fourth Test came to be played, there were no fewer than six of those Natal victors in the South African team. The result was a draw in favour of South Africa. In their second innings, South Africa declared at 309 for nine wickets, giving us the job of scoring 313 to win. After 133 had been obtained by Rhodes and myself for first wicket, it looked as if our side would hold out till stumps were drawn, and that was easily managed. Our total was 154 for five wickets, including 97 from me.

There was a visitor from England in our hotel, who was so keen on our winning that fourth Test that he promised to hand a five-pound note to any member of the England team scoring a century. At tea-time I was 93 and had a pretty confident notion that I was on a good thing. On resuming, I hit Blanckenberg for 4 in the first over, and I endeavoured to hit another 4 off the next ball, but I unfortunately dragged it into my wicket and—bang went five pounds!

From Durban we went by sea to Port Elizabeth. We were not landed there on the quay in the ordinary way, because the mail-boat was too large to go close in. Instead, we got into baskets that were lifted by a crane and then lowered into small boats. I never felt more like a bale of cargo. There the fifth Test took place, and again we won—this time by ten wickets. Thus the series finished. No century had been scored by me in any of the five Tests, but I had a 97 and a 92 to my credit; and my Test average was 63.

Although nothing very terrible happened to me during the tour, there were incidents which might have had most serious results, and which, indeed, were quite alarming at the time. For instance, I was motoring with Strudwick and Booth one day, when the driver, suddenly finding himself unable to pass a horse and trap, jammed on the brakes and overturned the car. Strudwick fell clear, and I was thrown over the wind-screen. Major Booth and the driver were under the car, and, as we two were unhurt, we managed to right the car, and, to our surprise, discovered that the two underneath were hardly hurt at all. The news reached J. W. H. T. Douglas that some of his team had been killed in a fearful motor accident; he rushed to the hotel, and there we were sitting on the verandah.

Strudwick was a Jonah in motor-cars. He and I were motoring in Bloemfontein one afternoon, when the driver knocked down a Kaffir, the car passing right over the man. The car was pulled up promptly, and the occupants looked back, expecting to see a much-injured victim. The Kaffir, however, got on his feet, apologised, and walked on. He must have been made of india-rubber.

It was at Bloemfontein that we had a distinctly unpleasant experience with the local authorities. We arrived there early one morning, and, although we half expected to be welcomed officially, nobody on the platform looked particularly official, and, being very tired with the journey, we were glad to go straight off to our hotel without any fuss. Unfortunately, the mayor had been at the station all along, at the far end of the platform. We were accused of having been discourteous; various social functions were abandoned; and rude remarks were made about our captain, J. W. H. T. Douglas, who had stayed behind at Kimberley and had not been on the train at all. When he arrived later, he went off to the mayor and apologised for our sins of omission, but the Dutch newspapers took care that the incident should not be regarded as closed. In contrast with that misunderstanding, we had wonderful hospitality shown to us in all the other centres. We motored, for instance, to the beautiful home of the late Sir George Farrar, one of the mining magnates, and he provided a day's splendid entertainment, with lunch, tea, tennis, croquet, etc.

A strange experience was caused to us by reason of industrial troubles at Johannesburg. Martial law had been proclaimed; we had to get permits to enable us to get about; and every night we were obliged to be in the hotel by nine o'clock. Anybody in the street after that hour was arrested by the military patrols, and night after night we heard the tramp of those patrols outside our windows. When our programme took us to Vogelfontein, no trains were running and we travelled by motor-cars, the trip being rendered none the pleasanter by stories told to us of cars being fired upon. However, we did not get arrested, and none of us was shot. The only interference with us was the order now and then to show our permits.

Of all my recollections of South Africa, the quaintest is of a ridiculous affair at Kimberley. A local resident suggested to one of our team that I was a queer chap. My friend replied: "Hobbs is all right; why do you call him queer?" "Well," said the stranger, "he was in an hotel last night and asked if anybody was going to buy him a drink, after which he borrowed a couple of pounds." My friend maintained that there was a mistake somewhere, but the next development was that I got a bill for three bottles of champagne from an hotel where I had never been. Just as I was showing that absurd bill to some of our fellows, in walked a chap who turned out to be a tailor. "Thank you, Mr. Hobbs," said he, "for the order that you gave yesterday at my shop." I had never seen him or his shop, and it was becoming clear to me that I was being impersonated by some ingenious impostor. Whoever he was, he got right away before he could be identified.

At last the time came to take our departure. Nothing much happened on the way back home. I had said good-bye to South Africa, and I have never seen it since—the land of wide-stretching veldt and long train journeys; the land of scorching cricket grounds and matting wickets; and, last but not least, the land of genuine lovers of the Mother Country and keen supporters of the greatest of all games.

CHAPTER XIV

1914 AND THE WAR

OF all the ups and downs of my life the most dramatic came in 1914. The year had started in the happiest fashion for me. I played in good style in South Africa in the first three months of 1914 and reached England feeling as fit as a fiddle, with every reason to anticipate a successful season. Moreover, it was the year for my benefit match at the Oval. Before, however, the 1914 season came to an end, the outbreak of the Great War had caused the Oval to be commandeered by the War Office, and the final matches of the season were cancelled. As for my benefit, the Oval was not available, and only the generous alternative arrangements made by the Surrey Committee saved me from a serious loss.

Certainly, the successful season that I had looked forward to largely materialised. There were two or three bad patches, but I scored eleven centuries, including the top score of my career up to that date—226 against Notts at the Oval on August Bank Holiday, the day before the country entered the war. Of my other scores, the highest were 215 not out at Leyton against Essex and 202 against Yorkshire at Lord's. In our first contest with Yorkshire earlier in the year at Bradford, I scored my first century against that county, making the first 50 in fifty minutes and lifting Rhodes for 6 twice in one over. My second innings produced an amusing incident. I smashed the clock on the top of the football pavilion with a hit for 6 off Drake. Instead of apologising for injuring the clock, I am sorry to say that I waved my bat exultingly. The smash had the effect of sending the clock back half an hour, and somebody made the remark at the time that "progressive cricket had put the clock back." In the same match, Birtles hit a "no-ball" and was caught at short leg; but, for some reason, he ran; Hitch returned the ball smartly, and Birtles was run out. Even a county player, it seems, could forget that, although you cannot be bowled by a "no-ball" or caught off one, you can be run out.

One of my centuries was obtained in our match against Kent at Blackheath. We were doing so well on that occasion that it looked as if we should beat Kent on that ground where a wet wicket had so often brought us defeat. Their first knock produced 349, and we hit up in reply the fine total of 509, Tom Hayward and I scoring 234 for first wicket. On the Saturday afternoon, they were only 100 ahead and had only three wickets in hand. Then the rain fell and saved their bacon.

Kent was to be the opposing side at the Oval on the days fixed for my benefit—August 10th, 11th and 12th. A very large crowd could be expected, for I was in very good form that season and Surrey was likely to win the County Championship. After my 226 on August 3rd, when 17,000 spectators thronged the Oval, what could prevent a bumper benefit in the week following? On August 4th, the Oval secretary asked for me, and I went to the office.

"I have bad news for you," he said. "The military authorities have commandeered the Oval."

However, the Surrey Committee gave me the option of postponing my benefit until after the war or of transferring it to the Lord's ground. I chose the latter course. Already I had a fixed guarantee from Surrey in case the gate receipts from my Oval benefit should be ruined through any cause, such as rain. At Lord's, there is an embargo against any collections on the ground; but, as a special favour in my case, this rule was relaxed to a certain extent, two or three of my professional colleagues from the Oval staff being permitted to stand inside the gates with collecting-boxes. The result was a very unsubstantial total.

Again the Surrey Committee came to the rescue in the kindest fashion. It was arranged, first of all, that the Committee should retain the gate-money; secondly, that I should have a new benefit after the war; and, thirdly, that the subscription lists should remain open. As a matter of fact, everything turned out all right in the long run, and I had no cause to regret the arrangement made. The Surrey Committee has always treated me in a very handsome manner, and my relations have always been most cordial with every member of the Committee and with the Committee as a body. No player who is loyal to them ever has any regrets.

The war having stopped the playing of two important matches, the M.C.C. had to decide what was to be done about the County Champion-ship. They resolved to award it to Surrey, which, on the figures, was the right decision. Fifteen years had elapsed since we had last held it, and it was very gratifying to find it once more in our possession. Our front position in that season was largely due to P. G. H. Fender's batting, bowling, fielding and slip catching. His batting average was 23, and he took eighty-two wickets at an average cost of 22 runs. I had a share in the Surrey success, as is shown by my batting average, which was as follows: Innings, 42; times not out, 2; aggregate runs, 2,499; highest score, 226; average, 62.47.

In the spring of 1915, the Surrey Committee

issued the following statement: "Owing to the war, cricket will be considerably interfered with in the coming season. The County Championship will not take place; but, in the event of the war coming to an early conclusion, it is hoped that some matches may be played in July and August." How curious it seems to-day to think that there was an impression abroad that the war might not be prolonged throughout the whole of 1915. First-class cricket vanished not only that year, but from 1916, 1917 and 1918. Even the cricket played in 1919 was not up to the old standard, although public interest in the great game reasserted itself as soon as we got going again.

I was only one of those numerous individuals who failed to realise, in the early days of the war, how serious the position was, and I did not join up for some time. In considering my financial outlook, I had to take into account my obligations to a wife, to four young children and to a widowed mother. For a time I worked on munitions in a factory, and I joined the Royal Air Force in 1916, serving for two and a half years. If it appears to anyone that I was slow to recognise the country's needs, I do not want to make excuses, and I state the nature of my circumstances because at the time those circumstances seemed to emphasise a duty to my family.

Saturdays were half-days at the munition factory, and I was given special leave to take certain Saturday mornings off, which privilege I utilised to travel to Bradford to play League games, returning the same night to London. I also recall a charity match at Catford in which I scored a century.

The war removed from the cricket field many fine players. Amongst those who died on the field of honour were several dear friends of mine and many young cricketers of great promise. I give some of their names in alphabetical order: Blacklidge (Surrey Club and Ground), Colin Blythe (Kent), Major Booth (Yorkshire), Alonzo Drake (Yorkshire), John Howell (Surrey), Kenneth Hutchings (Kent), Percy Jeeves (Warwickshire) and Myers (Surrey Club and Ground). Jeeves might have developed into one of the best all-rounders. John Howell, the brother of Miles Howell, of Surrey, would, in my opinion, have also been a great cricketer.

Post-war cricket saw many strange changes in cricket organisation. Two-day matches were tried, and the hours of play were altered, the start being fixed at 11.30 for the first of the two days and at 11 o'clock for the second day. Play was arranged to last until 7.30 p.m. on both days, which caused much inconvenience; when one had dressed and had a meal most of the usual forms of evening recreation were ruled out by the lateness of the hour. One result of this two-day system was a large increase in the number of unfinished matches. Out of twenty matches played by Surrey for the County Championship, no fewer than ten were drawn. In 1920, the three-day programme was restored, much to the satisfaction of all of us.

Perhaps the most notable difference between pre-war cricket and the cricket of to-day is the development of the commercial element. The numerous crises in the world of finance and the slumps in some of our biggest industries have made county secretaries nervous about gate receipts. What was to happen to the clubs if their coffers became empty? In some cases, prices of admission were doubled, but that policy may not improve the total takings, except in the case of specially attractive matches.

The falling off in the incomes of that class of society which provided cricket with the great amateurs of the past is partly responsible for the impression that the game has changed in character. Thus it has happened that one has heard grumblers declare that cricket has deteriorated, but elsewhere in this book I have endeavoured to prove how unjustified is all this pessimism. The future of English cricket is as much assured as that of any other great English institution.

CHAPTER XV

SOME POST-WAR CRICKET

WHEN 1919 arrived, the question arose whether cricket would recover from the effects of four years of neglect, and, if so, would it be revived quickly or slowly. Would it ever reach the high level of the past? The tumult and the shouting had died down. Bats were got out again; on the village green, as well as on the county ground, the crack of the willow was to be heard once more. Some of the old faces were missing. Would the public acclaim the old favourites who had survived?

I opened the 1919 season with two centuries—106 and 118 in the Surrey trial match. There were many Australians in England who had served in France and elsewhere and who were excellent cricketers. Before they returned to Australia for demobilisation, it was arranged that they should tour England as a cricket team, and they were invited to meet our county teams. There were no Test matches, because the team did not represent Australia officially. They played as the Australian Imperial Forces, and amongst them were some of the players who were destined to take part in Tests later on, such as

Jack Gregory, J. M. Taylor, H. L. Collins, W. A. Oldfield and C. E. Pellew. They drew gates wherever they appeared, and were a great attraction, being specially brilliant in the field. They helped enormously to stimulate interest in cricket generally. Surrey, in common with other counties, met this popular Imperial Service team, and I had the satisfaction of scoring 205 against them at the Oval, carrying my bat through the whole innings.

Only once up to that time had a century been scored twice in one season at matches between the Gentlemen and the Players. Dr. Grace had done it at Lord's and the Oval in the same year. Now, in 1919, I was to break that record by hitting up three separate centuries in the Gentlemen v. Players matches—120 at the Oval, 113 at Lord's, and 116 at Scarborough. Other scores of mine that year included 106 against Lancashire at the Oval, 102 against Lancashire at Manchester, 102 against Kent at Blackheath, and 101 for the Rest of England in an Oval match against the Champion County, Yorkshire. I headed the aggregates for the season with 2,594 runs; no other aggregate reached 2,000, but Holmes totalled 1,887 and Sutcliffe 1,839. Nevertheless, I was not top of the averages; that place went to George Gunn with an average of 63 for twenty-five innings, and "Patsy" Hendren came second with 61 for twenty-nine innings. My average worked out at 60·37 for forty-nine innings, with six times not out.

When the winter of 1919 was approaching, I was invited to go to South Africa as a coach, but I had other plans. For some time I had contemplated embarking in business, and I now carried out this idea and started an establishment to supply the outfit for cricket and other games. One result of this move on my part was that I came in for some curious criticism. Certain people said: "Hobbs will never be seen again at his best. Business worries will spoil his cricket." When I scored only 14 and 19 in the trial match at the beginning of the season of 1920, there was a chorus of, "I told you so," from these wiseacres. My answer was to score 114 in the first county match. That was against Northamptonshire, and I followed it up with 122 against Warwickshire. During the year, my top score was 215 in the match at the Oval against the Champion County, which this year was Middlesex.

Nevertheless, I do not regard that 215 as my best innings that season. The innings that stands out in my career at that time and gave me most pleasure was at Leicester, against Leicestershire, on a most dangerous wicket. Our captain, P.G.H. Fender, when he inspected the pitch, remarked that we should not want to bat more than once

12

on it. By good luck, we won the toss and went in. I played one of my most brilliant innings, completing a century in sixty-five minutes and altogether hitting up 134 in ninety-five minutes before lunch. My timing was accurate; I was hitting with vigour, and I exploited every variety of stroke. Our score was 309.

On the second day, P. G. H. Fender had to go to London, and I captained the team. When he came back, he was highly delighted to find the match over and won. We beat them by an innings, and did not have to bat twice on that nasty pitch. In Leicestershire's second innings, three of their players were absent, hurt, two of them by reason of the fiery nature of the wicket. Since then the Leicester pitch has been remedied, and to-day it has possibly no superior in the country. For years afterwards, Fred Boyington and Strudwick were fond of bringing up that innings of mine whenever comparisons were made on the subject of best innings and fast scoring.

My centuries that season numbered eleven in all, as had been the case in 1914. My highest scores were the 215 that I have referred to and 169 against Hampshire at Southampton. The eleven centuries included four in succession against Sussex, Leicestershire, Warwickshire, and Yorkshire. C. B. Fry scored six consecutive hundreds; I have not been able to beat his record, but I narrowly missed equalling it in 1925. My fifth innings produced 70, and, although that is generally considered an excellent total, I was not pleased with it.

A special interest for me attaches to the Warwickshire match, for I was put on to bowl and took five wickets for 21. A well-known local supporter was heard to remark: "I never expected to see Hobbs bowl; I came here to see him bat, but I never want to see him bat better than he bowled." One of the newspapers also had a comment. "Hobbs," it said, "has something more than mere length; he made the ball break quite sharply on a pitch which was nearly slow. He bowled maiden after maiden at the start." That year I made my highest aggregate up to that time, 2,827 runs, and my average was 58·89.

In July, I accepted an invitation to join the team for Australia, which was to set off in September. Before leaving England, we played the match at Wimbledon for the funds of local hospitals, and, in spite of rain that afternoon, those hospitals benefited, I am pleased to say, to the tune of a thousand pounds.

CHAPTER XVI

MY THIRD AUSTRALIAN TOUR

BRINGING button-holes of white heather for good luck, Mr. Leveson-Gower came to the station to say good-bye to Strudwick, Parkin and myself, when we set out for Australia in the autumn of 1920. The other members of the team, after the usual send-off from cheering crowds, had already left by boat from Tilbury; we three were taking the first part of the trip *via* Paris, catching the boat contingent at Toulon. Our train was dispatched in two sections; we were in the first section, and Mr. Leveson-Gower never discovered us. My wife, who had just seen us off, met him as he was going out of the station, and he gave her the white heather. Thus, as luck would have it, she presumably got the good luck.

On arrival in Paris, we took a taxi across the city to the terminus of the P.L.M. Railway. When I offered the fare to the driver, he said "*Encore*." "He wants you to sing, Jack," said Parkin. Instead of singing, I held out some cash and allowed the driver to help himself. I don't remember ever seeing a taxi-man look so pleased with himself.

We had an hour to wait at the terminus after

we had finished our dinner. Parkin wanted a drink, and, seeing some bottles in a shop window, he went in and pointed to one that looked as if it contained something tasty, if its bright colour was any indication. They poured out a glass; when he put it to his lips, he found it to be a sickly syrup entirely distasteful to him. However, an interpreter at the station put him on the track for what he wanted.

A couple of days after leaving Toulon, we sighted Naples, where we had a day ashore and took a car to Pozzuoli. Here we saw one of the most extraordinary wonders of nature—pools of lava seething in a turmoil like cauldrons of boiling water. Jets of steam shot out from the crust of the lava through vent-holes, and, when we chucked stones into one of these holes, the stones came hurling back at us like Mills bombs. It would happen like that when we had neither pads nor gloves. We picked some very luscious grapes as we drove through vineyards on our way back to Naples.

As before, a cricket match was arranged for us at Colombo. Dr. Gunesakara, who had played for Middlesex, and W. T. Greswell were in the opposing side. After we had gone ashore, a case of fever was discovered on board our liner, and we found the yellow flag hoisted when we got back. Next day eight of us were suffering horrible pains in our "tummies" as the result of eating prawns at our lunch ashore. I love Colombo and have spent many happy hours there; I have been several times, but always give the prawns a miss.

At Fremantle, we were put in quarantine for a week at a place known as Goodman's Point. We lived there in huts and occupied the time in bathing, fishing and football. Harry Howell was the keenest angler, and the most amusing of our catches were the blow-fish, for the blow-fish inflates itself like an air balloon when it is caught. Howell was christened "Blow-fish" and the name stuck. One day, when Parkin and some others were playing cards, Howell brought into the hut a dead iguana, and it was deposited by somebody in Parkin's cap, which was lying on the bed, holding his money. We went off to the next hut and awaited developments. Like myself, Parkin was terribly afraid of snakes. When he put his hand into his hat to pay out, he saw what he took to be a snake. There was a terrific yell. Later on, he was heard to swear that he would give a black eye to the fellow who had placed the reptile near him. It is not for me to say who that fellow was.

We had only one day's practice at the nets before our first match in Australia. That is what the quarantine had done for us; it had robbed us of a week's practice. The quarantine delay also caused the first match, which was at Perth, to be a one-day affair, instead of the three-day match originally planned. We scored 276 for eight to Perth's 119 for seven, and that ended the match. Makepeace hit up 117, and my score was 63.

The first Test was at Sydney. Australia went in and scored 267; we replied with only 190, of which my share was 49. Australia's second total was a splendid 581, Armstrong and Collins getting centuries. All we managed in our second knock was 281, my 59 topping the list of our performances. That meant a win for them by 377. Melbourne was the scene of the second Test. After Australia had scored 499, we had to bat on a wicket ruined by rain. Our reply was 251, out of which I scored 122 and "Patsy" Hendren 67. We had to follow on, but we only hit up 157. They won by an innings and 91. Then came a remarkable match at Adelaide—the third of the Tests. Australia won the toss as it had done already twice and scored 354. Our two scores were 447 and 370, and, in an ordinary match, those totals might be expected to ensure victory, but this was no ordinary match, for Australia's second knock produced 582. We were beaten by 119. Their best scores were 160 from Collins, 147 from Kelleway, 121 from Armstrong and 104 from Pellew. Ours included an excellent 135 not out by Jack Russell, and I scored a century.

Very early in Kelleway's innings, P. G. H. Fender missed him at slip off Howell. Not often is P. G. H. Fender guilty of such a lapse, but this proved very expensive. Most of Kelleway's play was deliberate stonewalling, and he took about seven hours over his 147. His policy was right enough for his side, but the crowd found it tedious and shouted "Rock of Gibraltar" at him. When he was at last dismissed, I said to him: "Well done, Charlie." He replied: "I've been slow." Said I: "I wish I'd done as much for England." A few hours later, I hit up 123, but it did not save us from defeat.

We also lost the fourth Test by eight wickets. Between the fourth Test and the final Test, a match was played by us at Sydney against New South Wales. The result was a draw. I had the misfortune to tear a muscle in my leg, whilst I was fielding, and had to retire. This injury was to have a strange sequel. I ought to have taken some weeks off for absolute rest, as my leg pained me considerably, but J. W. H. T. Douglas was most anxious that I should play in the fifth and last Test, and, after sampling my powers at the nets in the morning of the day of the Test, I agreed to play. It would appear to have been the right decision, because I scored 40 and 34.

Nevertheless, I gave away a lot of runs in fielding.

It was this faulty fielding on my part that caused one of the most peculiar incidents in my life. I was hobbling after a ball hit by Kelleway when some of the spectators jeered at me, because they saw that Kelleway had stolen a second run. We may take it that they were unaware of the nature of my injury. Kelleway, at the end of the over, said that, if he had remembered my bad thigh, he would not have taken the second run. As it happened, the jeering of the crowd was the subject of rebukes in cables sent to England by P. G. H. Fender and E. R. Wilson. Something that English newspapers gave of these cable messages was at once re-cabled to Sydney, and, when E. R. Wilson went in to bat on the following day, he was received with savage hooting from the crowd. Again, when he was out for 5, the cheering of the crowd was loud and prolonged. In the pavilion, his arrival was greeted by some of the members rising to hoot him. This was a most unusual procedure, for the members generally keep calm even when the crowd is hostile.

I had to follow E. R. Wilson to the wicket. Noble gave me the tip not to get rattled. The moment I appeared at the door of the pavilion, the spectators rose from their seats and cheered like mad, shouting, "Good old Hobbs!" They even sang "For He's a Jolly Good Fellow." This was undoubtedly intended to make it clear to me that any chaff directed at my fielding had been due to ignorance of my injured leg; they had never meant to be unfair to one of their favourites.

The cheering continued all the time I was walking to the wicket. I felt a bit wobbly, but showed no emotion. Not even did I acknowledge the cheers by raising my cap. Next day, a letter came to me from an Englishman, containing compliments on what he termed my "dignified bearing." After I had hit a 4 from the second ball, I felt entirely at ease, but it all remains fixed in my memory as an event that never happened to me before nor since. One moral from the whole affair is the lesson it teaches to those responsible for handling the news cabled from one country to another. By emphasising extracts in a sensational way, they give a distorted view of the facts and damage the relations between the two nations.

That fifth Test ended like the others. We scored 204 and 280; their scores were 392 and 93 for one wicket. It was a victory for them by nine wickets. Macartney contributed 170 towards their 392; no other century was obtained in that match. Macartney's average in the five Tests was actually 86·66. The characteristic that stands out when I think of his cricketing record is his brilliant, audacious play all the time right up to the end of his career. Most of us slow off; even Victor Trumper was a sedate player on the last tour on which I saw him. No one who was privileged to see Macartney's innings at Leeds in 1926 will ever forget the great treat that he gave us that day. I shall always remember him for his super-confidence, which brought him the title of "Governor-General."

So we lost all the Tests, one after the other. One explanation is that they had an exceptionally strong team, and their advantage in that respect was intensified by a number of calamities that befell the members of our team, one by one. Jack Hearne became ill at an early stage of the second Test and did not bat; he was absent from the three matches that followed. Waddington was also away ill part of the time. Makepeace damaged his thumb in starting up a car, and Russell was absent from the fourth Test on account of a thumb injury. Parkin had abscesses on the neck, and Howell hurt his toe. Hitch strained his leg, and, as has been already told, I tore a muscle in my thigh.

As a contrast with our failures in the Tests, we were top dog in some of the matches played against States. At Melbourne, against Victoria, they hit up 274, and we scored no less than 418 for three wickets. My score was 131 in three hours and a half. Then we got them all out for 85. Against New South Wales, we started with 235, including 112 from me, and got them out for 153, which was cleverly done, considering their strength. Our second knock produced 250, leaving them to get 334. However, they managed that task in fine style. Macartney and Collins hit up 244 for the first wicket, and they won a victory they well deserved by six wickets. At Too-woomba, a match that was treated as a first-class game provided us with an easy win. After we had declared at 288 for nine, they only put on 62 and 27. Our bowlers overwhelmed them, as is shown by the averages, which were: Wadding-ton, seven wickets for 29; Parkin, three for 31 and five for 5; P. G. H. Fender, two for 7; and E. R. Wilson, two for 13. Against New South Wales a second time, we scored 427 and 381, and they replied with 447 and 151 for two, the result being a draw. There was also a farewell match against South Australia at Adelaide, where we hit up the biggest total of our tour—namely, 627, which included 210 from Rhodes, 201 from Russell, and 106 not out from J. W. H. T. Douglas. South Australia hit up 195 and 369; we won by an innings and 63.

One of the Australian firms offered a pound for every run over a century scored by any Australian player in the second Test match. Gregory's score in that encounter was 100; he received exactly nothing. In another Test, there was a promise from a firm of a shilling for every hit to the boundary and of a pound for every 6; I picked up a few shillings from this offer. Then there was an Englishman in Melbourne who was good enough to give ten pounds to any of our team who scored a Test century in this particular Test, and ten pounds from him went into my pocket. On the other hand, an old Surrey member in Adelaide, who promised me fifty pounds if I hit up a century in the third Test, never paid up, although I scored 123.

That particular score produced a very pleasing letter from Lieut.-Colonel Sir Archibald Weigall, who was the Governor at that time of South Australia. It ran as follows:

"GOVERNMENT HOUSE, ADELAIDE

"MY DEAR HOBBS,
        "I hope you will accept this tiny souvenir of a perfect innings and as a slight recognition of the great pleasure it gave.
            "Yours sincerely,
                    "ARCHIBALD WEIGALL"

Enclosed was an opal tie-pin, which I have greatly valued ever since. Another gift came from an Australian business house, with a testimonial signed by cricket enthusiasts. It was a pipe. There was also a bat from friends in South Australia. It was of rough willow, with the bark left on the back and a painting on the front depicting eleven native birds called kookaburras. Mr. Albert Edwards, M.P., presented me with this bat at my hotel, made a very kind speech, and handed over a complimentary address. I told the assembled company that I was no speaker, but hoped that I could acknowledge the presentation by inviting them all to drinks. They agreed very promptly, and then refused to let me pay the bill for the drinks!

On the day before we set out for England, a letter came to me from Sir Willoughby Maycock, in which he enclosed a poetic effusion written by him in the style of Rudyard Kipling. I quote the last lines:

> So here's the best of luck to you, Hobbs,
> For we all admire your pluck, don't we, Hobbs?
> You've put up a gallant fight
> And we think it would be right
> To see you made a knight—
> Sir J. B. Hobbs.

Before I wind up my account of this tour, I must put on record a piece of foolery indulged in by "Patsy" Hendren in a match at Geelong. He was in the long field, after a ball that was travelling to the boundary. We could not understand how he picked it up; but when he threw it in, it burst. He had, in fact, thrown in an apple. We were obliged to laugh, but our captain, E. R. Wilson, did not appreciate the humour of the proceeding.

With us on our way back to England was the Australian team that was to play against us at home in the 1921 season. Naturally, we played quoits, tennis, etc., with them on board, but no England *v*. Australia spirit was introduced into those deck games. We got off at Toulon and came on through France. In Paris snow was falling, as a gentle reminder that we had really got away from the broiling heat of the cricket field "down under."

There was a crowd of some thousands at Victoria Station to welcome us home, although we had returned without the "Ashes." We were even mobbed by enthusiastic supporters, and a little damage was done to my opal tie-pin and to some brooches in my pocket. So generous is the British public that it is always ready to show recognition to its cricket favourites, even when no success has attended their efforts.

CHAPTER XVII

A YEAR OF ILL LUCK

I CAN apply only one epithet to 1921: it was for me a season of calamities. First of all came our series of defeats at the hands of our doughty Australian opponents; then a return of the trouble in my leg; and, finally, an operation and my withdrawal for a time from cricket and nearly all other activity. The season began quietly enough with the Trial match at the Oval, in which I scored 26. Then I played in a match early in May between the Australians and a team got together by the late Mr. Lionel Robinson. This was at Old Buckenham Hall, Norfolk. Our team was captained by A. C. MacLaren and contained J. W. H. T. Douglas, P. G. H. Fender, D. J. Knight, Pat Hendren, V. W. C. Jupp, and other formidable players. Rain prevented nearly all play the first day, and the Australians were all out for 136 on the second day. Then D. J. Knight and I opened the innings for our side. He was out l.b.w. for 1, and V. W. C. Jupp came in. Against some good bowling, we took the score to 125, when suddenly that muscle in my thigh gave out again, and I had to retire. Jupp said that he heard the muscle snap as he passed me between the wickets. Incidentally, I may add that I was well on the way to a century, and very few centuries were compiled that year against our Australian visitors. As for the match itself, A. C. MacLaren declared at 256 for nine, and rain put an end to the game after the Australians had put up about a couple of dozen.

Now came the problem whether the affected muscle would have to be sewn up; but, very fortunately, the specialist I consulted adopted an alternative remedy and sent me to Dr. Murray Levick for massage and electric treatment. Dr. Levick had been to the Antarctic with the Scott Expedition. He treated me for several weeks. I played in a little match in June at Maresfield and scored a century, and I hit up 49 for Surrey against Oxford University.

Then came a match between Surrey and Yorkshire at Leeds, in which I hoped to distinguish myself, because I wanted to be selected for the Test match in July. I was bowled for 1. This was most annoying; what was to be done about it? However, the second knock supplied the answer; I carried my bat through the whole innings for 172. From Leeds I returned to the Oval to captain the Players against the Gentlemen. We hit up 608 for eight, but my share of that fine total was only 3. Hardinge scored 127 and Hearne was only 1 short of a century. The

13

Gentlemen got 404, including 127 from the Hon. C. N. Bruce (now Lord Aberdare), and 201. We won by an innings and 3 runs—obviously my 3 runs.

Two Test matches had by this time been played. Australia had won at Nottingham by ten wickets and at Lord's by eight wickets, whilst I was powerless to render any assistance to my country, condemned by doctor's orders to be a mere spectator. Distressing as this was for me, worse was yet to come. The third Test match was on the same Headingley ground at Leeds, where I had compiled 172 the week before, and that score alone gave me every reason to believe that I was back in my old form. The day before the match, I felt a dull pain, but thought that it arose from some medicine that I had taken. It grew worse on the journey to Leeds, and Mr. Seth Pilley, a friend at whose house my wife and I stayed at Calverley, noticed my appearance and expressed concern.

The day of this Test match was July 2nd, 1921. In the morning, when I reached the ground, the Selection Committee called me in to their consultations, as they wished to have my opinion as to which of the bowlers should be left out. I suggested that, whatever they decided about the bowling, they ought to consider whether I should be left out. They said that, if I would stand the risk of playing, they would stand the risk of playing me. So, as the Australians went in first, I fielded. All day long, this dull ache was troubling me, but I stuck it up to tea-time. Then, as the pain was becoming more acute than ever, I had to give up, and C. Hallows, of Lancashire, fielded sub. for me, whilst I sought a doctor, who, after examining me, straightway ordered me to bed.

Next day was Sunday; I made a little improvement. Early on Monday, the doctor came and absolutely refused to permit me to play. I went to the ground to let them know what the doctor's orders were. H. K. Foster thought that I ought to go to London, but somebody mentioned that Leeds had a very eminent surgeon, Sir Berkeley Moynihan (now Lord Moynihan). I decided to go to him, and I was hurried off in a taxi to his private nursing-home. After examining me and feeling my side, he said sternly: "You will have to be operated upon to-day. If you go to London, I tell you emphatically that you go at your own risk. Moreover, if you go, the operation must be done to-day. Remember that." After a moment or two's thought, I asked him whether he would himself operate if I resolved to have it done there and then. He replied: "Delighted." My wife was fetched; very quickly we consulted together; a decision was arrived at; and, within a few minutes, I was on the operaitng-table, oblivious to everything—even to the great Test match.

Appendicitis was the trouble. Sir Berkeley carried out the operation so successfully that other surgeons came to inspect his handiwork. On the following day, he told me that mine had been a worse case than he had anticipated. "You would never have reached London," he added. "You could not have lived five hours." I wish to place on record my appreciation of his great skill. The accurate diagnosis of the nature of my malady and his prompt action saved my life. I also feel the warmest gratitude to him for his kindness and the consideration that he showed to my wife.

I had every attention and care in the nursing-home, where I stayed for between two and three weeks. Telegrams and letters came from all parts, one of the first being from the Surrey Club. There was one from "the Rest of the Surrey side"; they were playing a match at Taunton. A cable came from Geelong, in Australia, and another message ran as follows:

"Eight hundred working men at Rowton lodging-house, Hammersmith, wish you a speedy recovery."

One morning, Sir Berkeley Moynihan came to see me. As we were talking, he said: "Ah, Hobbs, cricketers and surgeons have to make their money whilst they can." I replied: "Quite right, but you get more innings than I do." I was thinking of the express speed with which he operated on a large number of patients. He replied: "We have to make our runs quickly." When I was well enough to quit the nursing-home, he gave me his photograph, with his signature, and the words: "In memory of a good innings and a great score." I have the score to this day!

There was no more cricket for me that season. It was the year of the famous hot spell, and it is quite possible that I might have scored ten centuries if I had been playing in what has always proved my best scoring weather. With my wife and family I went to Cliftonville for convalescence; my professional duties had, up to that year, always robbed me of a summer holiday with them. A county cricketer is not like a chemist or a cheesemonger; he cannot take his folk to the seaside for a fortnight in the summer.

The Surrey Club kindly sent me telegrams every day, so that I might follow the fortunes of my fellow-players; as there was no wireless then, I could not listen in to close of play scores. That third Test at Leeds was won by Australia by 219 runs, and with it the rubber. The fourth Test, perhaps because it took place at Manchester, was rendered a draw by rain. I came up from Cliftonville specially to see part of the fifth Test at the Oval. Mead knocked up a splendid 182, and Russell, who opened for England in my place, hit up a century. The Australians were, however, unbeatable, and the match was another draw.

As for the County Championship in 1921, it rested between Surrey and Middlesex, and they met to decide the issue at the end of the season. Surrey had a lead of 137 on the first innings; then Middlesex won by six wickets and retained the championship for a second year.

The annual match in aid of the hospitals took place at Wimbledon, and I took my team down, but did not play. There was a continuous demand on the ground for my autograph, and I signed willingly at first, because it brought coins to the fund; but it nearly caused me to collapse, and, after a time, I had to quit the ground and come back to the pavilion by another entrance, to avoid being overwhelmed by the friendly auto-graph-hunters.

When the 1922 season came round, I was glad to find that I was fit to play, and the proof of it was that I scored 68 and 74 in the Trial match. It was one of my best scoring years. My aggre-gate of 2,552 runs included ten centuries, of which the highest was 168 against Warwickshire. As I played in forty-six innings, and was not out five times, my average was 62·24. Hendren, how-ever, came out top with an average of 66·83 for thirty-eight innings, in five of which he was undefeated. One of the incidents that I can recall was when I hit a 6 at Bristol; the ball struck a girl at the ringside and laid her out. I was told later that she had recovered, but I never saw her and could not personally express my regret to her. Another recollection is connected with the match between the Champion County, Yorkshire, and the Rest of England. Yorkshire's total was 233 and ours 207. My score was 100, which was 1 more than all the runs scored by the others in our team. Those runs came to 99, and there were 8 extras.

When the end came of the season of 1922, the number of centuries to my credit was ninety-nine. To complete a century of centuries I had to wait till the following year.

A team went out to South Africa in the autumn, and I was asked to join it, but I felt obliged to decline the invitation that meant leaving my home and my business for another winter. It was bad enough to leave my wife and a baby in 1907; and to leave two boys, Jack and Leonard, in 1911; but now there was a daughter, Vera, and another boy, Ivor. Too much cricket obviously makes a player stale, whereas, after a winter's rest, you come back to the game fresh and keen, ready to do or die. I am of opinion that no player should go to the other end of the globe two winters in succession.

CHAPTER XVIII

MY HUNDREDTH CENTURY

EVEN to summarise all the matches in which I played would cause this book to run to a thousand pages, but I must find space for some description of the match in which my hundredth hundred was obtained. We went to Bath to play Somersetshire, but the match only began after five o'clock in consequence of rain, and it was adjourned after three overs for the same reason, without a run being scored. This was a Saturday, and some of us started for London at night, in order to spend Sunday at home. We got into the wrong train and had to get back to the main line. In the train was a parson, who asked me if I could tell him whether Hobbs had made his century. I replied: "Not he; he'll never get a century against Somerset." Later, we told him our names and he wished us success. He added: "Especially you, Mr. Hobbs; I shall look out for your century."

On Monday I was caught first ball and went back to the pavilion feeling disgusted. In the late afternoon we were in again and I scored 19 before stumps were drawn. At lunch-time on Tuesday, I had reached 50; and thereafter I plodded on, without knowing much about my total, because the score-board at Bath did not give any individual scores. After I had hit 6 and 4 in one over, however, I noticed Strudwick, near the scoring-tent, was holding up six fingers, and I tumbled to the fact that I was only 6 runs short of my 100. It was a tense moment; I felt terribly excited. I hit a single; then another; and another. My excitement grew as these singles came. There was no ball loose enough for more than a single. Now I was 97. Then I hit a single to cover point; it was the fourth consecutive single, but this time the return went away for two overthrows—the 100 was scored!

There was a tremendous burst of cheering all over the ground. It is not easy to describe the varying emotions that surged through my breast. I had achieved a feat that only twice before had been seen on the cricket-field. Only the famous W. G. Grace and my old hero, Tom Hayward, had ever done it. A hundred hundreds!

Congratulations came at once from J. Daniell, the Somerset captain, P. G. H. Fender and others. "It was a treat to watch you get them," said P. G. H. Fender. The very first telegram came from my first county captain, Lord Dalmeny. My thoughts turned to Kennington Oval, and I had a feeling of regret that my Surrey friends had not seen the gradual compiling of that 100. It was not the best of my centuries from the standpoint of performance, but I had never had to work so hard for one. Robson was a wonderful bowler; moreover, the wicket was slow, and the ball seems always to swing about in an exceptional way at Bath. Every ball needed playing with the greatest care and concentration. However, I had won through, and my excitement lasted all that day. Even at night I could hardly sleep, and kept thinking of my wife's delight and the pride of my eldest boy. Above all, I thought of my dear old father, who had given me so much encouragement in my young days and who had passed away before he could see his hopes for me realised.

That century was my first against Somerset, the only county against which I had never scored 100 up to that time, except Glamorgan, against whom we had only played once. It enabled Surrey to win the match. Although my century was slow, I managed to hit three 6's. It was a wonderful win and finish. After being 49 behind on the first innings, P. G. H. Fender declared at 216 for five in our second, leaving them plenty of time to get the 168 for a win. They failed by 11 runs to get them. For several weeks I had no more centuries, and the season was not a good one for me. On the August Bank Holiday I scored 100 at the Oval against Notts, but some of my scores at that period were quite small.

A visit during that year was paid to this country by a team from the West Indies, which had not as yet been promoted to Test Match rank. I played against that team at Scarborough in a match that had a somewhat sensational finish. H. D. G. Leveson-Gower had got together a very powerful side to meet them. In the last innings, we were left with 28 runs to get, but lost six wickets in getting them. It was very funny to me at the time; most of the amateurs had gone over to the marquee for refreshments, thinking naturally that they would not be wanted to bat. I was immensely tickled, as the wickets fell, to see them scampering out of the marquee, dashing across the ground to the pavilion, and rushing to get their pads on. There was a lot of leg-pulling afterwards. As we had won, it was most amusing, but it was not so laughable whilst the wickets were falling, for it really looked at one time as if the West Indians were going to bring off an extraordinary win.

In connection with leg-pulling, I remember something of the kind in a Gentlemen *v.* Players match at the Oval a few years ago. Overnight we had lost two or three quick wickets, and some of us schemed to give a shock to Jack Newman, who was behind the curtain engaged in putting on his pads, in readiness to go in next. We arranged that, when the next ball was bowled, we should startle him by all shouting out: "Bowled him!" We shouted, in accordance with our plan. Lo, and behold, the ball had really bowled the batsman; the joke was not on Jack Newman, but on us.

In the dressing-room, we occasionally used to adopt this method of keeping things alive, and, when a player was waiting to go in, he would hear the "Bowled him!" shouted out, and he would snatch his blazer off and bustle about, before realising that he had been had. On one occasion, at the Oval, we tried the joke on "Lofty" Herman, in a Gentleman v. Players match. He was busy writing, when he heard our shout. Off came his blazer, and he got his gloves and bat. "Patsy" Hendren walked out with him to distract his attention, giving him words of advice about his play. He went out on the balcony and down some of the steps before he discovered that no wicket had fallen. As he came back, roars of laughter greeted him from the members and the pros.

There seems to be a little curiosity as to what players do in their dressing-room to while away the time. Although some people think that we play cards, we do not whilst the game is on; cards are played, if at all, only on wet days. Players, for the most part, like to sit and watch the cricket. When we tire of that or we are out, we write

letters, sign bats and autograph-books or get the
signatures of other players. Some of us clean
up and oil our bats, preferring to do that ourselves rather than give the attendant the job. A
good bat is a treasured article. We look to our
boots, see that the spikes are in, sort out soiled
flannels, and pack or unpack in readiness for
returning home or for the next away match. A
bath or a rub down from a masseur is taken.
There are friends and other callers to be seen, and
it is sometimes a relief to get out in the field
to escape from visitors. Of late years, I have
always found plenty to do in the dressing-room.

My average that season dropped to 37·94. So
the year ended with a little disappointment; but,
as a set-off, there was the joy of recollecting that
glorious day when, following in Tom Hayward's
footsteps, I scored my hundredth hundred on the
beautiful ground of the ancient city of Bath.

The year 1924 was the one in which I first became associated with Herbert Sutcliffe as England's opening batsmen. We first opened together
in the first Test match against South Africa at
Birmingham. Our opponents put us in first, the
idea of their captain, Herbert Taylor, being that
it would be of advantage to his team to feel their
feet as fielders before they faced the bowling.
His policy didn't work; we piled up 438, and then
got them out for 34, thanks to brilliant bowling

by A. E. R. Gilligan and Maurice Tate. It shows how risky it is to put the other side in, instead of taking what the gods provide. Sutcliffe's score was 64 and mine 78; we hit up 136 for the first wicket. South Africa's second score was 390, but they were beaten by an innings.

That was the beginning of a friendship and partnership with Sutcliffe that remained unbroken, save in times of illness, until I retired from Test match cricket in 1930. Our partnership became a byword wherever cricket was played; incidentally, it was a second Yorkshire partnership, for earlier it had been Rhodes and Hobbs. I use the expression "byword" because we were so successful together, exceeding a century for first wicket fifteen times in Tests and twenty-six times altogether. The manner in which we ran our daring, short singles must have often caused the spectators to have their hearts in their mouths. Although we had many narrow escapes, only once were we caught napping; in all the hundreds of short singles, we were run out once, and thus we can claim that our policy paid.

Herbert is a great Test match player—one of the greatest that we have ever had. He has the temperament for a big occasion, if ever anyone had. We gave each other confidence; I had every trust in him, for his successes far outnumbered his failures. He was a good judge of the game, and many a time we had a word together as to the line to adopt against particular bowlers. On one occasion, after a bowler had sent up an exceptionally deadly over and had beaten me twice, Herbert walked along to me and said: "Stick it, Jack; he can't keep that up." That's where Herbert was so great; if he was beaten, he would go on playing his natural game, quite unruffled, just as if nothing untoward had happened. In that respect, he was the counterpart of Wilfred Rhodes. Many players, when a bowler has been bowling his deadliest and they have been beaten a few times, are tempted to give it up; that was never the case with Wilfred or Herbert.

What I admired in Herbert was his thoroughness. Evidently, his motto is: "What is worth doing is worth doing well." As an illustration, he was, a few years ago, quite an ordinary speaker, but recently I heard him make a speech on a big occasion, and it was a wonderful bit of oratory. I felt very envious of him.

In the second Test against South Africa, which was played at Lord's, I hit up 211. As Murdoch's score for Australia in 1884 at the Oval had also been 211, I missed by one run establishing a record up to that time in all Test matches in England. Had I been aware of my nearness to that record, I might have made a special effort for the required single, but players do not ponder over these figures when they are at the wicket. In fact, the spectators are much more likely to be working out the mathematics of addition and subtraction. My 211 did assist in constituting a record of another kind. As partners, Sutcliffe and I put on 268 for first wicket, and that was a Test record in England. It was not a world record, for Rhodes and I put on 323 in 1912 at Melbourne. In the 1924–5 tour, Sutcliffe and I put on 283 in the second Test at Melbourne.

When Sutcliffe got out, after that hefty start, in the second Test, Frank Woolley joined me, and we added another 142 in eighty minutes. At 531 for two, A. E. R. Gilligan declared, and, after a fair effort by South Africa, we won by an innings and 18. The third Test fell to us likewise—an easy victory at Leeds by nine wickets. The fourth was ruined by rain at Manchester; South Africa scored 116 for four wickets on the Saturday, and, when stumps were drawn at the end of the third day, the score-board still read: "South Africa, 116 for four." I was not in the team for this fourth Test, because the Selection Committee wished to include only those players who had expressed willingness to accept invitations for the coming tour in Australia, and I had not at that time decided whether I could go. By

HOBBS LEADING OUT THE ENGLAND TEAM, MANCHESTER, 1926

HOBBS AND SUTCLIFFE AFTER THE FINAL TEST, AT THE OVAL, 1926

HOBBS'S HIGHEST FIRST-WICKET PARTNERSHIP (SURREY *v.* OXFORD UNIVERSITY), AT THE OVAL, 1926

the time that the last of the five Tests was played, I had accepted for Australia, and, accordingly, I was in the team against South Africa at the Oval. but I only scored 30. Rain again interfered; South Africa hit up 342, and our reply was 421 for nine, after which the rain stopped the match.

My centuries in 1924 numbered six. One of my best innings was 203 not out against Notts at Trent Bridge. This was my first century of the season and it took me past Tom Hayward's total of 104 centuries. Whilst I realised that I was now second in the list to "W. G." in the number of centuries, I had felt all along that it was coming, and, therefore, did not regard it as an outstanding feat. When I was a youngster and Tom Hayward such a hero of mine, I should no more have thought of such a thing happening than of my becoming King of England. I felt that I almost owed Tom an apology for sort of pegging him back, but I had consolation in the knowledge that the honour still went to Cambridge and that, if anybody was to exceed his record, Tom would wish it to be me.

Another century of mine was in the Gentlemen *v.* Players match at Lord's. The big aim of every cricketer is to score 100 at Lord's in a Test match, and, after a century in any Test, the next biggest thing from a player's point of view is to score 100 in a Gentlemen *v.* Players match

14

at headquarters. This century was particularly pleasing, because the wicket at the start was very jumpy. I had a nasty period to overcome and batted so slowly that, in an hour and a half up to lunch-time, I scored only 18. My tactics were justified, for the wicket improved, and I went on to score 118. Roy Kilner hit up 113, and our total was 514, the Players winning by 231.

The invitation to join the team that was going to Australia was, in the first instance, declined by me because I did not want to leave my family and my business. A team was also going to South Africa under the captaincy of the Hon. Lionel Tennyson and at the expense of Mr. "Solly" Joel. I was asked by Mr. Tennyson whether I would go if my wife accompanied me, Mr. Joel defraying the extra expense of that arrangement. This would have, to a large extent, removed my difficulties, and I took the matter into serious consideration.

Then Mr. Leveson-Gower heard of the offer and reported it to Lord Harris. I was asked whether the news was correct, and I replied: "Yes, the privilege of going with my wife having been granted, I find it possible to go to South Africa, and that is why I cannot accept the invitation for Australia." The question was then put to me whether I would change over to the

Australian team if my wife was permitted to go with me. I was, of course, aware that the M.C.C. could not arrange to pay the additional expense entailed by my wife's going, but the privilege of taking her was important.

A new difficulty now arose. I said that I could not go if it involved turning somebody out of the team. Lord Harris suggested that one of the players could be transferred to the team for South Africa. That didn't seem to me fair. I replied: "An Australian tour and an African tour are very different. There is nothing like an Australian tour—nothing in all cricket." Ultimately, it was decided that I should go to Australia as an extra member of the England team and that my wife should also go. I should like to state, in justice to the M.C.C. and to myself, that the whole expenses incurred by my wife were paid by me and that I received no higher remuneration than any other player in the team.

CHAPTER XIX

MY FOURTH AUSTRALIAN TOUR

THERE was a strange feature about the team that set out for Australia in the autumn of 1924; we numbered as many as seventeen. One drawback to the plan of having so large a party was that six players would have to stand down each match, and some of them might never get into their real form by reason of certain enforced inactivity. That disadvantage was, however, off-set by the guarantee it provided that, in cases of illness or injury, there would always be reserve players available.

The team was captained by A. E. R. Gilligan, and we came to be known as "Gilligan's Men." J. W. H. T. Douglas, who found himself super-seded in the captaincy, served very loyally in his lower status. Nearly half of our number had never been "down under"; these new-comers were A. E. R. Gilligan himself, Freeman, Sand-ham, Sutcliffe, Tate, R. Tyldesley and Whysall.

Sensational cricket marked the tour from beginning to end. In the first Test, which was at Sydney, the match ran into the seventh day, which had never happened before. The "Aus-sies" started with 450, and then Sutcliffe and I put on 157 for the first wicket, but we could not keep on at that standard of run-getting and were all out for 298. Australia's second knock produced 452, leaving us with the stupendous task of getting 605 for a win. Manfully we shouldered the burden, Sutcliffe and I again hitting up a good lead for the first wicket—110. On we went, with centuries from Sutcliffe and Frank Woolley, until we passed the 400 mark, but the Australians were too far ahead and ultimately won by 195. It was the first time that 400 had been compiled in a fourth innings.

We had lost, but we had put up a brave fight. In my first innings, I scored a very important century, for now I had more Test centuries to my credit than any other player. I had beaten the total of six centuries, which had been scored by both A. C. MacLaren and Victor Trumper. The "Hillites"—that is to say, the crowd on the popular side—knew that I had beaten a record and rewarded me with a round of cheers. Sutcliffe had the distinction of hitting up a century in his first England v. Australia Test, and Ponsford did the same.

We travelled to Melbourne for the second Test. As in the first match, they won the toss and made a big first-innings total. This time it was 600, a record. When our turn came, Sutcliffe and I put on 283 for first wicket, and were batting during the whole of that Saturday. It was the first time that two players had carried their bats from morning to night. Monday brought a nasty jar for me; I was bowled by a full toss, Mailey's second ball that day. My score was 154, and Sutcliffe went on to 176. Our total was 479; excellent as that was, it was 121 short of the other side's. Another 250 was added to that 121 in Australia's second knock, which put them 371 ahead, to which we replied with 290—a second win for the "Aussies" by 81. The worthy Sutcliffe scored another century, following in the footsteps of Bardsley, who also scored two separate centuries in a Test match.

When Herbert Collins won the toss for the third time in the Adelaide Test, we decided to call him "Horseshoe" Collins. Luck did not, however, seem to be in the ascendant with him when the first three wickets of his side fell for 22 or when six players were out for 119. Nevertheless, his luck returned, for A. E. R. Gilligan and Tate had to retire, the first with a strained thigh and the other with a renewal of foot trouble. Freeman also was hurt and retired for a time. Then Ryder scored 201 not out. Nearly all of us had to bowl, but we could not prevent the last four wickets from putting on 370. Their total was 489, and we scored 365, out of which I scored 119 and Hendren 92. Then they hit up 250, so that we were confronted with the job of getting 375 for a victory. It was a most gallant struggle on our part. I was caught on the leg-side for 27 and had to ask myself whether that failure would affect the others. It did not; they marched ahead, and were only 27 behind, with two wickets to go, when, to add to the excitement, rain stopped play about three-quarters of an hour before the schedule time. I believe that, had we been able to play again that night, we might have won, because the Australian bowlers were very tired and exhausted. What a night of anxiety! What excitement at the start next day! Ladies in the grand-stand seemed in a state bordering on hysteria, and my wife reported having met Englishwomen so nerve-racked that one might imagine that they were waiting news from the seat of war.

When we had added 9, A. E. R. Gilligan was caught at mid-off. He had scored 30 and had taken nearly two hours over it; that shows the tension of the responsibility that he must have felt. Strudwick joined Freeman; there were 18 runs to be got. When 6 of the 18 had been scored, Freeman was caught at the wicket off a "teaser" from Mailey. Years afterwards, Strudwick, who was, of course, at the other wicket, said: "I can still see that ball going into Oldfield's hands off Freeman's bat. I never saw anything so dead certain." A tremendous burst of cheering greeted that catch; Australia had won the rubber, and the "Ashes" were still in their possession. In the grand-stand, the English ladies were weeping.

A. E. R. Gilligan took us round to the Australians' headquarters to tender our congratulations to the victors. At lunch, toasts were drunk, and there was a general expression of opinion that, on our merits, we ought not to have been so quickly defeated.

The tide turned. In the fourth Test, for which we returned to Melbourne, we won the toss, hit up 548, got the "Aussies" out for 269, and, when they were asked to follow on, they scored 250 for the second knock. It was a grand victory for us by an innings and 29. Sutcliffe scored another century, making four for the tour, but I was stumped very cleverly on the leg-side by Oldfield when I had got to 66. A curiosity in connection with the total for the Australians' second innings was that they had now scored 250 three times in succession, and in each case it had been in the second innings. The odds against such a coincidence in Test matches must be a million to one!

We had not won any Test match against Australia since August 1912, and my mind went back to my experiences on that earlier tour, when, by our splendid team-work, we had been victorious in four Tests out of five and had brought back the "Ashes" to dear old England. Not many changes had come over the scene in the dozen years that had passed. There were larger crowds in 1925 and larger grand-stands. Pros were now wearing gay sweaters, which were only worn by amateurs at the earlier date. Moustaches had vanished for the most part, including Frank Woolley's. We use spikes now only for batting and bowling; for fielding, rubber-soled shoes are less tiring. They heat the feet, but this is remedied by changing socks at lunch and tea intervals. Change shoes also from rubber to leather and back again. Otherwise it was the old scene repeated—the same enthusiasm on the part of the older spectators, the same hero-worship on the part of the youngsters.

I should prefer to end the chapter at this point, but the story of the fifth Test has to be told, and it had better be told briefly. We lost by 307. My scores were a "duck" and 13; Sutcliffe, who had been adding century to century, added now a "duck." The honours were with the enemy—especially with Grimmett for capturing eleven wickets for 82 in his very first Test match and with Oldfield for his wicket-keeping, rarely if ever surpassed in the cricket-field.

It was Oldfield who had been responsible for

my "duck," with a splendid catch wide on the leg-side off Gregory. I would not like the task of deciding whether the title of the greatest wicket-keeper should go to Strudwick, Sherwell or Oldfield. In Percy Sherwell, South Africa had a really great wicket-keeper—one who would compare favourably with the best in England or Australia. He was neat and trim in everything he did. Undoubtedly, Bert Oldfield was the best wicket-keeper of Australia in my time and is the best of those playing to-day. Here you have another fellow much like Struddy, so modest and unassuming is he. A characteristic of these two is their honesty; they would never do a wrong thing. I am sure that neither would appeal if he knew that the batsman was not out. Bert Oldfield was also a useful bat and many a time has been a thorn in England's side. When Australian wickets have been falling, he has come in, made a useful stand, and put up a good score. When keeping wicket his timing is perfect. He always wears big gloves, and they always seem to be in the right place to receive the ball, whether leg or off side. Strudwick, Sherwell and Oldfield were artists in all that they did—Sherwell perhaps the greatest personality; Oldfield the neatest; Strudwick the most amusing. The greatness of all three was in their true simplicity.

As regards our team, A. E. R. Gilligan made

an excellent captain, efficient, popular and gifted with a full measure of the tact that smoothed over difficulties. Maurice Tate's bowling was wonderful; he captured thirty-eight wickets during the tour, at a cost of 23 runs per wicket, thus eclipsing the performance by Syd Barnes in the winter of 1911–12. Sutcliffe shared with me four first-wicket partnerships of more than 100 runs, and I had the pleasure of bringing my aggregate of runs in Test matches to 2,398, beating the record of 1,931 held by A. C. MacLaren.

And so home to England. To see the welcome at Victoria Station you would think that "Gilligan's Men" had brought the "Ashes" back instead of leaving them behind us.

CHAPTER XX

MY BIG YEAR

MANY people, looking back over their past lives, can identify a particular year as the best that they have known. With one man it would be the year in which he married; with another the year in which he effected the biggest turnover on his business; with a club cricketer the year of his first century. My best was, without doubt, 1925. To begin with, although the team to which I belonged had been the losers in the great duel in Australia, I had achieved the fine batting average of 63·66 on the tour, and, apart from my centuries and first-wicket partnerships, had, as already stated, beaten A. C. MacLaren's record for the aggregate of runs in Test matches.

At the outset of the season in England, I had scored 113 centuries in first-class cricket and needed thirteen more to equal Dr. Grace's great record. After my return from Australia, I was feeling remarkably fit. I was in phenomenal form and started scoring centuries right away. In my first match at the Oval, I scored 34 and 47; thereafter the centuries followed in a series. Against Gloucestershire, in the second match, my score was 104; against Glamorgan I scored 109, and against Warwickshire 120. All those matches were at the Oval. Our fifth match was at Leyton against Essex; my score was 129. I did not play in Surrey's sixth match, but I hit up 189 in the seventh, which was at Nottingham against Notts.

There was nothing doing in the next two matches, which were against Leicestershire and Lancashire, and then I started on another lucrative spell, in which I just failed to get six centuries in succession. My scores were 107 and 87 against Essex; 104 and 143 not out against Cambridge University; and 111 against Somersetshire. Those four centuries at the Oval were followed by 215 at Birmingham against Warwickshire. Later on, at Lord's, I captained the Players against the Gentlemen; Herbert Sutcliffe and I put on 140 for first wicket, and I went on to score 140, which was the fifth century that I had hit up in the Gentlemen *v.* Players matches at Lord's. This was followed up with 105 against Kent at Black-heath—one of the few occasions on which we have beaten that county on that ground. It was a very satisfactory win by an innings and 69 runs.

That century at Blackheath was my 125th, and thus I now wanted only one century more to equal the Grand Old Man's record. At the time when the season started, I had no idea of over-taking the "W.G." record that year; it was only when I had put up six or eight centuries that the newspapers began to talk about it, and they implanted in me the determination to finish the task quickly. For some reason or other, the Press took it into their heads that the next century, the 126th, would be the big thing, because the record would then be equalled, whereas I thought that the 127th would be the big thing, because it would beat the record. Every match the papers expected me to get level with Grace. I felt that every eye in England was focused on me, and I began to get rather harassed. Surely there was plenty of time; it was bound to come sooner or later. The end of my career was not exactly in sight, but no, the Press wanted it at once, and I was expected to get it every time that I went to the wicket.

I well remember the next match at Brighton. There was a big army of reporters, with photographers galore, cinematograph apparatus, etc., and sore was their disappointment when I returned l.b.w. to Maurice Tate for 1, in the second over. Brighton has never been a lucky ground for me; I expected 100 there least of anywhere. On arrival in Brighton overnight, I received a trunk call and was asked what I felt like. I inquired: "What do you mean?" The answer was: "Oh, to-morrow's your Big Day, you know.' I said: "I don't agree; I have never got a century at Brighton yet, and I don't expect to get one now. It's not so easy as all that." There was nothing more to be said; so we rang off.

A little later in the evening, a Press photographer put in an appearance and wanted to know whether I would allow him to make a photograph of me in swimming costume on the beach. When I raised objections, he said rather apologetically: "You can get up early, Mr. Hobbs, before anybody's about, and you needn't go into the water." That was one of the few occasions on which I did not oblige a Press photographer.

About this time, the story of my life was being filmed, and I am afraid that I led the operator a rare dance, lugging his paraphernalia around the country. After the Brighton match, the weather broke down a bit, and I think that I was getting a bit stale. After such a phenomenal series of centuries, a reaction had set in, and the mental strain was beginning to tell. That equalling century wouldn't come; it became elusive, for there followed a somewhat lean period, in which I scored 22 against Kent, 52 and 38 against Gloucestershire, 54 and 1 against Notts, 49 and 4 not out against Middlesex, and 31 against Leicestershire.

Nothing would have pleased me more than to have hit up that century when batting against Notts on the August Bank Holiday at the Oval. This is always a big match—a great rally of cricket fans. We always had a large gathering of real Surrey partisans, many of whom never attended any other game during the season. It has ever been a source of very deep regret to me that I didn't score my 100th century, my 126th, my 127th, or my 150th, at the Oval, where always the crowd and the members have been such true friends.

I cherished the fervent hope that I might be able to compensate them in a way that would, I am sure, have proved a mutual pleasure by scoring my 200th century in their presence; but, alas, it was not to be. Many a time I have pictured the scene in my mind and felt that I could hear the tumultuous cheering that would have rung out if I had succeeded. As often as I think about it, a lump rises in my throat, but at such times I find comfort in the thought that I had the will to achieve; it was well that it was in my heart.

It seemed that a whole circus was following me round. The newspapers were working everybody into a state of fever heat. At the time I thought it comic that, after my 54 against Notts on the Bank Holiday, on the placards of one evening journal appeared the words in large type: "Hobbs Fails Again."

Straight from the match against Leicestershire at the Oval, I went to Taunton to play against Somerset on Saturday, August 15th, and the Monday and Tuesday following. On the Taunton ground I had never scored a century and had little hopes of managing it on this occasion. The Saturday was a beautiful day, and there was a fair crowd. Somerset won the toss and just before four o'clock they were all out for 167. Then Sandham and I walked out to open our innings; it was about ten minutes past four, and that left two hours and twenty minutes for play. The crowd had greatly increased, and obviously they had come in the hope of seeing this memorable century scored.

I felt fairly normal, although pardonably fidgety towards the end of the day, for I remember an incident that happened about six o'clock. I played a ball to mid-on and called for a run; then, seeing that there was no run in it, I tried to send my partner, D. J. Knight, back. Undoubtedly, I should have been run out, but D. J. Knight very sportingly crossed me and ran to the wicket to which the ball was being returned. He thus sacrificed his wicket for mine; otherwise

Lord's Ground.

MIDDLESEX v. SURREY.

SATURDAY, MONDAY & TUESDAY, AUGUST 28, 30, 31, 1926.

SURREY.	First Innngs.	Second Innings.
1 Hobbs	not out 316	
2 Sandham	c Hendren, b Haig 58	
3 Ducat	b Durston 41	
4 Shepherd	c and b Stevens 15	
5 D. R. Jardine	c and b Powell 103	
6 A. Jeacocke	run out 26	
†7 P. G. H. Fender	not out 1	
8 E. R. T. Holmes		
9 Peach	Innings closed.	
*10 Strudwick		
11 Fenley, S.		
	B 12, l-b 7, w , n-b , 19	B , l-b , w , n-b ,
	Total 579	Total ......

FALL OF THE WICKETS.

1-115	2-216	3-258	4-528	5-575	6	7	8-	9-	10-
1-	2-	3-	4-	5-	6-	7-	8-	9-	10-

ANALYSIS OF BOWLING.

Name.	1st Innings.					2nd Innings.				
	O.	M.	R.	W.	Wd. N-b.	O.	M.	R.	W.	Wd. N-b.
Haig	37	7	118	1	... ...	...	...	...	...	... ...
Durston	31	12	69	1	... ...	...	...	...	...	... ...
Allen	19	3	88	0	... ...	...	...	...	...	... ...
Stevens	22.3	1	95	1	... ...	...	...	...	...	... ...
Lee	8	1	44	0	... ...	...	...	...	...	... ...
Powell	27	4	109	1	... ...	...	...	...	...	... ...
Enthoven	10	1	37	0	... ...	...	...	...	...	... ...

MIDDLESEX.	First Innings.	Second Innings.
1 H. L. Dales	b Jardine 52	c Fender, b Holmes 4
2 G. T. S. Stevens	c Strudwick, b Holmes ... 2	c Fender, b Peach 63
3 G. O. Allen	c Shepherd, b Peach 21	c Jardine, b Fenley 17
4 Hendren, E.	not out 101	c Fenley, b Jardine 37
5 H. J. Enthoven	run out 1	b Fenley 5
†6 F. T. Mann	c Peach, b Jardine 3	not out 37
7 N. Haig	c Strudwick, b Fender ... 12	c Shepherd, b Fender ... 18
8 Lee, H. W.	run out 42	c Strudwick, b Holmes ... 31
9 Murrell	c Peach, b Fenley 20	c Fenley, b Peach 7
10 Durston	b Fender 0	b Holmes 1
11 Powell	c and b Fender 0	c Strudwick, b Holmes ... 4
	B 15, l-b 6, w , n-b , 21	B 11, l-b 3, w 2, n-b 1, 17
	Total 275	Total 241

FALL OF THE WICKETS.

1-2	2-37	3-112	4-120	5-125	5-147	7 248	8-275	9-275	10 275
1-5	2-31	3-115	4-122	5-156	6-188	7-209	8-224	9-229	10-241

ANALYSIS OF BOWLING.

Name.	1st Innings.					2nd Innings.				
	O.	M.	R.	W.	Wd. N-b.	O.	M.	R.	W.	Wd. N-b.
Holmes	14	2	41	1	... ...	15.4	2	49	4	1 ...
Peach	18	7	26	1	... ...	23	5	41	2	... ...
Fenley	24	4	76	1	... ...	23	4	66	2	... ...
Fender	23	5	76	3	... ...	14	2	38	1	1 1
Shepherd	9	5	22	0	... ...	8	3	12	0	... ...
Jardine	8	2	13	2	... ...	6	1	18	1	... ...

Umpires—Burrows and Chidgey. Scorers—Burton and Boyington.

The figures on the Scoring Board show the Batsmen in.

Play Commences 1st day at 12, 2nd and 3rd day at 11.15

Luncheon at 1.30 p.m. †Captain. *Wicket-keeper. Stumps drawn at 5.30 p.m.

THE SCORE CARD SHOWING HOBBS'S HIGHEST SCORE: A RECORD AT
LORD'S

TESTIMONIAL PRESENTED BY THE M.C.C. TO EACH MEMBER OF THE
1928–29 TOUR

another story of my 126th century would have to be written. Actions like that make cricket the fine game that it is and endear us to one another. Here was an amateur who was unable to come into the side until August sacrificing his wicket for a professional. I am everlastingly grateful to him for his chivalrous act.

At one period, I had hopes of reaching my century that night, but Somerset, with an eye on Monday's gate, had other ideas, and, towards the finish, bowled to keep me quiet.

At close of play, I was 91 not out. Over the week-end, those 9 needed runs were in my mind almost continually. There were columns of matter in the Press—pictures, long reports, comment by the yard, etc. Again the newspaper placards got busy; it was now: "Will Hobbs hit those Nine?" Nevertheless, I spent a very quiet Sunday, never leaving the hotel grounds, save to go to church in the morning. In the hotel I was given room No. 9, and Sandham was given No. 37. As I have said, I had a perfect horror of all nines, whereas thirty-seven was supposed to be my lucky number. Sandy, knowing my views about nines, generously changed rooms with me. I wonder if there is anything in it.

The window of the hotel dining-room overlooked the railway station, and, as I was sitting at dinner on the Sunday night, I was greatly amused to see a shoal of reporters and photographers streaming out of the station, when the train from London arrived. They had come to be in at the death, taking it for granted that I should get those 9, although it was by no means a cert.

15

I slept well that night and awoke fresh and fit. When I arrived at the ground, there was a huge crowd waiting at the gates to get in; but, evidently, the authorities had not sufficient entrances or gatemen, for the crowd was not all inside when the time came for me to continue my innings. J. Daniell, the Somerset captain, asked me if I would mind waiting until those outside had all been admitted, and so I had just the experience that was likely to make me more fidgety than ever—namely, the experience of hanging about, waiting for the critical moment. It is something like sitting in a dentist's parlour, thinking about the dentist's chair. However, as soon as I reached the wicket I was all right. A few minutes later, I had hit up the 9.

In my pocket was a telegram which I had written out. It was addressed to my wife and was worded as follows:

"Got it at last.—JACK."

When I had hit up the 9 runs, I signalled the groundsman and handed him the telegram. Before I knew where I was, the Somerset fielders were all round me, showering their congratulations, which I heard with difficulty, because of the vociferous cheering that surged up from all quarters of the ground. That telegram to my wife somehow got into the newspapers. It had no business to be made public, and I have often wondered how it came to be printed. It's a complete mystery.

Then P. G. H. Fender, the captain of our side, walked over from the pavilion with something in a glass. "Champagne," said the spectators to one another. Nothing of the kind; it was ginger-ale. P. G. H. Fender and I have often joked about the contents of that glass. As a matter of fact, I had become a teetotaller before that date, and I did not celebrate the event alcoholically.

It would be a great mistake to think that Somerset was kind enough to make me a present of those 9 runs. Robertson-Glasgow was bowling for all he was worth, and J. J. Bridges was working the leg-theory with such effectiveness that he beat me with it for 101.

Somerset, fortunately for me, scored 374 on that Monday, and Surrey needed 183 to win, which gave me a chance to get another century on the Tuesday and thus to beat the "W.G." record. I was successful in getting it, and we won the match. Here I have to chronicle another of those chivalrous actions of a colleague, for Andy Sandham, when he saw that there was a good possibility of the record-breaking century being obtained, hung back and gave me the opportunity of scoring that century before the 183 runs were knocked off that were necessary for a win. After the tumultuous reception of my equalising 100, this record-breaking produced a sort of anticlimax, for the Pressmen and the photographers and most of the spectators had departed!

Within three days of my beating the record of the Grand Old Doctor which had stood for so long a time, I was startled and amazed to receive from Balmoral Castle a letter from H.M. the King, through Lord Stamfordham, congratulating me upon scoring 127 centuries and on putting up the new record of fourteen centuries in one season. It is not given to everyone to receive such a letter from the King. I thought it very gracious on his part to notice my achievement and naturally was pardonably proud. It is another evidence of the very real personal interest taken by our King in the sports and pastimes of the people.

Although I had greatly rejoiced at having done something memorable, there was a little sadness in my mind at the thought of passing the Grand Old Doctor's figures, for during all my life the famous "W.G." had meant a lot to me. He had one outstanding natural advantage over me—his powerful physique. On the other hand, he had had to overcome technical difficulties in regard to wickets that did not exist in my case.

After my return to London, the B.B.C. authorities invited me to give a talk over the wireless on the subject of my 126th and 127th centuries. It was one of the most terrifying ordeals that I had ever faced up to then, far outweighing any Test match. It is rather absurd how we dread such an experience, for, after all, there is nothing in it; it is just a case of getting used to it. To me it was a peculiar sensation; whilst talking to thousands of people I felt as if I was talking to myself. On the next occasion of my appearance before the microphone, I felt quite comfortable by comparison.

The Surrey authorities very kindly allowed me to rest when the next match took place. I thoroughly needed that rest, and went to stay with a friend in Dorset for three days. I rejoined the team at the Oval for our match against Yorkshire on August 22nd. Surrey won the toss, and, directly I appeared out of the pavilion, I received a truly wonderful ovation. The members rose *en masse*; the people all round the ground cheered me loudly all the way to the middle. It was a remarkable reception—one that I remember most vividly to this day. When I reached the wicket, the Yorkshire players in a very sporty way gathered round me and gave me three cheers. I started off with three 4's in the first over, but was caught out to a brilliant catch at fine leg for 19.

A week or two later, playing at the Scarborough Festival for the Players against the Gentlemen, I scored 266 not out, which ranks as the highest score in all Gentlemen *v*. Players matches, and I wound up the season by knocking up 106 in the match between the Champion County, Yorkshire, and the Rest of England. Incidentally, in the second innings of that match, I completed 3,000 runs for the 1925 season—the only season in which I have attained that figure.

I have already referred to my 120 runs that year against Warwickshire. Sandham and I on that occasion put on 232 for first wicket. It was the hundredth of the series of my partnerships in which a century was scored. I was very pleased to have Sandham in with me on that occasion. He has been a splendid partner throughout many years, and he is undoubtedly a very fine player. It was unlucky that his career clashed with Herbert Sutcliffe's and mine; for, if he had come along at a different period, he would have opened for England more often than he has done. He has not been the luckiest of players. His benefit match in 1927 was partly ruined by rain, and I am very delighted to know that he is to receive another benefit during this 1935 season. May he have a bumper!

The Gentlemen *v*. Players match at the Oval was an unusually thrilling affair, well worth while for those who played and for those who watched. I was captain and declared twice. The Players batted first and hit up 403 for eight; my contribution was only 5. The Gentlemen followed with 458. In our second innings we compiled 252 for seven; I was run out for 51. That left the Gentlemen the task of getting 198 in one hour and three-quarters against some of the best bowling in the country. This they succeeded in doing, winning the match in the last over of the day. I recall that the very last ball sent down was a full toss from Alec Kennedy, one of the best and most consistent good-length bowlers in the game; it was promptly dispatched to the boundary, and the match was won and lost. Alec was most apologetic to me about that full toss, but I was glad to reassure him, for, although we had lost the match, we had done a good thing for cricket in making possible such a sporty finish.

I look back upon 1925 as my big year for many reasons. For the first time, I was top of the batting averages, with an aggregate of 3,024 runs in forty-eight innings; five times not out; 266 not out highest score; and average 70·32. I had set up a new record by scoring sixteen centuries in one season, the previous best being thirteen by C. B. Fry and Tom Hayward.

This period of prolific run-getting stands out very clearly in my recollection. It would, indeed, have been a great record if I had succeeded in scoring six consecutive centuries. As it was, in the match against Essex we led by 213 on the first innings and, instead of directing Essex to follow on, P. G. H. Fender decided that we should go in and get runs quickly. He gave us orders to go for runs, and I rattled up 87 in an hour out of 135. I well remember being out to a full toss, trying to hit it too hard or, as we cricketers say, making too much of a fuss of it. I was caught and bowled.

My innings of 215 against Warwickshire at Birmingham was very hard luck on Harry Howell, for a great local admirer had promised him a five-pound note if he got my wicket. This he ought to have got, for I was missed at second slip off his bowling in the second over of the day, when I had scored 8. I felt very sympathetic towards Harry, and said: "Hard luck, old man!" He never moaned, however, nor let it get him down. Seeing that I scored more than 200 after that miss, I have often wondered since whether I ought not to have offered him that fiver myself.

As a result of that year's performance, the Surrey Club organised a testimonial for me, heading the list of subscriptions with two hundred and fifty guineas. I was rather afraid that this would jeopardise my chances of a second benefit, and, when I mentioned my fears to them, they very generously granted me the Notts match on the August Bank Holiday in 1926. They also arranged that the testimonial list should be kept open, so that the two could join up. Without going into figures, I can say that it was very successful, although not to be compared with the wonderful benefits given to Yorkshire and Lancashire players in recent years. To give me the Notts match at the Oval was a delightfully generous act on the part of the Surrey Club, and I am the only player to whom they have accorded that great compliment.

My "ain folk" at Cambridge were also keen on celebrating my achievement in beating W. G. Grace's record. I was entertained at a dinner and concert at the Guildhall. Various suggestions were made at the time, one of which was that I should receive the Freedom of the Borough of Cambridge. Another proposal, however, was put forward that pleased me much more; it was to build a pavilion on Parker's Piece, to be called the Hobbs Pavilion.

Up to that time there was no proper accommodation there for home players or visiting sides. They had to dress in a tent or in a room in Tom Hayward's inn, which adjoins Parker's Piece. This Pavilion would remedy a much-felt grievance. Subscriptions began to pour in. Then the promoters found that the building would cost more than had been anticipated, as they wanted to do the thing well. There was a lull in the subscriptions, and a sort of stalemate ensued. However, a great cricket enthusiast and personal friend of mine, Mr. E. H. Church, came to the rescue, with the result that the Pavilion was completed. In April, 1930, Mrs. Hobbs and I went down for the opening ceremony. A very nice

Pavilion it is, too, and greatly appreciated by all cricketers who play on the world-famous Parker's Piece.

In September of that year, 1930, I took a side to Cambridge, including six Internationals, to carry out a promise that I would, when the Pavilion was finished, bring down a team to play for the benefit of the local hospital. The match was a thorough success and the crowd the biggest that I ever saw on Parker's Piece.

One outcome of that eventful season was that I was inundated with requests or offers of every sort and kind. The requests included the lending of my name to numerous advertisements. Amongst the offers were an invitation to appear on the cinema stage, as the preliminary to the showing of a film that I had made, and an invitation to appear in a big film with the promise of a suitable leading lady to play opposite. Another big offer was for my appearance at the Coliseum. Sir Oswald Stoll wrote to me, proposing a contract for £250 a week; I was, I think, to appear in some Cricket Scena, but the stage never appealed to me, and I remember receiving at that time a letter in which the writer congratulated me on not cheapening the Great Game.

CHAPTER XXI

CAPTURING THE "ASHES"

NOT only was 1926 another Test match year; it was the year in which, thanks to England's victory over Australia, the enthusiasm of the whole country was aroused on a scale never before witnessed in my time. The Australian team that visited us contained some old friends of ours and also some players who had not before been seen here. Grimmett, Ponsford, Arthur Richardson and Woodfull were new to Tests in England, and some of our side were also new-comers to Test cricket. For the first time, pro-fessionals were put on the Selection Committee, that important compliment being paid to Rhodes and myself.

The first Test match at Nottingham was almost a complete wash-out. Sutcliffe opened with me, and we scored 32 without loss before rain stopped the game for good. The second Test was at Lord's. A. W. Carr, who was our captain, lost the toss; the Australians went in and scored 338, more than half of which total came from Bardsley. He hit up 173 not out, carrying his bat throughout the whole innings—an achievement only attained twice before in all the England v. Australia matches.

The second day of that match produced a serious episode, although it had an amusing side. A hose-pipe had been left running in the middle

234

of the ground, and water had run across the centre of the pitch in a stream a couple of yards wide. At first ulterior motives were suspected. It was suggested that somebody had deliberately tried to flood the pitch, but the result of investigations afterwards revealed that one of the groundsmen had left the water running. When Sutcliffe and I opened our innings, the wicket was in excellent condition, with the exception of that wet stream. Jack Gregory tried to bump a ball, but it bounced on that moist patch and only crawled along, which made him rather annoyed. At lunch-time, we had scored 77 in seventy minutes, and we afterwards took the first-wicket score to 182. My score totalled 119, and I was criticised for taking a long time between 90 and 100, but Richardson was bowling "leg-theory" and Ryder wide on the off; I failed to see why I should indulge in risky play, because England was not yet in a safe position. A. W. Carr declared on the third day at 475 for three, and was blamed for providing the Australians with a valuable afternoon's batting.

In the course of the play on the second day of that match, "Patsy" Hendren scored his first century in a Test match against Australia. He went round beaming in a fashion that seemed to mean: "Haven't I the real Test temperament? Haven't I just?" Yes; certainly he had; we were all delighted with him. That was one splash in a fine series of big scores; it is a great thing for any player to make his first century against the Australians, especially at Lord's. Somehow I have always been interested in "Patsy". I have played with him in many matches and have watched his career with infinite pleasure. He is my ideal batsman. He has all the strokes, on all types of wicket, against all kinds of bowling. The power that he gets into that off drive of his is amazing. The ball appears only just to be pushed, and yet it travels through the covers as fast as another player's full-shouldered drive. His fore-arms must be possessed of great strength; that and his perfect timing must be the secret. As a fielder, he is excellent, picks up wonderfully and cleanly when moving at top speed, and returns the ball like lightning. He is of a most cheery disposition, a great humorist, popular alike with players and spectators on every ground that he visits. He is cricket's Prime Minister of mirth, and we all gather round to listen to his stories, he tells them so well. Perhaps his speciality is his nigger stories.

In the third Test, at Leeds, A. W. Carr won the toss, but put the enemy in because the wicket was likely to be sticky after the rain that had fallen. Bardsley was at once caught at slip off Tate—the first ball of the match—and Macartney was missed off the fifth. That looked like a justi-fication of A. W. Carr's decision to send the other side in. Macartney, however, after his escape, put a different complexion on the position of affairs by hitting up a century before lunch. Macartney's innings was a wonderful display. He afterwards said: "I felt like going for everything, and I went for it." Woodfull and Richardson also scored centuries, and the Australia total was 494.

Our first knock produced 294, and we had to follow on. However, we saved the game. My second innings score was 88, and, when I had reached 77, I heard some applause; it turned out afterwards that I had, at that point, beaten the record for the largest number of runs in the England v. Australia Tests—a record previously held by Clem Hill with 2,660 runs.

On the second day of the fourth Test, which took place at Old Trafford, our skipper, Carr, was ill with tonsillitis and could not play. The Selectors paid me the compliment of asking me to take command. P. F. Warner came into the dressing-room and said to me: "We have talked things over, and we would like you to lead the side." I replied: "You are doing me a great honour, but Mr. Stevens is in the eleven." G. T. S. Stevens was an amateur, but he was a new-comer. P. F. Warner's answer was: "We would like you to take it on, all the same." So I agreed, and the crowd gave me a most encouraging reception when I led the team out. The Press seemed as pleased as the public, and one newspaper later put out a placard: "Captain Hobbs 'Logs' 74." The kudos of being captain of an England team was, of course, very highly appreciated by me, but I soon encountered the worrying side of the position when Woodfull and Macartney hit up 192 between them. Woodfull was four hours at the wicket, and the match was a draw.

Personally, I prefer to see an amateur as captain, and most professionals prefer it, especially in International cricket, chiefly because of its social side and because of the natural dislike of professionals to boss their own fellows. At the same time, I cannot understand the policy of putting a young amateur, with practically no experience, to captain teams in county cricket for an odd match or two, when there are professionals in the side who are obviously more experienced and quite capable of taking over the leadership. Recent years have shown how eminently successful they can prove themselves in captaining sides; take, for instance, the case of Maurice Tate, "Patsy" Hendren, Frank Woolley and Herbert Sutcliffe.

On the whole, I do not think that captaincy has improved during my career. We are such sticklers for tradition in insisting on an amateur captain, regardless of the question whether he can pull his weight as a player or not. The time is coming when we shall have to change our views, because each year more and more amateurs find it difficult to afford the time for playing, and the day may not be very far distant when there will be no amateurs of sufficient ability to put into an England side.

The old Australian method was probably the most satisfactory. There the team was chosen first, and then the players in the team elected their own captain. That is better than the English system, where a player may obtain the position for no particular reason except that he is an amateur.

Before the last Test, there was the match against Notts at the Oval, which was given to me by the Surrey Club as my second benefit.

A. W. Carr had not got over his tonsillitis and came to captain the Notts players with his throat wrapped up. He was fulfilling a promise he had given to play in my benefit match—a very sporting act on his part. When the captains met to decide the order of going in, P. G. H. Fender took me out to toss the coin, out of compliment to me as beneficiare. The coin fell "heads." A. W. Carr was very hoarse, and I said as a joke: "Did you call 'tails'? I couldn't quite hear." Whatever the state of his throat he didn't swallow that.

The fifth Test was at the Oval. On the previous day a reporter came to interview me. He was not a specialist in cricket matters and put questions to me that showed that he had given no attention to what had been in all the newspapers for days past. Finally, he asked: "Will you be playing, Mr. Hobbs?" Such is fame!

A. P. F. Chapman was captain of the England team for this final Test. A. W. Carr had not distinguished himself against the googly bowling of Mailey and Grimmett, and his health had been unsatisfactory. Nevertheless, there was a great hubbub over the dropping of A. W. Carr. I fail to understand why the dropping of a captain should cause such a fuss. When Woolley or Hendren was left out of a team, no such uproar was created.

As our team succeeded in winning under A. P. F. Chapman's captaincy, the fuss died down. When A. P. F. Chapman in his turn was dropped out of the captaincy of the Test match at the Oval in 1930 and was replaced by R. E. S. Wyatt, there was another big fuss, which lasted a very long time because Wyatt's team was unsuccessful.

The fifth Test began at the Oval fairly well, for Sutcliffe and I put on 53 for first wicket, but I was bowled by a full toss from Mailey when my score was 37. I smile now when I think of that full toss. I had tried to place Mailey for 4, and I said to myself: "Fancy missing a thing like that!" I can still picture Tommy Andrews, who was fielding at silly point, raising his hands and exclaiming: "What a turn-up for the books!" Our total was 280, and Australia hit up 302. When Mailey went on in the second innings, I called out to him: "Now then, Arthur, play the game; no more full tosses." He replied laughingly: "All right, Jack." Sutcliffe and I had an hour's batting late on the Monday, and in the night there was a thunderstorm. On the Tuesday, as we patted the wicket after the first over, I said to Herbert: "Jolly bad luck that rain; it has cooked our chances." He agreed, and I said the same thing to Young, the umpire. If it had been a lighthearted affair on Clapham Common, the umpire would have said: "Cheer up, I'll do my best for you." But the Oval umpire had no such consoling reply. He only said: "Yes, it's hard luck."

I really thought that our chance was small. The Australians were on tiptoe, and undoubtedly should have got many of us out on that wicket before lunch. As the time went on and we were still there, the atmosphere became tense, especially amongst those behind the bowlers, where the spectators could see how much the ball was turning. Later on, when Richardson was bowling, with three or four short-legs, and making the ball turn and kick, the crowd, who thought that I must be caught at short leg sooner or later, heaved a big sigh of relief at the end of each over. I seemed to stick at the pavilion end, and Noble says that I kept there to give the idea that Richardson was difficult and encourage Collins to keep him on. The fact is that he was bowling so well that I couldn't get away.

At lunch-time, Sutcliffe and I had scored 161 altogether. Before going to lunch, we stopped to pat down the pitch. "Well played, Herbert," said I. "Well played, Jack," said he. In the interval, we were presented to the Prince of Wales. Then I turned the 97 I had already scored into a century, and the crowd kept on cheering for nearly a minute. Almost immediately afterwards, I was walking off to the pavilion, bowled by Gregory. Sutcliffe went on to 161, and we finished the day at 375 for six—in other words, 353 in front. That evening I dined at the Trocadero with a friend; everybody was talking about the match. Later, we went to a cinema and saw Sutcliffe and myself on the film patting down the pitch; but, as the "talkies" had not come into fashion, the audience could not know that the figures they saw were saying "Well played" to one another.

I was more excited that night than on any occasion, except, perhaps, when I had scored three centuries in successive Test matches in Australia. I felt that victory was assured, and that we two had done our share. Moreover, I

16

shared in the kudos of the victory, because
Chapman, during the match, had consulted
Rhodes and myself a good deal. On the last day,
I remember worrying Chapman to move Rhodes
from long leg to the gully, so that Geary might
be added to the slips, and Woodfull was caught
by Geary next ball. I recall this move because
it happened to come off so suddenly. The score-
board said 1 for one, and Australia's prospects
seemed to have vanished. So they had. Rhodes
took four wickets and Larwood three, and they
only scored 125. We won by 289. Then the
Oval crowd rushed at us, and we had to scamper
as fast as possible to avoid being mobbed. I was
cut off from the others and had to be protected
by the police.

It was hopeless to try to get the crowd to go
home. They yelled for us to come out on the
pavilion balcony. They were shouting for each
of us in turn. "We want Chapman." "We want
Collins." So it went on. "We want Hobbs."
"We want Sutcliffe." "We want Rhodes." We
had at last to show ourselves. There were many
thousands in the assemblage below us, and yet
it struck me as remarkable that, in that vast sea
of faces, I picked out my wife.

Next day I heard that it took hours for Sutcliffe
to get away from the Oval, but my wife and I
slipped off at the Vauxhall entrance, where a
friend was waiting with a car. Thus we got
quietly away from one of the most wonderful
scenes that the world of cricket has ever
known.

Quite apart from my share in the Test matches,

I had a good season in 1926, scoring ten centuries and only failing by 51 to reach an aggregate of 3,000 runs. In our match against Middlesex at Lord's, I had the satisfaction of scoring 316 not out—the highest score on that classic ground. It was one run more than the record, which had been gained in the previous year by Percy Holmes. In the match between Surrey and Oxford at the Oval, Andy Sandham and I put on 428 for first wicket, which is, I believe, the highest opening partnership for Surrey. At that time, it was the second highest first-wicket stand in all first-class cricket in England. Sandy scored 183; my contribution was 261. Some people thought that I made a mistake in batting so long just before a Test match. The players, when I arrived at Lord's for the Test match, said: "Well played; but aren't you tired?" Beyond feeling a wee bit stiff, I was quite all right. Even the King, when both teams were introduced to him during the Lord's match, spoke to me about my big score and asked if I was not tired. Looking back, I don't think that it was wise, although in this case it had no detrimental effect, for I managed to compile 119 in the Test.

On the general question of rest for players before a Test match, I am strongly of opinion that it is necessary. It certainly helps for fitness and keenness. Moreover, the players want time for their railway journeys. It seems to me to be very bad policy for a Test player to be playing in a county match on the day before a Test and then have to take a long journey by train. Since 1930, the Test matches in England have started on Fridays, so that this question has not arisen, as the players get two days' rest before a Test.

I had the pleasure of hitting up a century again in the Gentlemen v. Players match at Lord's. This match provided some very remarkable batting—1,218 runs for the loss of twenty-one wickets. My total was 163; Sutcliffe and Tyldesley hit up centuries, and A. P. F. Chapman scored one for the Gentlemen.

My average for 1926 was: Innings, 41; runs, 2,949; times not out, 3; highest score, 316 not out; average, 77·60. This put me top of the averages again, and it was higher than my 1925 average.

CHAPTER XXII

TWO YEARS IN ENGLAND

WE were able to return to the peaceful atmosphere of the County Championship in 1927, and we could thoroughly enjoy it, free from combats with Test teams from distant parts of the Empire. After a match at Lord's against M.C.C., in which I scored 61 and 13, I opened my season at the Oval with 112 and 104 against Hampshire. This was the fourth time that I had performed the feat of a century in each innings of a match. Jack Newman got 102 not out in both innings in that same Oval match.

Although I have said that we were free from Test cricket, there was a New Zealand team over here, and I scored 146 against that team. In the second innings, we tried to get 308 runs in three hours and ten minutes and were 24 runs short when stumps were pulled up, having lost eight wickets in the attempt. I was caught down at long leg for a "duck." That was the first time that I had the pleasure of playing against New Zealand.

My 142nd century was compiled against Kent at Blackheath. I scored 121, and it was my hundredth century for Surrey. Before that match I had managed to contract some form of skin trouble and had been absent from nine games. Just after I started playing again, the team was picked for the Gentlemen v. Players match at Lord's, and I was omitted. This was a grief to

245

me, because somehow I thought that I ought to have been asked whether I was fit. Therefore, my 121 against Kent—the match before the important event at Lord's—gave me great satisfaction. I was never more keen to get a century and never remember trying harder. Perhaps this sounds a trifle spiteful, but I am only human.

I recall with pleasure another century that year against Notts at the Oval on the August Bank Holiday. This century mark was reached before lunch, and worked out at a run per minute—in other words, 105 runs in 105 minutes. After lunch I went on to 131, and the innings was described by a well-known writer as "the best poem of 1927." Later in August, during an England v. the Rest trial match at Lord's, I tore a leg muscle and had to retire; my score at the time was 23. This trouble also caused me to miss a match or two.

My highest score that season was 150 against Yorkshire at the Oval. As this was Andy Sandham's benefit, it stands out in my memory. He had been my partner in many triumphs, and I was naturally anxious that he should do well, and the pleasure that I derived from my 150 was marred by the fact that the benefit was, as I said in an earlier chapter, spoilt by rain.

Altogether, it was rather a thin year for me. I failed to score 2,000 runs, but I did get seven centuries. My average was: Innings, 32; runs, 1,641; highest score, 150; times not out, 1; and average 52·93. I was well down the list—twelfth in fact.

I had a very successful year in 1928. It was

also a very busy year, for we had a visit from a West Indies team. For the first time, they enjoyed Test match rank. In one respect 1928 brought me bad luck, for I tore a muscle in my thigh again when chasing a ball to the boundary in the Gentlemen *v.* Players match at the Oval. This caused me to be absent from the big Lord's match. I turned out in the Test trial, England *v.* the Rest at Lord's, and the trouble reasserted itself, so that I was compelled, acting on the advice of a doctor present, to refrain from fielding again after tea. The outcome of this injury was that I was debarred from playing against the West Indians on the historic occasion of their first Test match in England. I was, however, fit enough to play in their second Test at Manchester, where I scored 53, and in their third Test at the Oval, where my score was 159.

In this Manchester Test, a ball was sent up higher than I have ever seen a ball go. It was hit by Constantine. Freeman looked round to see if anybody would tackle it and found that he had to go for the catch. It went through his hands on to his chest and nearly choked him; in addition, he had the mortification of reading in the papers next day that he missed an easy catch. A ball played by Roach in that match came to me at mid-off on my left side. I crossed the ball with my feet, picked up, and threw with a single action. Elliott accepted in fine style and swept Challenor, Roach's partner, out by yards. I felt pleased to know that I could still field in that manner—a manner that grows more difficult as the years pass.

Another match against West Indies I well remember. I was playing for Mr. Leveson-Gower's Eleven at Scarborough. The West Indians started their second innings on the last day 119 ahead, with only one man out. It looked long odds on a draw. V. W. C. Jupp and Maurice Tate, however, brought about such a collapse that we were left with only 211 to win, and those we knocked off for the loss of two wickets. I scored 119 not out. In all, I hit up three centuries against West Indies, as I had scored one against them when playing for Surrey at the Oval.

At Trent Bridge, Surrey had a great win against Notts, although the latter started off with 457, to which we only replied with 288. Instead of making us follow on, Carr elected to bat again and lost four wickets for 15. Next morning, they were all out for 50, leaving us 220 to win, which we managed in two hours and three-quarters for three wickets. I scored 114 in our first knock— my 150th century in first-class cricket. In the second knock, my score was a blob. Fender and Peach bowled superbly and turned a possible defeat into a magnificent victory. As with my 100th century, so with my 150th, it had not been scored where I wished—not at the dear old Oval amongst my ain folk.

Another important innings of mine, important chiefly for its speed, was for the Rest of England against the Champion County, Lancashire, at the Oval. My score was 150—the first hundred in an hour and three-quarters and the last fifty in just over half an hour. Sutcliffe got 139, bringing his aggregate to 3,000 for the year.

I had the splendid average of 82 that year, finishing second to Jardine with 87·15. Although I scored twelve centuries, three others beat me with thirteen—Hendren, Mead and Sutcliffe. My top score was 200 not out against Warwickshire at Birmingham.

CHAPTER XXIII

FAREWELL TO AUSTRALIA

ONCE more, and for the last time as a player, I was to see that wonderful land "down under" in the winter of 1928–9. We set off, a merry band; for the "Ashes" were in our possession, and we had every confidence that we could bring them back again from Australia to these shores. That was the determined feeling of the players and of the great assembly of friends who saw us off at Victoria Station in September, the rest having left in the usual way from Tilbury.

We were seventeen in the team, but twelve of us, staying in England for the match against the Champion County, caught up the *Otranto* at Toulon. When I got to Toulon, my wife reported that the *Otranto* had passed through a terrible thunderstorm the night before reaching Toulon; we had, fortunately, missed it by travelling overland through France; it had been a rather terrifying experience for those who came through it.

Nothing of very great interest happened on the way out, but we had the disappointment, on arrival in Australia, of finding that one of our number, Sam Staples, of Notts, would have to return to England, in consequence of the state of his health. My diary contains a few notes relating to the voyage. An entry under September 26th reads as follows: "Arrived Port Said; went on shore; tea at Casino hotel; a few locals came up with cameras and snapped me." A native gentleman from Ceylon got into the semi-final of the deck-quoits with me, and the ship's company gathered round to watch our match. My wife was asked by a lady if she could tell her the names of the two rivals, and when my wife supplied the answer, the lady's next question was: "Which is Mr. Hobbs?" That was rather severe, but I had a compliment at Colombo when another gentleman informed me that he had come eight hundred miles from Southern India just to see me play.

My diary has for November 30th: "Brisbane, Test Match commences; glorious weather; enthusiastic crowd; barrackers not too bad." Next day it runs: "Great day for M.C.C.; 521 all out; Australia, 44 for four." They got only 122 altogether. Gregory could not bat on account of a return of an old cartilage trouble. In the dressing-room, the doctor told him that he had finished with cricket, and he was so much upset that he wept. It was a sad end to a splendid career. I have heard that he has gone in for farming. Chapman decided not to let them follow on. We went in again and declared at 342 for eight, to which, on a sticky wicket, they replied with 66 only, giving us victory by the stupendous figure of 675.

In that Brisbane Test, I first met Don Bradman. Like Phil Mead, he is a great run-getting machine. He is above everybody as far as scoring runs is concerned. Whatever odds there may be on any other player getting a score, those odds are increased by fifty per cent when Don walks to the crease. The secret of his phenomenal success is his wonderful eye—a schoolboy eye, I have heard it termed—and his perfect timing. He is not a strongly built fellow; on the contrary, he is just the opposite, but the pace with which he sends the ball to the boundary is simply amazing. Perhaps his chief asset is his remarkable concentration. He never gets excited when he scores a century, for he can settle down for the second hundred almost as though he had just started his innings. He hits up 200 and 300 where other stars would get 100, and he seems to do it more often. He has strokes all round the wicket, and I really do not know which one to single out. A stroke of his that has always interested me is his leg stroke; the ball we glide down to long leg he gets the full face of the bat to and pushes it, with the result that it travels almost square at a very fast pace, bringing him many boundaries. Another feature of his play is the way he lies back to anything a trifle short from the slow bowlers and hooks it with terrific force. Don is also a wonderful field, can run fast, pick up cleanly, and has a speedy return, full toss to the wicket-keeper from any part of the field. I think the talk about his being conceited is all moonshine. Of course, that is always the first brickbat thrown at any successful player. Whilst he has every excuse for being a trifle cock-a-hoop, so magnificent have been his performances, I must say that I have always found him an exceedingly modest fellow, very retiring and preferring the quiet life.

My diary, referring to the second Test at

Sydney, says: "Beautiful day; beautiful wicket; although we lost the toss, we got nine out for 251." On the second day, 58,000 people assembled—a record up to that date. It was one of my very big days, because a presentation was made to me on the field. Through the agency of the *Sydney Sun*, a "Bobs for Hobbs" fund had been raised, and the amount subscribed, £46 in a wallet, was handed to me in front of the pavilion, together with the gift of a boomerang. Noble took me round the ground with him, and the cheering was mingled with "For He's a Jolly Good Fellow," which was taken up by each section of the vast crowd as we walked by.

The Australians were all out for 253, and we replied with the record total of 636. Their second innings produced 397, and we won by eight wickets. The feature of the match was Hammond's batting all the third day and into the fourth, until he had hit up 251, nearly reaching Foster's record of 287 in the early years of the present century.

Hammond is a really great bat, one of the very best exponents of the off-drive, very strong and powerfully built, as is evident from the force that he gets into his strokes. No type of bowling has any terrors for him. He started young, got off the mark early, made good and was an England player almost at once. I think that we have here a player who, given normal health and reasonable luck, will get more centuries than any of us. He would have played for England in 1926 but for a bad illness contracted on a West Indian tour. He is a really good change bowler, who could be top class if it wasn't for his batting. He is a brilliant fielder anywhere and one of the best slippers I have ever seen, if not the best. What is peculiar about Hammond's play is that you never see him hook. He doesn't believe in it and thinks it too risky. Perhaps he is right, because the hook brings about the downfall of so many of us. Instead of hooking, he steps back towards his stumps and forces the ball to mid-off or extra cover.

We were now two up, and the rubber seemed in sight. Before the third match, my wife and I paid a Christmas visit to friends at Warrnambool. It was a Christmas with picnics in bright sunshine, and tennis, whilst friends at home were eating their plum-puddings and gathering round the fire.

The third Test was at Melbourne. To their total of 397 we replied with 417, and then they scored 351, leaving us 332 to get to win on a wet wicket. My diary has the note: "We did not think we had an earthly." I realised, after an hour's batting, with Sutcliffe and me still there, that we had a chance, if we did not lose too many wickets that afternoon, as the wicket was drying fast. I decided to suggest to our captain that the order of our side should be changed to enable Jardine to go in. The only way to get a message to him was to signal for a new bat, and I think I was within my rights in adopting that method. If a message can be sent to a batsman, why not a message from a batsman? Jardine did well and Sutcliffe better, for he scored 135. We won by three wickets. There was some fine scoring in that match—200 from Hammond, 112 from Bradman and centuries by Kippax, Ryder and Woodfull. The crowd numbered 63,000 and broke the Sydney record.

I cannot help thinking that Jardine, in his day, was a great captain. The last Australian tour convinced me. He was a very deep thinker and had a cricketer's brain. He studied batsmen, their methods and their strokes. He had the key to all situations; he knew how to save runs and how to make batsmen fight for every run they got. Some of his moves were very clever. I feel, however, that he was never really up against it; England was always on top during the time that he had charge. Consequently, he never had a real opportunity of proving that he was one of the great skippers. As a batsman, he was a wonderful fighter. England never had a better Number 5; you could put him in when things were going wrong and be almost certain that he would stop a rot. In contrast with P. G. H. Fender, he was inclined to be too careful. In India, particularly, when things were going well, I have seen him go in and play as though England was in a bad way. Moreover, if the batsman at the other end was forcing the pace, he would stop him. He seemed to me to be more ready to make the game safe than to get in a winning position.

The funniest incident that happened to me during the Melbourne match was due to my taking the host of my Christmas visit into our dressing-room. When Sutcliffe lost his wicket my friend applauded, although he was also a friend of Sutcliffe. He forgot where he was and only remembered that he was an Australian. Our players were furious, especially Geary. Having taken Geary aside and explained the position, I was glad to get away quickly with my offending guest.

Sutcliffe and I opened our innings in the fourth Test at Adelaide and put on 143. Hammond was 119 not out. In our second innings, Hammond did even better and scored 177. At the end, Australia had 348 to get, and they managed to get so near that, with seven wickets down, they only needed 41. Excitement was intense; runs still came. Then Bradman and Oldfield dashed for a run as the ball came to me at cover. Duckworth took my return splendidly, and Bradman was out. A voice from the crowd was heard near the end. "Bertie," it said, "if you get those runs, you'll sure go to Heaven!"

Melbourne was the scene of the fifth Test. One would have thought, when we started with 519, that we were safe to add another to our bag of successes, but Australia scored 491, and our second knock produced only 257. Thus the "Aussies" were set a not very formidable task, and, for the loss of five wickets, they hit up 287, which gave them a well-earned victory. When Australia wanted only 4 to win, "Patsy" misfielded a ball, thinking that he could collar it as a souvenir, and Chapman, fielding sub, pulled up a stump as his mémento of the last Test. The idea of both was that the ball was sure to go to the boundary, but it didn't. So we had the amusing spectacle of Chapman replacing the stump.

Amongst the scores in this match were 142

from me, 137 from Maurice Leyland, 123 from Bradman and 102 from Woodfull. "Patsy" was unlucky in failing by five to get a century, but Leyland was more unlucky, for he lost a wallet with £65 in it. My 142 had a very jolly sequel in the evening of the day on which it was scored. My diary says: "When I walked into the hotel dining-room, the orchestra struck up 'See the Conquering Hero Comes,' and followed by playing 'For He's a Jolly Good Fellow.' The guests at the tables rose up and joined in." One of those guests was a famous English actress; she came right across the room and gave me a kiss! It was most embarrassing. I will not give her name away.

We were back in England by April, 1929. Since the war, it has been the practice of the M.C.C. to award the professional players cash bonuses according to merit and the success of the tour. This year, in addition, as a memento of our successful tour, each member of our team received from the M.C.C. a testimonial in a gold frame, the first time that such a gift was presented by that club. The inscription ran as follows: "The M.C.C. in general meeting assembled records its gratitude to the members of the English team and its high appreciation of the conduct and play of each member during their Australian tour 1928–9, whereby they have sustained the credit of cricket." Special mention was made of Mr. Chapman's captaincy and of the services of Mr. Toone, the manager. Then the memento added the name of each player. I value this gift very highly as a happy link with the M.C.C.

17

Mr. Toone was afterwards knighted in recognition of his management of this and former tours.

Another memento of that visit "down under" was a gift to each of us by Mr. James Ferguson, a member of the Surrey Club for thirty years. He came to Naples to meet us and made the presentation there in a little speech on board, in which he suggested that it was a strange sight—"a Scotsman giving away things." I have met many Scotsmen who make jokes against their own nation. One of the best Scotch stories I have heard is of a golf match in which a Scotsman, playing with his daughter, said: "Maggie, your mother tells me that to-day's your birthday. I've been considering very carefully what to give you, and I've decided to make you a present of the next hole."

CHAPTER XXIV

MY TEST CAREER ENDS

THE South Africans were our cricket guests in 1929 under the captaincy of H. G. Deane. What a charming fellow he was, highly popular, one whose personality went to the hearts of players and spectators alike. He led his side well, with tact, ability and sound judgment. Previously he had been a fearless hitter, but on this tour he was somewhat subdued; possibly the cares of captaincy had something to do with it. He retired rather prematurely; it was regretted by all who played against him that he disappeared so early.

Trying to catch P. G. H. Fender at cover point in the Test trial at Lord's, I fell and injured my shoulder. In jumping up to catch the ball, I sort of fell sideways, and, coming down, lost my balance. Thereafter I missed many matches, and, because of my inability to throw with full power, I was unable to play in the first four Test matches. However, I scored ten centuries in the 1929 season and finished up top of the averages. The figures were: Innings, 39; times not out, 5; runs, 2,263; highest score, 204; average, 66·55. That 204 was against Somerset at the Oval.

Just before our match against Kent, a paragraph in a Kentish newspaper asked the question whether Jack Hobbs would elect to play for England or would pile up his average by playing against Kent. This was a very unkind way of putting it and quite unjustified. In my first innings against Kent, I looked more like damaging my average, for I got only 5, but I did improve it in my second knock to the extent of 155 not out. The fact was that I was fit to bat, and Surrey could hide me or nurse me in the field; moreover, I could go careful myself, so that Surrey were willing to play me with all my disadvantage. To play for England, however, is a very different matter; one cannot there be a passenger in the field. The Selectors knew the position and were not prepared to play me. I dare not let my arm come over or attempt to throw at any pace. I did play in the fifth Test and scored 52. That match was notable for the fact that Sutcliffe got a century in each innings. This fifth Test was a draw, which had been the result of the first and second. The third and fourth were won by England—by five wickets at Leeds and by an innings and 32 at Manchester. The rubber was ours.

Brilliant weather came for the opening of the 1930 season, but it broke up in mid-June and thereafter became what is known in some quarters as "cricket weather." It was a case of "rain stopped play," but I made hay while the sun shone. I started well, scoring a century in each innings against Glamorgan at the Oval—137 and 111 not out. This was the fifth time that I accomplished the feat, equalling C. B. Fry's record. During my second innings, Surrey's annual general meeting was taking place in the pavilion. I remember Mr. Leveson-Gower telling me afterwards that he was very grateful for my score, because there was some delicate business on the agenda, but the members were all excitement and were more interested in peeping through the windows to watch me get the double century than in attending to the business before them. My success put them all in a very happy state of mind.

I scored five centuries in 1930, the highest being 146 not out at the Oval for Surrey against the Australians. An interesting score was 40 against Middlesex at the Oval, because that 40 took me past W. G. Grace's aggregate of 54,896 runs. It was one more of the great Doctor's records which I had latterly become very keen to overtake. A record that, perhaps, gave me still greater pleasure was obtained by my score of 106 at Hastings against Sussex; it completed the list of centuries in home and also away matches against every county. Writing without the book, I do not know whether this has been accomplished by any present-day batsman.

The final series of Test matches in which I played came in this year 1930. For the last time in my long career I was to play the Australians. No team from "down under" ever put us so much on tiptoe. They had an uproarious reception at Victoria Station, and some of us attended the performances at the Coliseum and the Hippodrome, where the "Aussies" were guests and had tremendous receptions. At the former place of entertainment, Tom Webster, the famous cartoonist, presented the team with a wire-haired terrier as a mascot, announcing in his speech that it had instructions "to bite anybody who got Jack Hobbs out in the first over."

Four days were fixed for each Test, except the

last, which was to be played out to a finish, unless the rubber had previously been decided. Much may be said for or against this novelty. The authorities will probably consider four days enough for any match on English grounds. The first Test was at Nottingham, and I hit up 78 in my first innings, which pleased me, because I had thought that I was past usefulness in Test cricket. At meetings of the Selection Committee, I had suggested standing down for someone younger, but had always been overruled.

We scored 270 and the Australians 144. Our second knock produced 302, including 74 from me. After getting 58, Sutcliffe had a blow on the hand that caused him to retire and to be an absentee from the second Test. We won by 93. On the intervening Sunday, the deadly enemies fraternised, for the Duke of Portland entertained both teams at Welbeck.

Woolley went in with me in the second Test, which was at Lord's. I was caught after just breaking my "duck"; but Duleepsinhji hit up 173, and our total was 425. Woodfull and Ponsford opened for Australia and were going strong when the King arrived, play was stopped, and both teams were introduced to him. Immediately play was resumed, Ponsford was out for 81. The interruption may have unsettled him; if so, the King that day got his first Test wicket. The opening partnership had realised 162. Woodfull declared at the record-breaking total of 729 for six. Bradman's score was 254 and Woodfull's 155. Some of them got out through speeding up; batting normally, they might have topped the thousand. We started our second innings 304 behind, and the match was easily won by the "Aussies" by seven wickets, in spite of a century by Chapman.

Bradman's 334 was the sensation of the third Test, which was at Leeds. We kept saying to each succeeding 50 and 100: "Well played, Don," until it became monotonous. Hammond knocked up 113 for us, and we reached 391 in reply to their 566. I had only scored 29 when I was caught by à-Beckett. This catch caused a lot of comment. A silly point and a silly mid-on were fielded to Grimmett, and à-Beckett was at silly mid-on. Some people jeer at two fieldsmen being allowed so close apparently to the wicket, but, when you bat on a pitch of the slowish type like that at Leeds, the ball is apt to "bite." In going out to hit, you take a big risk, and it is in the hope that you will hit that the silly point is played. The safest method for the batsman to deal with slow spinners under these conditions is to play right forward at the pitch of the ball and smother the break or play back and wait for loose ones to come along. The Australian bowlers were keeping a perfect length, and Grimmett was exploiting all his tricks, and making the ball talk. I tried to turn a leg-spinner to the on side, but edged it and cocked it back towards à-Beckett. Instantly he threw himself down full length and held the ball low down, tumbling completely over and coming up with it held in silent appeal to the umpire. I stood my ground, not knowing quite what had happened. If I had been sure I was out, I would not have stayed a moment.

Then I asked Oldfield: "Did he catch it, Bert?" He answered: "No." If Oldfield had said that I was out, I would have accepted his verdict. As the umpire at the bowler's end could not see what occurred, the decision was transferred to the square-leg umpire. He gave me out, and I accepted the decree without a word. In the dressing-room later, I apologised to the Australians for not having gone out immediately.

At a late stage in the Leeds match, England appealed against the light; this action on our part some newspaper critics most unfairly condemned. If the Australians had appealed in the same circumstances, there would have been no such criticism. It was for the umpires to decide; they allowed the appeal, and the condemnation was thus a rebuke to the umpires. Sutcliffe asked me what I thought about the light, and I replied: "Not very good; if Grimmett goes on again at the dark end, we will appeal." Grimmett has a low trajectory, and there was a steep stand behind him. He went on at the dark end; I appealed because I was at Grimmett's end at the time. If he had gone on at the other end, we would not have appealed, because no big shadowy stand faced us there, and there was no storm-cloud above it. Our critics were in the big stand, looking on the bright side of things, and could not possibly appreciate the true conditions as they were in the middle. I might say further that we had instructions to appeal if we thought it necessary.

Sometimes, when a telegraph messenger is seen trotting out to a batsman, the cynics say: "He's taking him the winner of the two-thirty." That's nonsense; it is probably a wire of congratulation. I have had many. In this Leeds match, Don Bradman received a message at the wicket that an Australian admirer had given him £1,000. Some message, what!

We had much to put up with that summer. It was all we could do to cope with the Australians, and we sometimes felt that we hadn't our own people behind us. Much of the criticism, when we appealed against the light at Leeds, came from old first-class cricketers commissioned by newspapers to report the Tests.

Manchester saw the fourth Test. There was much rain, and a draw was the result. The score of the " Aussies" was 345 and ours 251 for eight. The fifth Test was a vastly different affair. It was a fight to the finish, and England was beaten fairly and squarely by an innings and 39 runs. Had we won that Oval match, not a grumble would have been heard, but, as it was, the Selection Committee came in for much unkind comment. That Committee is always in an unfortunate position and cannot defend itself. The deposition of A. P. F. Chapman was criticised, and, as a member of the Selection Committee, I must take my share of the responsibility for that step. As I look back, I think that we made a mistake in leaving him out, but we did it for the best, and, if we had won, nothing would have been said. He is a very popular captain; he knew his men, and he also knew the Australians. The sole idea of the Selection Committee was to strengthen the England batting.

The Selection Committee was unanimous in

its decision against the continued appointment of Chapman. It was stated by some stunt writers that Arthur Carr was at the meeting when the decision was taken. That is not true. Nor is it true, as was alleged, that our team was captained from the pavilion by the Selection Committee. Chapman's successor, R. E. S. Wyatt, had full powers, and was in unrestricted command. One newspaper hinted that there would be a demonstration against Wyatt. Actually he had a most cordial welcome; when he went into bat, the crowd stood up and signified by loud clapping their disassociation from the bitter criticism of that newspaper.

That was my last match for England. I did not know beforehand that any tribute would be paid to me, although I became a bit suspicious when I approached the middle, because the Australians were all clustered near the wicket, instead of going to their positions in the field. Suddenly, Woodfull's voice rang out: "Three cheers for Jack Hobbs!" Off came their green caps, and they gave the cheers in the most cordial way. I could only answer: "Thank you very much, you chaps." Since that day, I have often wished that I had gripped Woodfull's hand. I had the impulse to do so, but I was afraid that the spectators would think that I was "playing up." So I drew back.

Woodfull was the one man to plan such a surprise. I shall never forget the incident. It went right to my heart; it still goes to my heart whenever I think of it, and in a large measure compensates me for that tragic failure in my last Test innings, when I played on after scoring only 9 runs.

CHAPTER XXV

I VISIT INDIA

AT the end of the 1930 season, the Maharaj Kumar of Visianagram visited my shop in Fleet Street to order some bats, and asked me, in a casual way, if I would like to go to India. Just as casually I replied: "Yes, one of these days I would like to come out." Lo, and behold, in about another week, everything was arranged for Mrs. Hobbs and myself to visit India in October.

He came to see me during the match at the Oval between the Champion County and the Rest of England. I suggested that he might like to take Herbert Sutcliffe as well, particularly as the latter had been disappointed over a tour of South Africa with the M.C.C. team. I ought to explain that the Maharaj Kumar was getting together a team to tour and play a series of matches in India and Ceylon. Naturally I thought that it would be nice to have Herbert there, so that too much responsibility would not fall upon myself, for at that time I had no idea of what sort of side he was getting together. As it turned out, it was a really good side, including several of the best Indian players. The outcome was that Herbert joined us. The Maharaj Kumar promised us an enjoyable trip and that we should see some of the real old Indian cities.

Right nobly did he carry out his word. We had a marvellous trip. Nothing was too good for us; he entertained us lavishly. We saw more of Indian private life than many of the British had seen, who had lived in India a lifetime. To anybody who, like myself, had not seen anything of Eastern life, it was like going into a new world.

Amongst the hundred and one exciting and thrilling experiences, those that stood out most were the ancient Indian cities of Jaipur and Agra, and the trip to the Taj Mahal, which I shall never forget. I would not venture to describe it; its grandeur fairly takes your breath away. On an early morning trip down the Ganges at Benares, where the Maharaj Kumar's Palace was situated, I was fascinated to see the thousands upon thousands of Hindoos bathing in their Sacred River, with the funeral pyres along the bank cremating their dead. Other cities that we visited were Delhi, including a visit to the Viceregal Lodge; Calcutta, where Sir Stanley Jackson, who was then Governor of Bengal, entertained us to lunch; Bangalore; Hyderabad; and Madras. Then we went on to Colombo.

Whilst at Benares, Herbert and I had a couple of days' shooting. It was my first experience of big-game shooting. I brought down a zamba; he was a huge fellow. I felt thankful that he fell from my first shot and did not move. Herbert had the good fortune to bag a splendid panther. Never again! Hunting of any kind makes no appeal to me; when I revisited India in 1933, I accepted no shooting invitations. I remember our getting up very early on the second morning of our shoot, leaving the cars as day was breaking, and splitting up into parties of two. I had one fellow with me, who said, as we walked along in semi-darkness: "There's water here. Look out; we might see some bear." Such a cold shiver ran down my spine. I said to myself: "I hope to goodness we don't."

Herbert and I had, I am pleased to report, a very successful tour, each making four or five centuries. My chief successes came in Ceylon. During my trips to Australia, we had stopped each time for one day at Colombo. I had always longed to spend a holiday in Ceylon; and, now that anticipation was a realisation, I got one. We were there for a whole month. How I enjoyed it! We had a thoroughly great time. One match up in the hills I shall always remember. The nights were icy cold, and there was scorching sun by day. Yet it was never unbearable; it was such a dry heat, so healthy and invigorating.

On another visit to India, three years later, when we were again staying at Benares, Mrs. Hobbs and I had the most terrifying experience of our lives—an experience that falls to the lot of few people. We had two earth tremors in one week. At lunch at the Visianagram Palace, we heard a rumbling, which I thought, at first, to be a passing lorry. The rumbling increased to such an extent that, on the spur of the moment, I imagined that a railway train was passing very close. Then the chandeliers began swaying; glasses and crockery started tumbling from the tables; bits of plaster fell from over the doors. Somebody exclaimed: "It's an earthquake!" Everyone made for out of doors. At the time, we were on the first floor, and I shall never forget taking the trip down those stairs with my wife, for every moment we expected the palace to fall in upon us.

Later in the week, we had another shock—this time in the middle of the night. This was much more terrifying, because we knew what it was. We could hear the uncanny howls of jackals, who seemed to answer one another in chorus, setting up a terrible din. We slipped on our dressing-gowns, rushed downstairs, and got out in the grounds. Our alarm was intensified by hearing, in the distance, the plaintive wailings and moanings of the natives, which sounded like a riot.

During my first Indian tour, I had a lot of quite unsought publicity, merely because I objected to playing cricket on Sunday. When invited to make the tour, I had lost sight of the fact that all the big matches there were played on Sunday. Consequently, as I didn't play on that day, we had a break in the match and played Saturday, Monday, and Tuesday, instead of Saturday, Sunday and Monday. This caused, I believe, some inconvenience, but often a one-day match was arranged on the Sunday against another side, to provide our team with a game. I should like to place on record how readily the Maharaj Kumar respected my convictions and fell in with my wishes. He never at any time brought the slightest pressure upon me to play.

I was astounded at the publicity that my attitude towards Sunday cricket got. It was quite unsought. Perhaps the Press had no better news copy just then. I received cables and letters from every kind of religious organisation the world over, congratulating me on my stand for Sunday observance. I believe that it caused quite a stir at the time.

Quite apart from the religious issue, there is no excuse for a professional wanting to play Sunday cricket. I do not think that he should; he has enough of it all the week. He cannot get the best results if he plays on Sunday, because one day's rest each week is essential, and to insist on it is only fair to his county or club. I know of the case of a professional who was not out for his county on a Saturday night and played on the Sunday; he made a big score and was, consequently, so tired and stiff on the Monday that he soon got out.

I can understand the point of view of the fellow whose work prevents him from getting his game of cricket during the week. There is something to be said for him, but nowadays some of the big games are being played on Sundays. It is not so much the fact that you play yourself that has to be considered as the fact that you thereby employ other people and rob them of their day of rest.

The modern trend is spoiling our Sunday; it is not what it used to be. I don't hold with it; call me old-fashioned if you like. I look upon Sunday as a day of rest; I enjoy it that way. Some people can't settle; they must be on the go, here, there and everywhere.

I have never played Sunday cricket and never shall. It has been a great source of pleasure to me and to my wife that our boys have never had to be requested not to play on that day. My early religious atmosphere brought me up to respect Sunday, to remember the Sabbath Day and keep it holy, to make it a day of rest for mind, body and spirit.

HOBBS AND HIS FAMILY

THE MAHARAJ KUMAR'S TEAM AFTER WINNING THE GOLD CUP AT SECUNDERABAD

CHAPTER XXVI

MY LAST COUNTY MATCHES

RAIN again interfered with cricket in 1931.
It was a disastrous year for Surrey, the
gates suffering to such an extent that they lost
more than £3,000 on the year's working. New
Zealand paid us another visit and were given one
Test. They made a good show at Lord's, scoring
469 for nine declared in their second innings,
enabling them to effect a creditable draw. C. S.
Dempster hit up 120 and M. L. Page 104. As a
consequence they were given two more Tests
on the dates when they were due to meet Surrey
at the Oval and Lancashire at Old Trafford.
They lost the Oval match by an innings; Dempster was unable to play. The Manchester match
was spoilt by rain. Dempster had an average of
86·50 in the Tests and 59 for the tour. There
was no doubt about his being a first-class bat; he
held the same position in New Zealand as
Headley held in the West Indies. Although
short, he is sturdily built and gets a lot of power
into his strokes. He was really good. As I write,
Dempster is qualifying for Leicestershire, and I
am confident that he will, in a year or so, loom
large in English cricket.

I played against New Zealand at Scarborough
for Mr. Leveson-Gower's Eleven and scored
153. Sutcliffe and I put on 243 for first wicket in
three hours and ten minutes. T. C. Lowry, the

18   273

captain, on his return to New Zealand, paid me the great compliment of describing that innings as the best played against them.

During 1931, I hit up ten centuries, and my average was: Innings, 49; runs, 2,418; highest score, 153; times not out, 6; average 56·23. Perhaps the best innings I played that year was the 144 in the Gentlemen *v.* Players match at Scarborough. Herbert and I again made a great start, putting on 227 in two hours and forty minutes. This was the twenty-fifth time that we had shared in a century opening partnership and the seventh time that we had exceeded the 200 together for first wicket. My 133 against Yorkshire at the Oval was notable for the fact that it was on a wicket that was doing a bit; I carried my bat right through the innings. I was the first to reach 1,000 runs that season, and I recall it with pride because at the time I was forty-eight years of age.

My innings at Scarborough was the last I played there. It severed a very cordial association; I had had good times there and made many friends. Scarborough was a happy hunting-ground for me. It was one of my favourite wickets; the ball always comes along at a nice pace, not too fast, although fast enough to enable you to bring out all your strokes, and just slow enough to let you exploit the hook shot to anything a trifle short. The Scarborough Festival is the only one that pays. It is excellently run; the cricket is very keen, played in the right spirit, and thoroughly enjoyable. There is always a band. The crowd flocks there, many making it their annual holiday. Mr. Leveson-Gower has for years been the organiser and has made it a great success; from the profits he has much improved the stand accommodation and the general amenities of the ground.

In the winter of 1931–2, I gave a sitting to Mr. Leonard Fuller, the artist. The portrait was passed for the Royal Academy by the Committee; but, unfortunately, it was thrown out by the Academy's hanging committee, which means, I believe, that there wasn't room for it or that it didn't fit in. I am a bit hazy about these things. Two years later the same portrait was accepted; I was hung.

1932 was an ideal cricket season, practically fine throughout—a big contrast with 1931. The India Eleven were our guests and were, for the first time, given a Test match at Lord's. The Indians had some splendid players in their side, but suffered from the length of their programme. They were very stale at the finish and thoroughly had had enough of it. In their own country, they are not used to playing match after match week after week; they play week-end cricket only.

Although a torn leg-muscle kept me out of a few matches, I again had a fair season, with an average as follows: Innings, 35; runs, 1,764; highest score, 161 not out; times not out, 4; average, 56·90. The 161 not out was at Lord's; it was my last Gentlemen v. Players match on that classic ground—the Mecca of the game. I carried my bat. I remember Jardine, who captained the Gentlemen, graciously complimenting me on "a great personal triumph"; those were his very words. This innings undoubtedly saved the Players from defeat. I batted in all for five hours, and, but for slight lameness, I would, I think, have got a few more runs.

In that match, another of the Grand Old Man's records went west—namely, the record of fifteen centuries in Gentlemen *v*. Players games. I have now scored, in those games, seven centuries at Lord's, six at Scarborough, and three at the Oval. It is only fair to say that Grace scored seven centuries at Lord's, which is really the only match that counts in this series. Naturally, I was very bucked; it was a great thrill to have such a successful wind-up in big matches.

I also broke another record in 1932 in scoring 113 and 119 not out against Essex at the Oval. It gave me a total of six double centuries, beating the previous record held by C. B. Fry. If I might be allowed to say it, this was a pretty good season for a man in his fiftieth year.

At the end of 1932, I entered upon a new sphere, accepting an engagement from the *Star* newspaper, of London, to go to Australia with the England Team, to describe the Tests and other important matches. It was a pleasant thought to be able to renew old acquaintanceships "down under" and to see again the cities and towns where I had always had so many friends and such an enjoyable time. I jumped at the chance. At first I was, I must confess, rather nervous of the ordeal, because on occasions it might involve adverse criticisms of those who had been my colleagues on the field. Although I have been criticised myself, and justly so, I never get any pleasure out of blaming people. I prefer to look for the good. However, on the whole, I was satisfied with the way I got through. Only on one occasion did I get into hot water; it was when I criticised Herbert Sutcliffe's innings in the second Test. Then it was simply on a question of tactics. I want to make it clear that it was Herbert's friends who took exception to my criticism. We players are, I think, apt to be very sensitive and too prone to go up in the air when something adverse is said about us, forgetting the hundred and one nice things said about us by the very same journalist.

During the last match at Melbourne, I went up to the Press seats, which were in the grandstand, to say good-bye to my friends of the Press. It had already been stated in the papers that I was leaving for England that day. Many of the spectators in the stand must have seen it, for, when I came down the stairs, they gave me quite an affectionate ovation. I felt very much embarrassed, as this was a different experience; you can stand cheering when you have made a big score, but here I had done nothing. I bolted out of sight as quickly as I could.

I did not go over to New Zealand with the team, but Mrs. Hobbs and I, on the way home, spent a most enjoyable week with a friend at Cairo.

A season of record-breaking weather came in 1933. For fear of catching a chill after returning from Australia, I did not play in the first four matches. I kicked off with 221 against West Indies, batting in all for six hours and a half.

I recall feeling very stiff for a day or two afterwards.

Another century that gave me very great personal satisfaction was before the August Bank Holiday crowd at the Oval—133 against Notts. It was always a wonderful crowd to me, so generous in its plaudits. They gave me a great ovation as I walked back. A newspaper cutting in my album says: "The crowd of 15,000 people seemed to rise in a body, and the rousing cheers were sustained until the next man, tripping down the pavilion steps, arrived at the crease." This was my last hundred at the Oval. If I had realised that fact, I would have taken twice the time in getting back to the dressing-room, for those cheers were just lovely.

In all, I scored six centuries, which included 101 on our bogy ground, Blackheath. My figures were: Innings, 18; runs, 1,105; highest score, 221; average, 61·38. Again, at the end of the season, I accepted another engagement from the *Star* to go with the England team abroad— this time to India—to cable descriptions of the Tests and principal matches.

Whilst in India, I received the following cable from the President of the Surrey Club:

"Hobbs, Bengal Cricket Association, Calcutta. Do you agree to appeal being made to Surrey Club Members to subscribe for new main entrance to Oval, completing new wall, as a tribute to your services to England and Surrey cricket, with gates to bear your name. Best wishes New Year. Leveson-Gower."

I read it and re-read it. I could hardly believe my eyes. First of all I thought: "What joke is this?" When it dawned upon me that it was true, I felt overwhelmed. My feelings I shall never be able to describe. That my Club should think me so worthy stirred me to the depths. To me service had always been the highest ideal, and throughout my career I had striven humbly to serve my Club and all who loved and watched cricket. I replied to the effect that I was overwhelmed, that I was glad to agree, and that I thanked them sincerely for so great a compliment.

Next season, 1934, the gates were opened by the President, Mr. Leveson-Gower. I think it is a wonderful tribute. I cannot, even at this late stage, describe what is in my heart. It is a very great honour that they did me. When you come to think of all the great players that Surrey have had—men who have added lustre to the amateur and professional history of Surrey cricket, it hardly seems possible that I should be singled out for this very great compliment. I shall always cherish the happiest recollections of this token of affectionate regard, and to all the members who subscribed I tender my sincerest thanks.

Every time I go to the Oval, as I often will as the days come and go, these gates will, as I pass through them, remind me anew of all the happy years spent in the service of the Surrey Club and intensify my thoughts of those years. They are a link that naught can sever. When I think that many are honoured after death, it is a great comfort to me to know that I shall be able to enjoy this honour whilst I live.

If it had not been for a wonderful ovation at Old Trafford in 1934, I should have wished that I had finished in 1933, seeing that I am now not to get the 200 centuries. To be fair to the Lancashire members and to the crowd, it was grand; the occasion was George Duckworth's benefit match, and he had specially requested me to play. I made 116 in the first innings and 51 not out in the second. The great crowd gave me a special cheer when I took the field with the Surrey team, and, when I went in to bat later in the day, they rose *en masse* and gave me a tremendous ovation, which lasted all the way to the wicket.

Next day, after getting my hundred, as I returned to the pavilion, the crowd on the steps started up "Auld Lang Syne." This was altogether too much; I hurried to the dressing-room. I think that I can honestly say that I have been more popular on the Old Trafford ground than on any other, outside the Oval and possibly Lord's. In my experience, the Lancastrians are a warm-hearted and sporting people, who always see and applaud the good in the other side. Real cricket is always that way. This truly Lancashire ovation and the cheers that the Australian players gave me at the Oval in my last Test innings stand out in my mind above all else.

I opened the season with 50 against the M.C.C. at Lord's. Against Sussex, at Horsham, I looked like getting another century and saving our side from defeat, but I foolishly ran myself out. My last appearance at the Oval was against Somerset on June 16th, 18th and 19th, when I did nothing, scoring only 15. I did not play again until

Surrey's last match, when, upon a request from Glamorgan and against my better judgment, for I was short of practice, I turned out at Cardiff and on a sticky wicket took a blob l.b.w. What a finish to my Surrey career! The irony of it all was that, after a long spell of beautifully fine weather, we should get rain there.

I played in two matches in the Folkestone Festival, scoring 24 and 18 in a Gentlemen *v.* Players match and 38 in a match between an England Eleven and the Australians. I discovered this season that, more than ever, my powers had waned; stamina was one thing, but the chief difficulty was that my timing was at fault. I thought that I was hitting at the ball just as hard, but it made no pace off the bat.

I was very anxious not to go on too long and become an object of sympathy, as so many of us do. At the same time, there were numbers of people who, when I talked to them about retiring, pooh-poohed the idea. If I may say so without being conceited, I recognised that I was a bit of a draw in some places, but I knew better than any of the critics could tell me that I could not perform as well as formerly. The only urge to go on was to be the first to score 200 centuries and thus to delight my friends and wind up on a good top note. Even now that I have announced my retirement, I get many letters, saying that it is a pity, that I have made a mistake, and that I should have gone on. For myself, however, I am certain that I have got out of the game not any too quickly as it is.

I know that I have failed to deliver the goods

at times, but one must make allowances for the bowler; a snorter is always likely to come along. Then, again, other factors count, and we are expected to be fit at all times, but we are only human. I should like here to reveal a little secret; all my life I have suffered a great deal from severe headaches, and sometimes I have taken the field or batted when I hardly knew how to hold up my head. On one occasion we won the toss, and when I went in to bat I had a real beauty of a head. After a little running, I was terribly afraid of being sick. The skipper of our opponents very thoughtfully and sportingly suggested a runner, which I gladly and gratefully accepted. Next week, I was horrified when an article by one of the players in the match was sent me, in which he wrote something about my audacious request for a runner. I never let on, nor did I reply that the suggestion very kindly came from his skipper.

One of the penalties of my success all through my career has been a large amount of correspondence. Evening after evening has been fully occupied in replying to my many correspondents. I have never felt on top of it. I have always felt it a duty to reply to a letter; my conscience would not let me tear up a letter, even if an answer was not demanded. I felt that every one had to be answered, and I have been compelled to sacrifice much of my family life in replying to letters.

You may wonder what all this correspondence has been about. For years, my postbag has averaged considerably more than a hundred letters a week, apart altogether from business letters and letters from friends in all parts of the world. Here are a few general headings: Applications for articles for school magazines, contributions to symposia, hints on cricket, autographs, photographs; requests for old bats; lyrics or verse in my honour; information about new gadgets for cricket; questions about how to become a professional cricketer; invitations to open bazaars, to give lectures, to take the chair at brotherhood meetings or address them, to become president or vice-president of clubs, to present cups or medals or prizes, to kick off at football matches, to attend dinners or dances, to take charge of a stall at a fête, and to read the lessons in church. This list takes no account of letters from admirers and cricket "fans."

Even since my retirement I have still been receiving shoals of letters, most of them very interesting. Here is a specimen:

"DEAR MR. HOBBS,

"In view of your retirement from County Cricket, which is universally regretted, and of the possibility that you may be writing reminiscences, I must relate this incident which I heard in the stand at the Oval about three years ago. You were just walking out to bat, when a proud father, in an awe-struck voice, said to his small boy aged about seven: 'Look, there's Hobbs.' With just the merest glance at you, the boy said, 'Oh; what's Mrs. Hobbs like?' Such is fame! With best wishes for many more happy years of club cricket.
        "Yours truly,
                "HERBERT J. CHAPMAN."

One of the most remarkable requests made to me was that I should let my name go forward as Parliamentary candidate for a South London constituency. I received this letter in Clapham, where I was living at the time. I was not interested in politics, and never have been to any great extent. Perhaps I had better explain how the impression got about that I was a Liberal. There was a by-election going on at Northampton at the time, and the agent of one of the candidates wrote to ask me to go down and speak for his man. Naturally I declined, as is my rule with all invitations to speak. Without knowing which party the candidate represented, I ended my letter by wishing his man success. It turned out that the agent had an eye to business and circulated the slogan: "Jack Hobbs wishes Mr. —— success." It is only fair to say that, afterwards, the candidate was gracious enough to send me a written apology for the use of my letter in that way by his agent. Thus the idea got abroad that I was a staunch Liberal, and for several years afterwards I was bothered with invitations to talk to young Liberal leagues, Liberal societies, Liberal meetings, and women's Liberal associations.

CHAPTER XXVII

LOOKING BACK

IT is often said that travel is a great educator; well, this was never more true than in my case. In the first place, I was tremendously interested in going round my own country with the Surrey team in my early days; it was all so novel. I enjoyed especially visiting the big towns. When I first got my place in the team, most of our week's tours started on a Sunday. We all met at the Oval and all drove together in one conveyance to the railway station. To me it was like a small boy going to a treat.

We had a saloon carriage on the train; the time always passed pleasantly, and we were very happy together. Some of us chatted; others played cards. There was plenty of fun and leg-pulling. I well remember one instance in my Club and Ground days. Whilst waiting at a station for the train to come in, I noticed a number of my colleagues laughing. I could not make out what was amusing them until, when the train came in, I went to pick up my bag and discovered scores of station labels of all parts of the country stuck all over it. My hat, it looked a pretty fine sight. Fortunately, many of them were still wet and I was able to pull quite a number off.

On another occasion, at the end of a day, we were all in the dressing-room, and drinks were ordered. One chap, who was a teetotaller, ordered a ginger-beer, but Tom Hayward ordered a gin and ginger-beer. The drinks were brought in. Tom had a good pull at his, before discovering that there was no gin in it. He queried and looked across to the teetotaller. The latter had demolished his drink and said to Tom: "Fancy me not noticing that; it's one of the nicest ginger-beers I've ever drunk."

When I first joined the team, Fred Boyington was our scorer. He was a most lovable old chap and always travelled with us. It was part of his duties to look out trains and book hotels. Fred was a great talker, as well as a great character. If there was a youngster in the party, he loved to get him in the corner of the saloon and recount his experiences. Lo and behold, if anyone was cornered, there was no hope of his getting away until the train stopped and very little hope of getting a word in. I was cornered once and only once; never again!

At first, I was rather nervous of Fred, for he was a bit "bossy"; but, later, as I grew up, I didn't perhaps show him the respect that I ought to have done. Fred had a flair for economy, was very particular about his clothes, and took great care of them. I used to take a great delight in knocking off his hat and kicking it. He was very much annoyed; but, as I used to buy him a hat occasionally, he said very little. I could take liberties where others could not; for, if anybody else did it, he would read them the Riot Act.

Once, at Bradford, there was a hobbing iron in the dressing-room. Fred had a hat, a new, light-weight bowler, which he thought a lot of and felt very dandy when wearing. This hat was placed over the hobbing iron, and we started the anvil chorus on it with a hammer. The hat was like the lid of a pepper-box after we had finished with it, but we straightened it out, and Fred wore it. We should have to buy him another hat later; but, in the meantime, Fred stormed and raved. He preached us a sermon on the colossal waste, reminding us of the proverb, "Waste not, want not." He urged the need for practising strict economy and for looking after our money, for otherwise we should come to want what we wasted.

The subject of hats reminds me that Bill Hitch had once just bought a brand-new bowler, and, with Bert Strudwick and myself, went to a cinema in Leicester. All of a sudden, Bill turned to me and said: "Jack, there's a smell of burning about here." So there was; a little later, we discovered that Bill had dropped a cigarette into his bowler, which he was nursing on his knee, and had burnt a hole right through it.

I loved touring the old country; it was a great joy and a real treat to stay in the various hotels. I enjoyed my food in those days, especially the hotel food; breakfast, and dinner at night, were my delights.

Fred Boyington, the economist, never believed in paying for seats at a theatre or cinema, if there was the slightest chance of his arranging to get an invitation. When we were on tour, he was never backward in going to a manager privately and begging seats for the whole team. Only once was he bitten; it was when we were playing at Northampton. Fred came into the dressing-room at lunch-time and said: "Boys, it's all right to-night; invitation to the new cinema." Seven or eight of us went; we sat there in blissful ignorance, enjoyed the show and came away, leaving Fred to write a letter of thanks. Imagine our surprise when, a few weeks later, we got a bill for so many seats at such and such a figure. Fred said that it was a mistake, but we had to pay. Needless to say, Fred had a pretty rough time for some days afterwards.

It was a great thrill going to cricket grounds that I hadn't seen before. Worcester, particularly, charmed me. It is a beautiful ground, the river Severn skirting it and the cathedral overlooking it. Then there were Nottingham, Leeds, Old Trafford and Sheffield—grounds which I had read so much about, but had not seen, and upon which so many famous players had trod. Feelings of great awe welled up within me at the thought of following in their trail, and yet, whilst I was delighted to visit and to play upon those grounds, they had nothing like the same place in my affections as the Oval.

The Oval had the reputation of being too big and too hard to the feet. I got to love it. It was, you see, my home ground. I had my own lockers, with every comfort and convenience to hand, with somebody to look after us who knew our individual needs and a hundred and one other amenities, to say nothing of the delightful wicket —the batsman's paradise. Then, again, I was able to get home after the day's play.

Everywhere one went the circle of one's

THE HOBBS GATES AT THE OVAL

THE AUSTRALIANS CHEERING HOBBS ON HIS ARRIVAL AT THE WICKET IN HIS FINAL TEST

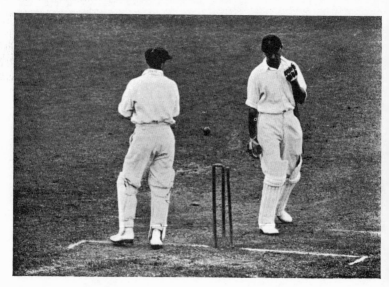

HOBBS'S LAST TEST INNINGS: PLAYED ON!

friends was ever widening: it was a case of always meeting old friends and making new. I was privileged to form friendships in those early days which have endured staunch and true and deepened with the march of time, and which will continue until the end. Almost in every county I have good friends who have always wished to entertain me during my visits, but, for the most part, I felt that it was my place to stay at the hotel with the team.

Two of the tit-bits of going round the country in those days were trips to Scotland and to Matlock. In Scotland, I saw the Forth Bridge and the gorgeous country around Edinburgh. It was some years later when I went to Glasgow and visited Loch Lomond, the scene *par excellence*, outstanding of all the sights that I have seen. The Sunday trip to Matlock and the Peak district came when I was playing Yorkshire, Lancashire, or Derbyshire. Two other trips that stand out in my memory were to Liverpool Docks and to Ireland, to play at Bray, a few miles from Dublin.

What has impressed me most about England is its wonderful country-side, its beautiful, fresh greenness, its small paddocks, in comparison with Australia, India and South Africa, the compactness of the towns and their nearness to one another. It is only when you go to those other vast countries that you realise how small England really is. Then there are the beautiful streams and rivers. When you travel from south to north, you are able to realise the enormous work and industry carried on there.

19

Another big thing is the superiority of travel in England as compared with that of the Dominions—the permanent way, the fine rolling-stock, the smoothness and comfort of the trains, with less noise and nothing like the same heat and dust to contend with. The more I travel in other parts the more I am reminded of Blake's poem, in which he rightly refers to "England's green and pleasant land."

In my opinion, English cricket-grounds are the most pleasant to play upon. Whilst we have no grounds, except Lord's, to compare with those of Adelaide, Sydney and Melbourne, our English grounds are, for the most part, very compact, with excellent wickets and out-fields. They compare favourably with any others, are nicer to play on and are softer to the feet. Unfortunately, a lot of dressing-room accommodation could be improved.

The Australians, on their big cricket-grounds, are able to play football, as their turf is not so easily damaged, and so they have a much bigger income to build stands, score-boards, etc. At Melbourne, a few years ago, they spent £90,000 on a new members' pavilion. With the possible exception of Lord's, none of our grounds could raise such a sum.

English crowds undoubtedly bear comparison with any others in the world. Visitors to this country can be sure of a fair deal. Of course, some crowds get a little partisan. It is only natural, but they are never very unkind about it. I certainly have no complaints; on the other hand, I have every reason to be grateful for the generous way in which they have received me. They show a worthy example of true sportsmanship, always ready to applaud good play by the home team and opponents alike. There is an innate sense of fair play.

African and Indian crowds compare with English crowds. My experience is that they are always ready for a fair deal to both sides. When playing in South Africa or India, I thought that there seemed as many shouting for England as for the home team. Australian crowds come in a different category. There are two sides to every question, and one must try to see the other man's point of view. One must allow for the fact that Australian crowds have been brought up to the idea of barracking in all their games, and I wish to stress this very strongly. The views of the two countries on this point will never agree.

I think that too much has sometimes been made of this barracking. Pages have been written, and we have perhaps been over harsh to the barracker, but we cannot get away from the fact that it is a form of intimidation. When entering the arena, one cannot help feeling most uncomfortable at the personal remarks aimed at one. It is apt to get you down, unless you have the skin of a rhinoceros. It doesn't fit in with our idea of sportsmanship and it cannot be pleasant to other spectators to sit beside fellows with raucous voices shouting all day long: "You'll never get them out." These others want to enjoy the cricket. The players want to enjoy it, too, and to do their best.

Our cricket crowds are, for the most part, quiet, but we get a line as to what barracking is like and as to the atmosphere of an Australian cricket ground from some of our football crowds. They are pretty noisy and hostile. You expect a crowd to stick up for its own team or county and to be somewhat biased, but I fail to see how they claim the right to be bitter and personal.

I am glad to see that the Australian authorities have promised to deal with barracking. It ought to have been dealt with years ago, out of courtesy to the wishes of visiting teams. The Australian newspapers have also been sinners somewhat in this respect; hitherto they have defended barracking when they should have condemned it. If the Press had given a lead, the crowd would, I am sure, have had different ideas. However, it is better late than never.

I have no personal complaint. The crowds have been great friends to me; I delight to play before them. It is only right to add that it is the popular crowd that makes the noise; only on rare occasions do you hear barracking from members.

I am a notoriously bad sailor. I don't know why it is; I have tried every known remedy and listened to hundreds of suggestions to "take this, take that." The fact is that what suits one doesn't suit another. I am certain that, if anyone could find a universal cure, there is a fortune in it for him. I have been told by a doctor that there is something in my ears which the movement of the boat affects; this upsets my balance and the nerves of my stomach. I am just as bad now as ever; in fact, I have given up trying cures, and, whenever I get a rough spell and the boat begins to move a bit, I take to my cabin and stay there until the sea becomes calm. It has always amazed me how fellows like Wilfred Rhodes and Syd Barnes never feel the slightest movement of the boat and have never been sea-sick, whereas I have never been able really to enjoy a sea-voyage. Although I may be below decks and I can see nothing, the boat has only to give one slight lift and I am aware of it immediately, and it makes me giddy.

I have always envied good sailors and the way in which they can enjoy a sea-voyage. Mind you, I don't say that I am bad all the time. A sea-voyage to Australia is a treat that many people would give their ears for. When an English team goes to Australia, it does the voyage in the best part of the year. There are days and days going through the tropics when the sea is like a lake.

I always look forward to the Suez Canal, where I am sure of 10 hours—it used to be longer—free from all movement, followed by three days in the Red Sea, where seldom is there any rough weather. The Canal was so full of interest, and it was a wonderful education, especially on my first visit. A modern liner can only be described as an up-to-date floating hotel. My first trip was in the *Ophir*, a ship of about 7,000 tons, much smaller and less up-to-date than a modern liner. I remember that I had an inside cabin and no port-hole. I had a very bad spin, being sea-sick for days on end.

Liners have grown out of all knowledge the last few years. When I first sailed away, ships of 9,000 tons odd were the biggest that could get through the Suez Canal, but it has since been greatly widened and deepened, and ships of 20,000 tons and more can pass through, which means that passengers are able to enjoy the luxurious comfort of a really modern liner. Every cabin has a port-hole, and ventilation by the Punkah Louvre air system; many have hot and cold running water, roomy beds instead of bunks, and ample wardrobes for clothes. These liners mostly burn oil fuel, which means practically no dust and none of the old discomfort involved in coaling at ports. They have plenty of bathrooms, spacious corridors, lifts connecting all decks with the dining-room, sumptuously fitted saloons and public rooms, broader decks, and a big space provided for the playing of all kinds of deck games. There need never be a dull moment afloat.

The two principal lines making the Australian trip are the Orient and the P. & O., and you cannot make a mistake if you travel on any of the ships of either company. You are assured of every attention and courtesy, excellent and well-varied food, and first-class service. Days and evenings are well planned and catered for; there is always plenty to do or you can rest, as you will. From commander to lift-boy, all are bent on your comfort and complete happiness and enjoyment throughout your journey.

I mostly travel overland to the south of France. On occasions I have been able to arrange a night in Paris, although nowadays it is possible to take the boat-train from Victoria about midday, travel right through via Folkestone or Dover, cross the Channel, and entrain from Boulogne or Calais direct to either Marseilles or Toulon without changing, completing the entire journey in, roughly, twenty-four hours. Taking advantage of this route means a week less at sea.

Paris! What a city of places of interest—boulevards, well-appointed hotels, renowned for warmth, courtesy and cuisine. I can never forget the rides in taxis, the breathless speed, and the perpetual tooting. I thought Toulon—a naval base—a very fine harbour.

I will wind up these travel experiences with a Ceylon anecdote. We were on a motor trip to Kandy in 1921. Pulling up for refreshments, we saw an elephant appear with his keeper. Our local friend suggested that Strudwick should be photographed on its back. "Struddy" was game. The elephant was made to kneel down for "Struddy" to mount, and the keeper prodded the animal to make it rise. To our surprise, a second or two afterwards, we saw "Struddy" disappear over its side. I would have given any money to have got a snap of the look on old "Struddy's" face as he passed from view. I shall never forget that look on his face as long as I live. It takes a lot to frighten "Struddy", but he properly had the wind up that time. He told me afterwards that what most frightened him was that he had visions of falling on the spike of the mahout's prodding gadget. Here we had melodrama and farce mixed, and the native kiddies standing round were tickled to death; they fairly shook with merriment.

EPILOGUE

DURING March I went to Cornwall for a health trip. On my arrival home to complete this story, my wife handed me a letter that had come whilst I was away, which she had not sent on, thinking to keep it for what she knew would be a most pleasant surprise for me. Here is the letter:

"8, NORTHWICK HOUSE,
"ST. JOHN'S WOOD ROAD, N.W.
"*March 25th*, 1935

"DEAR HOBBS,

"The Surrey County Cricket Club Committee have to-day received your letter to the President of February 25th last.

It is quite unnecessary to say that your decision to retire was received with very deep regret, not only because the County will be deprived of the services of the greatest batsman of his time—to say nothing of your fielding at cover point—but also because your fine, manly, and modest example both on and off the field will be even more missed than your outstanding achievements with the bat.

The Committee feel that your retirement should be marked in some special manner, and have, therefore, under the powers they possess, appointed you a Life Member of the Club.

The number of Life Members is confined

to five only, is the highest honour the Committee can confer, and they hope that for many years to come, though they will not see you on the Field, they will be able very often to welcome you in the Pavilion as a member of the Club.

"H. D. G. Leveson-Gower
"*President, Surrey County Cricket Club*
"*On behalf of the Surrey Committee*"

I can only leave you, my readers, to imagine my feelings on discovering that Surrey deemed me worthy of so signal a mark of their good favour.

It will be a proud moment when I attend the annual dinner of the Surrey Club in May, when I am to be presented with an elaborately designed book, containing, after a foreword by E. V. Lucas, the names of all the subscribers to the Hobbs Gates. A copy of this book will be placed in the Pavilion, to be permanently on view to the members.

I have often been asked whether, if I could have lived my life over again, I would have been a cricketer. The answer is "Yes." I have had a good deal of fun from the game, and I assert that no other walk in life could have provided me with the same happiness. It has been a wonderful life; I have enjoyed every minute of it.

I have made some wonderful friends, not only at home, but abroad. It is quite remarkable when I think of the number of friends I have in England, Ireland, Wales, and other parts, who have wished me well and given me kindly encouragement and yet have never seen me. They have supported me through thick and thin and considered that I could do no wrong. How they wanted me to get those 200 centuries! I could cry when I remember that I have disappointed them.

Throughout my thirty years on the playing field I have always had a wonderful Press. I count myself exceedingly fortunate to have had such a good Press; it has been a real encouragement, a great help and support in my career. I have had criticism when it was deserved, praise when it was merited.

Everyone must recognise how much the efforts of the Press help to make the game; in all that has been written about the subject in general and about myself in particular, the game has been pre-eminent.

Amongst newspaper men I have many true friends. To all the scribes of the great game I owe a debt of gratitude, and welcome this privilege of tendering my cordial thanks.

Elsewhere I have mentioned the names of a few "Aussie" friends, but, if I begin to give the names of English, Scottish, Irish and Welsh friends, it is difficult to know where to leave off. I must, however, express my esteem and sincere thanks to Mr. Ken Lockhart for the grand holidays in Cornwall he has given me, helping to keep me fit, to Messrs. Arthur Richards, Rowland Williams, E. H. Church, Jack Lyne, Alex Gauld, Jack Mears, Seth Pilley, George Simpson, Arundel Kempton, Andrew Kempton, and

S. P. Foenander, for their friendship and great interest.

It is with a heart filled with gratitude that I say to them and to all who have cheered me on: "Fare you well." To all who would play cricket I can pass on no better thought than that expressed in that beautiful motto:

"Keep your word;
Keep your temper;
Keep your wicket up."

THE END

APPENDIX

HOBBS'S records, centuries, Australian Test Innings and his first-class and Test averages are set out in the following pages.

These records have been compiled with the aid of "Wisden's Cricketers' Almanack," and have been supplied to the publishers by The Cricket Reporting Agency.

HOBBS'S RECORDS

Total runs to the end of 1934 season	61,221
(In 1930, Hobbs beat W. G. Grace's record aggregate of 54,896)	
Total runs v. Australia in Test Matches	3,636
(Hobbs played in 41 Test Matches against Australia)	
Hundreds in first-class cricket	197
Hundreds in Test Matches	15
Hundreds in Test Matches v. Australia	12
(Also a record)	

Hobbs and Rhodes, first-wicket record partnership in England v. Australia Test Matches—323 at Melbourne in 1911–12.

Hobbs and Sutcliffe, first-wicket record partnership in Test Matches between England and South Africa—268 at Lord's in 1924.

The innings of 211 made by Hobbs at Lord's in 1924 is the record highest score in England v. South Africa Tests.

Hobbs has taken part in 168 partnerships of three figures for the first wicket—a record number.

His 428 with Sandham v. Oxford University at the Oval in 1926 is the highest first-wicket partnership for Surrey.

Hobbs has to his credit the unparalleled feat of having made two separate hundreds in a match on six occasions.

His highest aggregate in a season is 3,024 runs in 1925.

His 266 not out at Scarborough in 1925 is the highest individual innings in matches between Gentlemen and Players.

His 16 hundreds during the season of 1925 is a record for first-class cricket.

Hobbs claims the highest score ever made at Lord's—316 not out for Surrey v. Middlesex at Lord's in 1926, and the highest innings of his career.

Greatest number of aggregates of more than 2,000 in a season—17.

Most centuries in Gents v. Players matches—16.

Record first-wicket stand, Gents v. Players, at Lords—263, with H. Sutcliffe in 1926.

Test Averages

	Inn.	N.O.	Total.	H. Score	Av.
Australians ..	71	4	3,636	187	54·26
South Africans ..	29	3	1,562	211	60·07
West Indies ..	2	0	212	159	106·00
All Tests ..	102	7	5,410	211	56·94

HOBBS'S TWO CENTURIES IN A MATCH

1909	May 20, 21, 22, for Surrey v. Warwickshire, at Birmingham ..	160 and 100
1925	June 17, 18, 19, for Surrey v. Cambridge University, at The Oval	143* and 104
1925	August 15, 17, 18, for Surrey v. Somerset, at Taunton ..	101* and 101
1927	May 7, 9, 10, for Surrey v. Hampshire, at the Oval	112 and 104
1930	April 30, May 1, 3, for Surrey v. Glamorgan, at The Oval ..	137 and 111*
1932	June 11, 13, 14, for Surrey v. Essex, at the Oval	113 and 119*

* Signifies not out.

HOBBS'S HUNDREDS

Year	Date	Venue	Match	Score
1905	May 4, 5, 6	The Oval	Surrey v. Essex ..	155
	June 1, 2, 3	Leyton	Surrey v. Essex ..	102
1906	July 23, 24, 25	The Oval	Surrey v. Worcestershire	162*
	July 12, 13, 14	Leyton	Surrey v. Essex ..	130
	May 21, 22, 23	Worcester	Surrey v. Worcestershire	125
	Aug. 30, 31, Sept. 1	The Oval	Surrey v. Middlesex	103
1907	July 29, 30, 31	The Oval	Surrey v. Worcestershire	166*
	June 27, 28, 29	The Oval	Surrey v. Warwickshire	150*
	July 25, 26, 27	Southampton	Surrey v. Hampshire	135
	Aug. 22, 23, 24	Worcester	Surrey v. Worcestershire	110
1907–08	Feb. 1, 3, 4	Melbourne	M.C.C. Team v. Victoria	115
	Jan. 18, 20, 21	Launceston	M.C.C. Team v. Tasmania	104
1908	May 7, 8, 9	The Oval	Surrey v. Hampshire	161
	Aug. 17, 18	The Oval	Surrey v. Kent ..	155
	July 6, 7	Northampton	Surrey v. Northamptonshire	125
	June 8, 9, 10	Nottingham	Surrey v. Nottinghamshire ..	117*
	July 23, 24, 25	Blackheath	Surrey v. Kent ..	106
	June 25, 26, 27	The Oval	Surrey v. Oxford University	102
1909	May 6, 7, 8	The Oval	Surrey v. Hampshire	205
	June 10, 11, 12	Bournemouth	Surrey v. Hampshire	162

* Signifies not out.

Hobbs's Hundreds—*contd.*

Year	Date	Venue	Match	Score
1909	May 20, 21, 22	Birmingham	Surrey v. Warwickshire	160 and 100
	May 10, 11, 12	The Oval	Surrey v. Warwickshire	159
	Aug. 12, 13, 14	Bristol	Surrey v. Gloucestershire	133
1909-10	Mar. 11, 12, 14, 15	Cape Town	England v. South Africa	187
	Jan. 8, 10, 11	Durban	M.C.C. Team v. Natal	163
	Dec. 4, 6	Cape Town	M.C.C. Team v. Western Province	114
1910	June 9, 10	Derby	Surrey v. Derbyshire	133
	June 27, 28	The Oval	Surrey v. Oxford University	119
	Aug. 25, 26, 27	Leicester	Surrey v. Leicestershire	116
1911	July 10, 11, 12	Lord's	Players v. Gentlemen	154*
	Aug. 14, 15	Leicester	Surrey v. Leicestershire	127
	Sept. 7, 8, 9	Scarborough	M.C.C. Australian XI v. Lord Londesborough's XI	117*
	July 31, Aug. 1, 2	The Oval	Surrey v. Lancashire	117
1911-12	Jan. 12, 13, 15, 16, 17	Adelaide	England v. Australia	187
	Feb. 9, 10, 12, 13	Melbourne	England v. Australia	178
	Dec. 30, Jan. 1, 2, 3	Melbourne	England v. Australia	126*
1912	July 15, 16, 17	Manchester	Surrey v. Lancashire	111
	June 24, 25, 26	Lord's	England v. Australia	107
	May 27, 28, 29	Nottingham	Surrey v. Nottinghamshire	104
1913	Aug. 21, 22, 23	Worcester	Surrey v. Worcestershire	184
	June 12, 13, 14	The Oval	Surrey v. Scotland	150*

	July 19, 21, 22	The Oval	Surrey v. Middlesex	144*
	May 15, 16, 17	Northampton	Surrey v. Northamptonshire	136*
	Aug. 18, 19, 20	Birmingham	Surrey v. Warwickshire	122
	Aug. 11, 12, 13	The Oval	Surrey v. Kent	115
	May 19, 20, 21	The Oval	Surrey v. Gloucestershire	113
	June 16, 17, 18	Southampton	Surrey v. Hampshire	109
	Aug. 25, 26, 27	Bristol	Surrey v. Gloucestershire	107
1913-14	Nov. 21, 22	Port Elizabeth	M.C.C. Team v. Cape Province	170
	Jan. 17, 19	Kimberley	M.C.C. Team v. Griqualand West	141
	Jan. 14, 15	Vogelfontein	M.C.C. Team v. Eleven of Transvaal	137
	Jan. 30, 31, Feb. 2	Johannesburg	M.C.C. Team v. Transvaal ...	131*
	Dec. 20, 22, 23	Johannesburg	M.C.C. Team v. Transvaal ...	102
1914	Aug. 3, 4, 5	The Oval	Surrey v. Nottinghamshire	226
	June 13, 14, 16	Leyton	Surrey v. Essex	215*
	Aug. 13, 14, 15	Lord's	Surrey v. Yorkshire	202
	May 28, 29, 30	The Oval	Surrey v. Warwickshire	183
	June 18, 19, 20	The Oval	Surrey v. Hampshire	163
	July 9, 10, 11	The Oval	Players v. Gentlemen	156
	July 18, 20	The Oval	Surrey v. Lancashire	142
	Aug. 31, Sept. 1	The Oval	Surrey v. Gloucestershire	141
	Aug. 6, 7, 8	Worcester	Surrey v. Worcestershire	126
	July 30, 31, Aug. 1	Blackheath	Surrey v. Kent	122
	May 25, 26, 27	Bradford	Surrey v. Yorkshire	100

* Signifies not out.

20

Hobbs's Hundreds—contd.

Year	Date	Venue	Match	Score
1919	May 31, June 2, 3	The Oval	Surrey v. Australian Imperial Forces	205*
	July 3, 4, 5	The Oval	Players v. Gentlemen	120*
	Sept. 4, 5, 6	Scarborough	Players v. Gentlemen	116
	July 14, 15, 16	Lord's	Players v. Gentlemen	113
	June 30, July 1	The Oval	Surrey v. Lancashire	106
	July 25, 26	Blackheath	Surrey v. Kent	102
	Aug. 15, 16	Manchester	Surrey v. Lancashire	102
	Sept. 15, 16, 17, 18	The Oval	Rest of England v. Yorkshire	101
1920	Sept. 13, 14, 15	The Oval	Rest of England v. Middlesex	215
	July 7, 8, 9	Southampton	Surrey v. Hampshire	169
	Sept. 6, 7, 8	Scarborough	Players v. Gentlemen	138
	June 9, 10	Leicester	Surrey v. Leicestershire	134
	Aug. 14, 16, 17	The Oval	Surrey v. Kent	132
	May 8, 10	The Oval	Surrey v. Warwickshire	122
	July 3, 5, 6	The Oval	Players of the South v. Gentlemen of the South	115
	Aug. 25, 26, 27	Northampton	Surrey v. Northamptonshire	114
	June 19, 21, 22	Sheffield	Surrey v. Yorkshire	112
	June 5, 7, 8	The Oval	Surrey v. Sussex	110
	June 12, 14, 15	Birmingham	Surrey v. Warwickshire	101
1920–21	Nov. 12, 13, 15, 16	Melbourne	M.C.C. Team v. Victoria	131
	Jan.14,15,17,18,19,20	Adelaide	England v. Australia	123

	Dec. 31, Jan. 1, 3, 4	Melbourne	England v. Australia	122
1921	Nov. 19, 20, 22	Sydney	M.C.C. Team v. New South Wales	112
1922	June 25, 27, 28	Leeds	Surrey v. Yorkshire	172*
	July 12, 13, 14	Birmingham	Surrey v. Warwickshire	168
	June 3, 5, 6	Nottingham	Surrey v. Nottinghamshire	151*
	June 7, 8, 9	Leicester	Surrey v. Leicestershire	145
	June 17, 19, 20	The Oval	Surrey v. Gloucestershire	143
	July 19, 20, 21	Lord's	Players v. Gentlemen	140
	May 27, 29, 30	Bristol	Surrey v. Gloucestershire	139
	Aug. 26, 28, 29	Lord's	Surrey v. Middlesex	126
	Aug. 12, 14, 15	The Oval	Surrey v. Middlesex	112
	May 20, 22, 23	The Oval	Surrey v. Essex	102
	Sept. 15, 16, 18, 19	The Oval	Rest of England v. Yorkshire	100
1923	Aug. 11, 13, 14	The Oval	Surrey v. Middlesex	136
	May 5, 7, 8	Bath	Surrey v. Somerset	116*
	Aug. 4, 6, 7	The Oval	Surrey v. Nottinghamshire	105
	Sept. 6, 7, 8	Scarborough	Players v. Gentlemen	105
	July 14, 16, 17	The Oval	Surrey v. Lancashire	104
1924	June 28, 30, July 1	Lord's	England v. South Africa	211
	June 7, 9, 10	Nottingham	Surrey v. Nottinghamshire	203*
	June 18, 19	The Oval	Surrey v. Derbyshire	118*
	July 16, 17, 18	Lord's	Players v. Gentlemen	118
	July 9, 10, 11	The Oval	Surrey v. Gloucestershire	105

* Signifies not out.

Hobbs's Hundreds—*contd.*

Year	Date	Venue	Match		Score
1924	Aug. 2, 4, 5	The Oval	Surrey v. Nottinghamshire	..	105
1924–25	Jan. 1, 2, 3, 5, 6, 7, 8	Melbourne	England v. Australia	..	154
	Jan. 16, 17, 19, 20, 21, 22, 23	Adelaide	England v. Australia	..	119
	Dec. 19, 20, 22, 23, 24, 26, 27	Sydney	England v. Australia	..	115
1925	Sept. 2, 3, 4	Scarborough	Players v. Gentlemen	..	266*
	June 24, 25, 26	Birmingham	Surrey v. Warwickshire	..	215
	May 30, June 1, 2	Nottingham	Surrey v. Nottinghamshire	..	189
	June 17, 18, 19	The Oval	Surrey v. Cambridge University 143* and 104		
	July 15, 16, 17	Lord's	Players v. Gentlemen	..	140
	May 23, 25, 26	Leyton	Surrey v. Essex	..	129
	May 20, 21, 22	The Oval	Surrey v. Warwickshire	..	120
	June 20, 22, 23	The Oval	Surrey v. Somerset	..	111
	May 16, 18, 19	The Oval	Surrey v. Glamorgan	..	109
	July 13, 15, 16	The Oval	Surrey v. Essex	..	107
	Sept. 12, 14, 15, 16	The Oval	Rest of England v. Yorkshire		106
	July 18, 20, 21	Blackheath	Surrey v. Kent	..	105
	May 13, 14	The Oval	Surrey v. Gloucestershire	..	104
	Aug. 15, 17, 18	Taunton	Surrey v. Somerset	..	101* and 101
1926	Aug. 28, 30, 31	Lord's	Surrey v. Middlesex	..	316*
	June 23, 24, 25	The Oval	Surrey v. Oxford University	..	261

	July 3, 5, 6	Southampton	Surrey v. Hampshire	200
	Aug. 7, 9, 10	The Oval	Surrey v. Middlesex	176*
	July 14, 15, 16	Lord's	Players v. Gentlemen	163
	June 26, 28, 29	Lord's	England v. Australia	119
	May 12, 14	The Oval	Surrey v. Gloucestershire	112
	June 16, 17, 18	The Oval	Surrey v. Cambridge University ..	108
	Aug. 21, 23, 24	The Oval	Surrey v. Yorkshire	102
	Aug. 14, 16, 17, 18	The Oval	England v. Australia	100
1927	Aug. 20, 22, 23	The Oval	Surrey v. Yorkshire	150
	Aug. 3, 4, 5	The Oval	Surrey v. New Zealand	146
	July 30, Aug. 1, 2	The Oval	Surrey v. Nottinghamshire	131
	July 9, 11, 12	Blackheath	Surrey v. Kent	121
	Sept. 3, 5, 6	Scarborough	Players v. Gentlemen	119
	May 7, 9, 10	The Oval	Surrey v. Hampshire 112 and 104	
	Aug. 8, 9, 10	Birmingham	Surrey v. Warwickshire	200*
1928	Aug. 11, 13, 14	The Oval	England v. West Indies	159
	Sept. 14, 15, 17	The Oval	Rest of England v. Lancashire ..	150
	May 9, 10, 11	The Oval	Surrey v. Gloucestershire	124
	May 12, 14, 15	The Oval	Surrey v. West Indies	123*
	Sept. 8, 10, 11	Scarborough	Mr. H. D. G. Leveson-Gower's XI v. West Indies	119*
	July 18, 19, 20	Northampton	Surrey v. Northamptonshire	117
	May 26, 28, 29	Nottingham	Surrey v. Nottinghamshire	114

* Signifies not out:

Hobbs's Hundreds—contd.

Year	Date	Venue	Match	Score
1928	July 28, 30, 31	The Oval	Surrey v. Kent	109
	Aug. 22, 23, 24	The Oval	Surrey v. Yorkshire	105
	Aug. 29, 30, 31	The Oval	Surrey v. Leicestershire	101
	May 2, 3, 4	Lord's	Surrey v. M.C.C.	100*
1928–29	Mar. 8, 9, 11, 12, 13, 14, 15, 16	Melbourne	England v. Australia	142
	Jan. 25, 26, 28, 29	Adelaide	M.C.C. v. South Australia	101
1929	July 17, 18, 19	The Oval	Surrey v. Somerset	204
	May 4, 6, 7	The Oval	Surrey v. Hampshire	154
	Sept. 4, 5, 6	Scarborough	Mr. C. I. Thornton's XI v. South Africans	151
	July 13, 15, 16	Blackheath	Surrey v. Kent	150*
	Aug. 14, 15, 16	Weston-super-Mare		
	Aug. 21, 22, 23	Cardiff	Surrey v. Somerset	134
	July 27, 29, 30	The Oval	Surrey v. Glamorgan	128
	Aug. 28, 29, 30	The Oval	Surrey v. Kent	118
	Aug. 31, Sept. 2, 3	Lord's	Surrey v. Leicestershire	115*
	June 1, 3, 4	The Oval	Surrey v. Middlesex	111
1930	June 18, 19, 20	The Oval	Surrey v. Essex	102*
	April 30, May 1, 2	The Oval	Surrey v. Australians	146*
	Aug. 6, 7, 8	Hastings	Surrey v. Glamorgan	137 and 111*
			Surrey v. Sussex	106

Year	Date	Ground	Match	Score
1931	Aug. 27, 28, 29	The Oval	Surrey v. Leicestershire	100
	Sept. 9, 10, 11	Scarborough	Mr. H. D. G. Leveson-Gower's XI v. New Zealanders	153
	June 3, 4, 5	The Oval	Surrey v. Warwickshire	147
	Sept. 5, 7, 8	Scarborough	Players v. Gentlemen	144
	Aug. 22, 24, 25	The Oval	Surrey v. Yorkshire	133*
	May 13, 14, 15	The Oval	Surrey v. Somerset	128
	May 20, 21, 22	The Oval	Surrey v. Sussex	117
	June 10, 11, 12	The Oval	Players v. Gentlemen	110
	July 8, 9, 10	The Oval	Surrey v. Glamorgan	106
	July 1, 2, 3	Chesterfield	Surrey v. Derbyshire	105
	Aug. 19, 20, 21	Taunton	Surrey v. Somerset	101*
1932	June 11, 13, 14	The Oval	Surrey v. Essex	113 and 119*
	July 13, 14, 15	Lord's	Players v. Gentlemen	161*
	June 18, 20, 21	Taunton	Surrey v. Somerset	123
	Aug. 27, 29, 30	Lord's	Surrey v. Middlesex	111
1933	May 27, 29, 30	The Oval	Surrey v. West Indies	221
	Aug. 5, 7, 8	The Oval	Surrey v. Nottinghamshire	133
	June 21, 22, 23	The Oval	Surrey v. Cambridge University	118
	July 26, 27, 28	The Oval	Surrey v. Somerset	117
	July 15, 17, 18	Blackheath	Surrey v. Kent	101
	June 14, 15, 16	The Oval	Surrey v. Warwickshire	100
1934	May 26, 28, 29	Manchester	Surrey v. Lancashire	116

* Signifies not out.

HOBBS'S FIRST-CLASS AVERAGES

	Inns.	Times N.O.	Runs	Highest Inns.	Av.
1905	54	3	1,317	155	25.82
1906	53	6	1,901	162*	40.44
1907	63	6	2,140	166*	37.54
1907–08 (Australia) ..	22	1	876	115	41.71
1908	53	2	1,904	161	37.33
1909	54	2	2,114	205	40.65
1909–10 (S. Africa) ..	20	1	1,194	187	62.84
1910	63	3	1,982	133	33.03
1911	60	3	2,376	154*	41.68
1911–12 (Australia) ..	18	1	943	187	54.94
1912	60	6	2,042	111	37.81
1913	57	5	2,605	184	50.09
1913–14 (S. Africa) ..	22	2	1,489	170	74.45
1914	48	2	2,697	226	58.63
1919	49	6	2,594	205*	60.32
1920	50	2	2,827	215	58.89
1920–21 (Australia) ..	19	1	924	138	51.33
1921	6	2	312	172*	78.00
1922	46	5	2,552	168	62.24
1923	59	4	2,078	136	37.78
1924	43	7	2,094	211	58.16
1924–25 (Australia) ..	17	1	865	154	54.06
1925	48	5	3,024	266*	70.32
1926	41	3	2,949	316*	77.60
1927	32	1	1,641	150	52.93
1928	38	7	2,542	200*	82.00
1928–29 (Australia) ..	18	1	962	142	56.00
1929	39	5	2,263	204	66.55
1930	43	2	2,103	146*	51.29
1931	49	6	2,418	153	56.23
1932	35	4	1,764	161*	56.90
1933	18	0	1,105	221	61.38
1934	18	1	624	116	36.70

* Signifies not out.

312

HOBBS'S TEST INNINGS
v. AUSTRALIA (41 Matches)

1907–08	Second Test (Melbourne)		83 and 28
in	Third Test (Adelaide)	..	26 and 23*
Australia	Fourth Test (Melbourne)	..	57 and 0
	Fifth Test (Sydney)	..	72 and 13
1909	First Test (Birmingham)	..	0 and 62*
in	Second Test (Lord's)	..	19 and 9
England	Third Test (Leeds) ..	..	12 and 30
1911–12	First Test (Sydney)	..	63 and 22
in	Second Test (Melbourne)		6 and 126*
Australia	Third Test (Adelaide)	..	187 and 3
	Fourth Test (Melbourne)	..	178
	Fifth Test (Sydney)	..	32 and 45
1912	First Test (Lord's)	..	107
in	Second Test (Manchester) ..		19
England	Third Test (The Oval)	..	66 and 32
1920–21	First Test (Sydney)	..	49 and 59
in	Second Test (Melbourne)		122 and 20
Australia	Third Test (Adelaide)	..	18 and 123
	Fourth Test (Melbourne)	..	27 and 13
	Fifth Test (Sydney)	..	40 and 34
1921 in England	Third Test (Leeds) ..	..	Absent ill
1924–25	First Test (Sydney)	..	115 and 57
in	Second Test (Melbourne)		154 and 22
Australia	Third Test (Adelaide)	..	119 and 27
	Fourth Test (Melbourne)	..	66
	Fifth Test (Sydney)	..	0 and 13
1926	First Test (Nottingham)	..	19*
in	Second Test (Lord's)	..	119
England	Third Test (Leeds) ..	..	49 and 88
	Fourth Test (Manchester) ..		74
	Fifth Test (The Oval)	..	37 and 100
1928–29	First Test (Brisbane)	..	49 and 11
in	Second Test (Sydney)	..	40
Australia	Third Test (Melbourne)	..	20 and 49

* Signifies not out.

313

Hobbs's Test Innings—*contd.*

1928–29 in	Fourth Test (Adelaide)	..	74 and 1
Australia	Fifth Test (Melbourne)	..	142 and 65
1930	First Test (Nottingham)	..	78 and 74
in	Second Test (Lord's)	..	1 and 19
England	Third Test (Leeds) ..	..	29 and 13
	Fourth Test (Manchester) ..		31
	Fifth Test (The Oval)	..	47 and 9
	Total Runs—3,636—a Record.		

SOUTH AFRICA (19 Matches)

1909–10	First Test (Johannesburg)	..	89 and 35
in	Second Test (Durban)	..	53 and 70
S. Africa	Third Test (Johannesburg)		11 and 93*
	Fourth Test (Cape Town)	..	1 and 0
	Fifth Test (Cape Town)	..	187
1912	First Test (Lord's) ..	..	4
in	Second Test (Leeds) ..	..	27 and 55
England	Third Test (The Oval)	..	68 and 9*
1913–14	First Test (Durban) ..	..	82
in	Second Test (Johannesburg)		23
S. Africa	Third Test (Johannesburg)	..	92 and 41
	Fourth Test (Durban)	..	64 and 97
	Fifth Test (Port Elizabeth)	..	33 and 11*
1924	First Test (Birmingham)	..	76
in	Second Test (Lord's) ..	..	211
England	Third Test (Leeds) ..	..	31 and 7
	Fourth Test (Manchester)	..	did not bat
	Fifth Test (The Oval)..	..	30
1929 in England	Fifth Test (The Oval)..	..	10 and 52
	Total Runs—1,562.		

	WEST INDIES (2 Matches)		
1928 in	Second Test (Manchester)	..	53
England	Third Test (The Oval)	..	159
	Total Runs—212		

Total Runs in all Test Matches: 5,410—a record.

* Signifies not out.

HOBBS'S TEST AVERAGES

	Inns.	N.O.	Runs	Highest Inns.	Av.
1907–08 (Australia) ..	8	1	302	83	43·14
1909 (Australia) ..	6	1	132	62*	26·40
1909–10 (South Africa)	9	1	539	187	67·37
1911–12 (Australia) ..	9	1	662	187	82·75
1912 (Australia) ..	4	0	224	107	56·00
1912 (South Africa) ..	5	1	163	68	40·75
1913–14 (South Africa)	8	1	443	92	63·28
1920–21 (Australia) ..	10	0	505	123	50·55
1924 (South Africa) ..	5	0	355	211	71·00
1924–25 (Australia) ..	9	0	573	154	63·66
1926 (Australia) ..	7	1	486	119	81·00
1928 (West Indies) ..	2	0	212	159	106·00
1928–29 (Australia) ..	9	0	451	142	50·11
1929 (South Africa) ..	2	0	62	52	31·00
1930 (Australia) ..	9	0	301	78	33·44

* Signifies not out.

315

INDEX